D1498119

THE WINE AND THE WILL

THE WINE

&

THE WILL

Rabelais's Bacchic Christianity

Florence M. Weinberg
SAINT JOHN FISHER COLLEGE

Wayne State University Press
Detroit 1972

Library of Congress Catalog Card Number 78–181450
International Standard Book Number 0–8143–1464–3

Permission granted for Rabelais, *The Histories of Gargantua and Pantagruel.*
Translated by J. M. Cohen.
Penguin Books Ltd., 21 John Street, London WC 1.
Copyright © J. M. Cohen, 1955.

Library of Congress Cataloging in Publication Data

Weinberg, Florence M.   1933–
    The wine and the will.

    Bibliography: p.
    1. Rabelais, François, 1490 (ca.)–1553?—Religion and ethics.   I. Title.
PQ1697.R4W4   843'.3   78–181450
ISBN 0–8143–1464–3

I could imagine that a man who had something precious and delicate to hide would roll through life, coarse and round like an old, green, heavily-laden winecask: the subtlety of his modesty would will it so.

Nietzsche, *Beyond Good and Evil*, Aphorism 40

To K. W. and O. G. B.

Contents

7

Illustrations

Preface

S *erio ludere:* Michelangelo used this oxymoron to describe his grotesques; it could serve as a motto for Erasmus's *Praise of Folly* and for the works of Rabelais as well. Many Renaissance artists and writers consciously used the technique of serious play, convinced that an absurd symbol provides both an excellent memory device and an effective defense against the "caphars." *Serio ludere* was primarily a hermetic device to communicate a hidden message to a few happy initiates. Rabelais's famed gallic humor, grotesque and obscene episodes, have always provoked hearty laughter, and yet most readers have felt, uneasily, not only that he is funny but that his bewildering wealth of orphic and cabalistic allusions, classical and contemporary references, might also mean something more than a display of useless erudition. Many of these readers, among them myself, believe that Rabelais has a consistent and coherent message which can be reached by an examination of his themes and metaphors.

I shall attempt to investigate certain depths beneath the bright surface, certain resonances beneath Rabelais's play. I have not forgotten that Rabelais is funny, but I do not dwell upon the mechanics of his wit. To be sure, nothing can be more rewarding than a metaphysical or literary study of the mechanisms of wit, humor, and irony when undertaken by authors like Hegel, Solger, Jean Paul, Bergson, or Freud. But nothing can be more deadly and self-defeating than pedantic enumerations of instances where wit, humor, and irony may be found in a literary work. Rabelais wished first to capture his audience with his ribald wit, then he hoped to convey a serious message beyond the guffaw.

His audience, like that of any famous preacher of the time, varied from the popular to the courtly, from the barely literate to the Christian humanist. He chose a form for his book that would appeal to a wide range of readers: a mixed genre, the mock epic, seemingly chaotic in structure, which stands in marked contrast to epic, lyrical, and dramatic poetry of the time, all directed to very specific audiences, feudal, courtly, or *grand-bourgeois*.

A monk trained by the Franciscans, Rabelais appreciated bawdy stories in themselves and for their effect upon an audience; he was a Neoplatonist, familiar with hermetic tracts and the great legacy of classical literature; he was a Pauline stoic who recommended indifference to the annoyances of this world. He was all these things at once: a Renaissance humanist, who was a physician of the sick bodies and ailing souls of his "flock," his patients and his readers. His books were meant as a consolation in both the initial effect of hearty laughter and their inner meaning. This meaning would have been readily intelligible to the Christian humanists of his time. I believe that these contemporaries did understand him, but that they did not comment upon their friend's work, since to break silence would have exposed him to more persecution than he actually did endure. His enemies were more vocal. Their pronouncements on Rabelais's atheism and license have been the legacy handed down to later critics, until, in the nineteen-twenties, Etienne Gilson began a reaction to the notion that Rabelais was secretly undermining Christianity, or that his books amount just to five, or, as some think, four, volumes of good, dirty fun.

By examining one metaphor, *wine,* and one theme, the *will,* I hope to open up an approach which can be further explored by the reader himself. Many other metaphors remain to be investigated, many areas of Rabelais's work remain untouched, since no such vast storehouse can be exhausted by a limited effort like the present one. The metaphor of the wine is central and recurs with obsessive frequency throughout the five books. Pursuit of the meaning of this important symbol has led to the heart of Rabelais's Christian message, which he repeats again and again in a protean multiplicity of parables, riddles, and poems.

In this book I owe a great debt to those scholars who redirected Rabelaisian criticism: Gilson, Febvre, Screech, to mention only a few. I utilize their work and build upon it. I have endeavored to give credit to them where credit is due, but if, in the opinion of the reader, I have omitted an occasional reference or acknowledgment, I beg his indulgence.

My repeated references to all five books of Rabelais will raise in many minds the question of the authenticity of the *Cinquiesme Livre*. In this connection, I should like to refer the reader to the appendix of G.M. Masters's *Rabelaisian Dialectic and the Platonic-Hermetic Tradition,* which provides a convenient summary of the present state of scholarship on this point, and which adds further evidence in support of the authenticity of book five. Against a tradition begun by two near-contemporaries of Rabelais, whose claim that the fifth book is not by Rabelais has never been proven, Masters points out that there have been a number of lengthy and detailed studies by scholars universally accepted as reputable authorities. Marty-Laveaux, through stylistic analysis, concludes that Rabelais left fragments which were later collected and edited. Tilley considers the last sixteen chapters unquestionably genuine and accepts chapter four as well, but with less certainty. Sainéan's analysis in *La Langue de Rabelais* (Paris, 1922–23), leads to the conclusion that, with the exception of four short interpolations, all of book five is authentic. Abel Lefranc, satisfied with the evidence his colleagues had brought together, believes the fifth book to be Rabelais's work (*Ed. cr.* 3: xli). To Masters's list, I would add Leo Spitzer. In his article "Rabelais et les rabelaisants," *Studi Francesi* 12 (1960): 423, he concludes on the basis of a purely stylistic study that the last sixteen chapters, the *Dive Bouteille* chapters, are one of the most beautiful examples of French prose and could only have been written by Rabelais. Among those not convinced of the authenticity of book five are Saulnier, Plattard, Lote, and Screech. The opinions of these scholars are not lightly to be dismissed, but none has, to my knowledge, produced convincing arguments proving the total inauthenticity of the work. Most rely on the unfinished "feel" of certain passages, and on the bitterness of the religious attacks in book five, which have little of the lightheartedness usually associated with Rabelais. None of them has yet published a full-scale study to back up his doubts.

My own position with regard to the *Cinquiesme Livre* is confirmed by Masters's study of the consistency of the hermetic and Neoplatonic allusions throughout the five books. I believe that the *Isle sonante* and the last sixteen chapters are from Rabelais's hand. The intervening chapters and the prologue to book five no doubt existed at least in draft form. Rabelais may not yet have polished them when he died, but they were then published, perhaps with a few short interpolations, by a disciple. The internal evidence of style and the use of symbol and metaphor in the *Dive Bouteille* chapters ally them very closely with his abbey of Thélème.

Various methods are combined in solving some of Rabelais's enigmas. *Explication de texte* in the tradition of Erich Auerbach is coupled with iconographic investigation and research into his etymological games. Among the masses of classical and Christian sources which the editors of the Edition critique have brought together, a number have been exploited for the light they throw upon Rabelais's text. The approach is not purely literary, for it often strays into intellectual history. The combination of these two disciplines has proven helpful in reconstructing a sixteenth-century background on which to project solutions to long-standing riddles, explanations which would otherwise seem absurd or farfetched to a twentieth-century mind.

I wish to express my gratitude to a number of scholars connected with the University of Rochester who have assisted me with valuable advice: Professor Jules Brody, for his painstaking reading of the manuscript and valuable suggestions on style, structure, and bibliography; Professor Frederick W. Locke for extremely useful references to interrelations between Greek myth and Hellenistic and early Christian thought; Professor Marvin B. Becker for guiding me to essential but lesser known Renaissance texts and authors; Professors Norman O. Brown and Alfred Geier for fruitful discussions of myths and etymologies; Professor Eleonore M. Zimmermann for her encouragement during the early stages of composition; Professor Philip R. Berk for his lucid reading of the manuscript, his helpful comments, and for his abundant bibliographical advice; and Professor Kurt Weinberg for his constant encouragement and his etymological, stylistic, and bibliographical guidance.

Among other friends who were eminently helpful in the compilation of source material, I should like to thank in particular Professor Henri M. Peyre of Yale University, Professor Edward P. Morris of Cornell University, and Dr. Nancy S. Struever, of Hobart College. I am deeply indebted to Mr. Franklin J. Enos for his generosity and skill in photographically reproducing the illustrations included in this work. Finally, I wish to praise the efficiency and good will of the bibliographical and interlibrary loan services of the Rush Rhees Library, the University of Rochester.

A Note on Translation and Abbreviations

To widen the circle of my potential readers, and to achieve smoother reading of the text, I quote Rabelais in English whenever I can. I use J. M. Cohen's translation (see Bibliography for complete reference). When he is in my opinion inaccurate, I supply my own translation. Where the actual wording of a text is in question, as opposed to its general meaning, I quote in French and follow with either a translation or a paraphrase in English. Direct quotations from Rabelais are followed by letters and numbers in parentheses. The letters, G, P, TL, QL, CL, refer to *Gargantua, Pantagruel, the Tiers Livre, Quart Livre,* and *Cinquiesme Livre;* the numbers (G. xiv. 48) refer to the chapter and page. Quotations in English refer to the paging of Cohen's translation except where I have translated. I supply book and chapter, but give no page reference, e.g. (TL. xxi; my trans.). Occasionally, I have only slightly revised a translation by Cohen, substituting certain words of my own. In such cases, my substitutions are enclosed in brackets. Quotations in French and paraphrases or allusions to a Rabelaisian text refer to the Boulenger edition of 1962, chosen because of its handy, portable format.

Ed. cr. refers to the Lefranc edition of Rabelais's works, and *Ed. Scr.* refers to M. A. Screech's edition of the *Tiers Livre* (see Bibliography for complete references).

PART I
The Wine

Introduction

Rabelais's Heritage

Rabelais's Christian Background

For over half a century, the liveliest debate among Rabelais scholars has centered around the problem of Rabelais's religious beliefs.

Abel Lefranc, whose efforts renewed a wide interest in Rabelais studies, believed that Rabelais professed a secret atheism, and that his hidden message is an attack on Christianity (Ed.Cr.3:xl–lxx). Since the time of Lefranc, distinguished scholars have maintained the opposite view. Etienne Gilson, by analyzing a number of characteristic expressions, proved that much of Rabelais's thought derived from the orthodox scholastic or Franciscan traditions.[1] Lucien Febvre accepted Gilson's analysis and went further to assert that it is anachronistic to believe atheism possible in the sixteenth century.[2] Verdun L. Saulnier and M. A. Screech followed Gilson and Febvre and deepened their insights: Rabelais was undoubtedly a Christian in good standing with Rome, yet he belonged to a movement which hoped to reform abuses inside the Church without destroying the unity of the Christian world.[3]

Rabelais's ideas on the Christian life, far from being *sui generis,* form part of the mainstream of Christian thought, a tradition which produced earlier great theologians like Nicholas of Cusa, and reformers like Erasmus. Thoughts of reform were not limited to a privileged few, the truly great thinkers, for in the north of Europe during the last decades of the fifteenth century, entire monastic groups based their daily lives on a reformed, revitalized Christianity. Their northern piety, often oversimplified under the label *mysticism,* did not, like the rapture of San Juan de la Cruz, exalt the believer to ineffable realms of divine ecstasy. It remained closer to day-to-day experience, and could be called mystical only in that it sought to establish direct communication with the divine, placing God and creature in a frank "mind-to-mind" relation.[4] Many northern theologians (Meister Eckhart, Wessel Gansfoort, Sebastian Franck) hoped to return to the *simplicitas* of the early Church, approximating the spirit that prompted the several reforms of the Benedictine order and inspired St. Francis of Assisi. The ideal of *simplicitas* — which, however, had undergone many highly sophisticated interpretations — took its place beside the traditional ideals of poverty and humility.

Erasmus, heir of northern mysticism, narrowed Christianity down to the *simplicitas* of the Sermon on the Mount: purity of heart. The Stoics, who like Socrates held purity of heart as their ideal, could all qualify for Erasmus as "Christians." Erasmus's ideas exerted a decisive influence on a group of Christian humanists in France, the Evangelicals, whose members included Marguerite de Navarre and Guillaume Budé. They hoped to reform ritualistic and purely formal worship in favor of scriptural readings and direct prayer to God. As a member of this group,[5] Rabelais criticizes abuses within the Church and suggests rather extreme remedies: do away with monasticism as practiced in his day and "Papimania" (G.xl, lii–lviii; QL.xlviii–liv). Like many of his fellow Evangelicals, he recommends direct communication with God (e.g., QL.i). But he never repudiates the Church altogether; he hopes, through the influence of powerful friends in Rome and of his protectors the Cardinal Jean du Bellay and his brother Guillaume, seigneur de Langey, to overwhelm his enemies in the Sorbonne who resist reform and who condemn each of the books of *Pantagruel* as it appears on the market. Although his difficulties with certain Church factions make it increasingly hard for him to follow the ideal of *simplicitas* or the Pauline and stoic contempt for the world so prized by the Evangelicals, Rabelais probably never considers joining any Protestant group. His reaction against the Protestants increases in violence as it becomes plain that their extremism has dimmed his hopes for a more moderate Evangelical reform from within; finally he will attack Calvin outright.[6] As his hopes fade, his tone through books four and five becomes more somber; his humor appears more labored; he is less able to practice *simplicitas* in the way he best loves to formulate it: Pantagruelism, "a certain lightness of spirit compounded of contempt for the chances of fate" (Prologue QL.439). But despite the grave and sometimes even pessimistic undercurrent in the last books, Rabelais seeks to serve his ideal to the end. His readers are repeatedly invited to drink and to share his merriment; "Pantagruelizing, that is to say, drinking freely and reading about the horrific deeds of Pantagruel" (G.i; my trans.). He promises ineffable, incalculable benefits, hoping to convey divine wisdom through laughter. Perhaps it would be appropriate to call him a laughing mystic.

Humanism and the Hermetic Tradition

Rabelais weds Evangelical Christianity to the Renaissance humanism imported from Italy by his most admired mentors. His Neoplatonism, too, derives from the Christian tradition: from the writings of Paul, from the Gospel of John, from the Greek Fathers of the Church, from St. Augustine; and also from his extensive classical readings either in the original texts or in digests by Erasmus (the *Adages*), by Ficino, or by Pico della Mirandola. Rabelais's Neoplatonism, implicit throughout his books, is rarely formulated explicitly, but it becomes overt enough to have aroused much scholarly comment in the medical advice of Rondibilis (TL.xxxi–xxxiv), and in the Guillaume du Bellay chapter of the *Quart livre* (QL.xxvii).[7] Here, the discussion of "daemons" and heroes as superhuman creatures in the ladder of being shows a Christianity heavily colored by classical ideas of the structure of the universe.

Plato's dictum that the sensible world is illusion, and only the Idea is real, led centuries of thinkers to seek the way out of the Cave. The hermetic tradition, closely linked with Plato's thought, continues unbroken to the time of Renaissance humanism, feeding on the belief that the ancients, both classical and Jewish, possessed the keys to eternal truths, since they lived nearer to the creation and the original blessed state.[8] In an age in which experimental science was in its infancy, natural phenomena seemed mysterious, doubly so when ancient pronouncements, whose relevance and purpose had become obscured by the passage of centuries, were believed to hint at a reality totally distinct from phenomenal appearance. The high purpose of the

Florentine circle and of such disciples as Cornelius Agrippa was to rediscover this wisdom of the ancients, and to reinterpret it for the initiate. The keys to nature's secrets were believed to be hidden in the Cabala, in Egyptian hieroglyphics, in the *Corpus Hermeticum* — in all ancient scriptures, from every ancient culture.

Closely paralleling the hermetic tradition in its assumption that true meaning is always hidden meaning, Christian exegesis used figural interpretation as a means of reconciling contradictions in the Bible, or of explaining passages which appear vulgar or obscene.[9] This firmly established tradition remains unbroken into the sixteenth century; thinkers like Nicholas of Cusa, never suspecting that such a procedure might be considered "medieval," engage in lengthy anagogical or allegorical interpretations of biblical passages. According to this tradition, the great men of this world only seem great, since they will be humbled in the next; activities which *appear* pleasant are harmful illusion; in short, nothing is what it seems. This pervasive assumption governs every human effort to represent life not only in theology but in literature as well. The reader of medieval and Renaissance sermons, stories, and poems was expected automatically to crack the "bone" of any obscure text in order to extract the "marrow." Rabelais's contemporaries, whether clerical or lay writers, openly approve hermetism as a means of shielding holy things from the vulgar. Cornelius Agrippa notes that the ancients were always anxious to conceal divine sacraments by covering them with enigmas. Mercury, Orpheus, and seers like Pythagoras and Socrates presented their truths enigmatically, as did Christ himself, since only his disciples could understand him.[10]

In the anonymous preface to the 1527 edition of the *Roman de la Rose,* the reader is invited to dig beneath the surface, because "great benefit [from the hidden moral meaning, lies] . . . hidden beneath the outer crust of the text." The author illustrates with a parable drawn from Ezekiel 17:3–6 who tells the reader that if the eagle had stopped at the bark of the tree on Mount Lebanon, he would never have found the marrow. Likewise, if we do not dig further than the crust of literal meaning, we will only be able to enjoy fables or stories without profiting from the spiritual marrow, inspired by the Holy Spirit.[11] Another text from which Rabelais undoubtedly draws many *topoi* of his Prologue to *Gargantua,* Erasmus's *Sileni Alcibiades,* depends almost entirely on anagogical and hermetic patterns:

> If you remain on the surface, a thing may sometimes appear absurd; if you pierce through to the spiritual meaning, you will adore the divine wisdom. . . . The parables of the Gospel, if you take them at face value — who would not think that they came from a simple, ignorant man? And yet if you crack the nut, you find inside that profound wisdom, truly divine. . . . In both the domains of nature and faith, you will find the most excellent things are the deepest hidden, and the furthest removed from profane eyes.[12]

These contemporary texts, chosen because of their remarkable resemblance to Rabelais's own words, openly sanction the hermetic approach. It is possible that Rabelais did not know these contemporary writings, and that he stood apart from all the other Evangelicals of his time in rejecting their approach to the world, choosing instead to mock his friends' ideas. It seems far more likely that he knew about and contributed to the predominant intellectual movements of his day, which blended Evangelical ideas on *simplicitas* — that return to "simple" Christianity — with Neoplatonic hermetism.

Chapter 1

Rabelais's Hermetism

R abelais's uniqueness has been recognized by generations of critics, but it would be little short of miraculous if he had remained untouched by the predominant bias of his time. His early education in two conservative Franciscan monasteries, La Baumette and Fontenay-le-Comte, would have laid a good foundation for his humanism, since the medieval exegetical exercises in which he engaged would have led him to think anagogically and to write a complex, hermetic style. His formation, closely paralleling that of Erasmus, prepared him to accept the older man's ideas, as well as those of more radical Renaissance thinkers. Still, many critics argue that Rabelais's work presents no consistent message, much less a hidden one. Most of their arguments are based on the Prologue to *Gargantua,* where Rabelais presents his material in syllogistic thesis-antithesis-synthesis form.[1] The thesis contains a strong statement of hermetism both explicitly and in allegorical terms. Rabelais recalls the circumstances of Plato's *Symposium* when Alcibiades, while praising his mentor Socrates, compares him to a Silenus. Rabelais describes a Silenus as a little box, painted on the outside with happy and frivolous figures, but containing the finest drugs: balm, ambergris, cardamum. He presents this simile because he hopes his reader will not judge his work by the frivolity of the surface. Like the Silenus, it contains a precious "drug" within. Rabelais compares the reader who will seek out this true meaning to a man who, in great suspense and expectation, opens a bottle of wine, or to a dog who diligently gnaws and sucks on a marrow bone. Like the tippler and the dog, he will be rewarded by a revelation of what

Rabelais means by the Pythagorean symbols in his work. He promises to make plain the "high sacraments and dread mysteries" concerning religion, politics, and economic life.[2]

The antithesis, considerably shorter, begins with a strongly anti-symbolic statement, telling the reader that if he believes Homer intended all the allegories attributed to him by later writers, or that Ovid's *Metamorphoses* really prefigures the Gospels, he then does not even approach Rabelais's own opinion.

The synthesis which follows has left most Rabelais scholars in doubt as to his real opinion: if the reader cannot believe what all the allegorizers have proposed, then he should not worry about allegory in Rabelais's work, since it was composed without a thought for such things, while the author was actually occupied with eating and drinking.

Rabelais has done his best to disarm his critics, for, taken at face value, each of his statements appears to cancel out the others, leaving the critic unable to approach Rabelais's opinion "by a hand's or a foot's length." On the surface it would appear that the problem remains insoluble, as it has for centuries, and one is left wondering why Rabelais went to such pains to promise glorious revelations, if he had merely written down, between belches, the fantasies conjured up by the fumes of wine.

But the weight of cultural evidence (i.e., our knowledge that hermetic and even allegorical writing was at the time an accepted and dominant genre) rests on the side of Rabelais's thesis. A number of critics have argued this side, saying that Rabelais was forced to disavow serious intentions to avoid persecution by heresy hunters. Masters also examines this prologue and concludes that Rabelais, in disavowing the allegorical interpretation of Homer by Plutarch and others, and of Ovid by the Christians, disavows only those who injudiciously force Christian interpretations upon the ancients rather than trying (as the Florentine Neoplatonists did) to find out their intrinsic meaning.[3] He hopes the reader will prove judicious, not credulous. Yet another piece of evidence may be produced in support of the thesis of the Prologue to G, for its essential message is repeated explicitly and without contradiction in the Prologue to P: "Each man . . . can surely teach [these chronicles] to his children . . . like a religious Cabala;

for there is more fruit in them than a heap of crude swaggerers may think" (Prologue to P; my trans.).

A detailed examination of the allusions and metaphors used throughout the Prologue to G should further clarify Rabelais's intentions by awakening in the mind of the twentieth-century reader the more obscure associations which a sixteenth-century mind would have recognized. The accumulated weight of evidence should then provide an answer to Rabelais's first enigma. The deeper resonances begin immediately after his salutation to his boozers and syphilitics, with the evocation of a Silenus and the drugs inside: the Container and its Contents.

The Hermetic Metaphor of the Outer and the Inner: The Container

Walter Ong, building on the theories of Lucien Febvre and Marshall McLuhan, traces the development of a new spiritual climate, during the last years of the fifteenth century and throughout the sixteenth, that brought with it a substitution of visual or spatial metaphors for auditory ones in the representation of abstract relations. This substitution became widespread with the advent of typography and the topical logic of Peter Ramus. According to Ong, books in general are seen as places where certain ideas are kept, like boxes whose contents are suggested by a sort of pharmacist's label, the title.[4] Ong's reconstruction of the sixteenth-century idea of the book fits Rabelais's conception of his work with astonishing precision, since he uses the metaphor of an apothecary box containing precious drugs to describe his apparently frivolous books.

Like a virtuoso, Rabelais produces countless variations on a single basic theme; the container and its contents, the outer and the inner. Whether or not he owes to Erasmus's *Sileni Alcibiades* the initial impulse to use this metaphor, it is certain that Erasmus's idea struck a profoundly responsive chord in his nature.[5]

The Prologue to G opens with a scene drawn from Plato's *Symposium,* a banquet where heavy eating and drinking take place, but where, despite the banality of the main topic (love), divine wisdom is imparted. Rabelais exploits the Platonic device, that true wisdom is present within apparent debauchery; the symposium conceals the divine feast. Rabelais's affinity with Plato may be due to his delight in Socratic irony, in which the humble metaphor is invariably exploited to suggest sublime meaning. His reference to the *Symposium* continues with a description of Socrates' absurd and Silenus-like appearance, which hides his truly divine nature. Silenus is then compared to (or identified with) frivolously painted caskets containing precious substances. The relation of the outer to the inner needs scarcely any comment here: like the earth which hides precious gems, the ugly or ridiculous "box" contains the precious drugs of superhuman understanding. Rabelais introduces two further metaphors involving containers and contents: the toper with his bottle and the dog gnawing his marrow bone. The wine stands in the same relation to the bottle as the marrow to the bone; in both cases, precious substances, hard to get at, lie within a worthless container. The legend on Gargantua's tomb, *Hic bibitur* (G.i.8), uses the same wine metaphor to indicate the spatial relation of the "outer" to the "inner." The reader is invited to "drink" the contents of the book lying beneath the inscription and the nine symbolic flasks, but it is a hidden, "buried" content, difficult to fathom.

The most persistent "container" metaphor is either the wine bottle or wine cask, both of which are in turn compared with other containers. Frère Jean calls his garbled biblical quotations "breviary stuff": the breviary is identified as a wine bottle bound in leather like a book. The breviary bottle of the "Ancien Prologue au Quart Livre" is described in a manner strongly reminiscent of the apothecary box: painted outside with hooks (*crocz*) and magpies (*pies*), it contains two compartments, one for white wine and one for claret. Like hieroglyphics, the *crocz* and *pies* inform us symbolically that only a master craftsman can produce a masterpiece, and only a true boozer can be a man of courage. Both containers serve a similarly serious purpose: one contains breviary stuff, wine, or the heady message of the Scriptures; the other, precious drugs; both are painted with comic figures that like hieroglyphic letters stand for something else which is at once serious and profound.[6] The breviary bottle makes its last major appearance in book five, where the "joyous gloss," filled with liquor, interprets the inscrutable pronouncement of the *Dive Bouteille* to the one who swallows the contents. Bacbuc sinks a large bottle in the form of a book into the fountain while she tells the pilgrims that, just as in their world preachers and doctors feed them through the ears with beautiful words, here they may assimilate wisdom through the mouth. She urges them not to *read* her chapter and *examine* its gloss, but to *taste* the chapter and *swallow* the gloss (CL.xlv.882). The contents, which explain the divine mystery of *Trinch!*, assure the entrance of the holy spirits by the most direct means: through the mouth.

In the barrel metaphor of the third Prologue, Rabelais elaborates the idea that his barrel-bottle-books contain divine wisdom. By analogy with the tub of Diogenes, Rabelais describes his work as a barrel of wine which he then compares to a cornucopia of joy and to Pandora's "bottle." At the same time, he contrasts it to the "tub" of the Danaids which contains despair, not good hope.[7] As Rabelais invites all good tipplers and gouty folk to come when thirsty to his barrel, he reassures them not to fear that the wine will run out, as it did at the wedding of Cana, in Galilee, since no matter how much wine is drawn, the same amount will be poured in from the top. The barrel will remain inexhaustible because the wine flows from a living and eternal source (Prologue to TL.). The miraculous barrel closely resembles the font of living water in John 7:37–38: "If any one thirst, let him come to me and drink. He who believes in me, as the Scripture has said, Out of his heart shall flow rivers of living water." The wording, the message, the sequence are the same in both passages, and the "Saulveur" stands as ultimate source for the "wine" in both. He is the speaker in John 7; His presence in the Prologue is suggested by the reference to the *nopces de Cana*, where He transformed water into wine.[8]

Seekers of Hidden Wisdom

The Tippler

Three of the five prologues (four of six if we include the "Ancien Prologue au Quart Livre") begin with a dedication to *beuveurs*, "boozers," as well as to the gouty and poxy. These are, no doubt, the patients whom Dr. Rabelais wishes to entertain with his droll stories. As a churchman and member of a preaching order, Rabelais could have conceived of his entire "congregation of sinners," his reading public, as spiritually ailing patients. But the illustrious boozer is much more than an ailing sinner: he is a seeker, thirsty for knowledge. *Beuveur* is equated with *philosophe* by Pantagruel who, astonished at Panurge's apparent wisdom, exclaims: "Since the last rains you have become a great guzzler — I should say philosopher" (TL.viii; my trans.). The equation guzzler = philospher is linked to Plato's *Symposium,* where all the philosophers present were hearty boozers. The ability to philosophize depends on drinking as well as on maturity in the Prologue to TL: "Now you are not young; and so you are equipped to philosophize — vinously and not vainly, and therefore metaphysically — and so to be raised at once to the Bacchic Council" (p. 281).[9]

Rabelais's boozers must be philosophers *and* "devout and honest people [*gens de bien*], drinkers of prime vintage and those gouty folk who owe homage to no man" (Prologue to TL; my trans.); they must incarnate the paradox of "wholesome disease," i.e., they must be sinners sincerely seeking a cure, as in the numerous biblical texts where the thirsty sinner craves righteousness.[10] Philo designates the true student of wisdom (*illi qui exercitatione disciplinarum vescuntur ac delectantur*) as a member of a society for sharing wine (*societas compotantium vinum*), since wine functions as the drink of Wisdom.[11] The merrymakers at the symposium form just such a society of wisdom seekers, imbibing knowledge in frivolous disguise. Plato furnishes an archetypal example of *serio ludere* in suggesting the equivalence between merriment and wisdom.

The tippler who seeks true wisdom slakes his thirst with the wine which is equivalent to the marrow in the bone, which is in turn identical to the precious drugs within the Silenus box and to the divine wisdom of Socrates, that Erasmian saint. The boozers, then, are those who truly seek. To these and to no others, Rabelais wishes to speak.

The Dog

Rabelais finds an equally "ridiculous" incarnation for the true seeker in the metaphor of the dog with his marrow bone. He ironically brings forward Plato in support of his choice because "He is, as

Plato says in the second book of the *Republic,* the most philosophical beast in the world." The explicit reference to Plato provides a vital clue to the way in which the canine metaphor should be understood:

A dog, whenever he sees a stranger, is angry; when an acquaintance, he welcomes him, although the one has never done him any harm, nor the other any good. Did this never strike you as curious?

The matter never struck me before; but I quite recognize the truth of your remark.

And surely this instinct of the dog is very charming; your dog is a true philosopher.

Why?

Why, because he distinguishes the face of a friend and of an enemy only by the criterion of knowing and not knowing. And must not an animal be a lover of learning who determines what he likes and dislikes by the test of knowledge and ignorance? [12]

The dog stands as a figure of the true lover of learning. Socrates' context, as usual, is ironic but serious in real intent; he is describing the qualities necessary in a guardian of the Republic. The guardian must combine the physical vigor of the dog, his swiftness and strength, with his intellectual prowess, philosophy, and spirit. To the qualities named by Socrates, Rabelais adds devotion, care, fervor, prudence, affection, and diligence. Here is a serious model for imitation of the same variety as the Silenus-Socrates; the dogged seeker of wisdom finds his reward at last in a bit of pure essence. No doubt by association with this seeker, Rabelais, in his Prologue to TL, introduces Diogenes the cynic, and relates a story about him to help the reader along in his cups and conversation. Diogenes was such a rare and joyful man that Alexander the Great (though a pupil of Aristotle) would have preferred to be Diogenes, if he were not Alexander.

The association between the dog and the cynic, natural enough in itself, was probably taken directly from Erasmus's *Sileni Alcibiades,* since Rabelais uses approximately the same words. Erasmus's passage further indicates the link between Silenus, Socrates, and Diogenes: "Another Silenus was Diogenes, whom the mob considered a dog. But it was about this 'dog' that a divine observation was made by Alexander the Great, the fine flower of princes, it seems, when in his admiration for so great a soul he said 'If I were not Alexander, I would wish to be Diogenes,' though he ought all the more to have wished for the soul of Diogenes, for the very reason that he was Alexander." [13] Diogenes, Silenus, and Socrates stand for Rabelais and his work as well as for the seeker (and possessor) of true wisdom. The link between Diogenes with (or inside) his barrel and Rabelais's own barrel full of wit and wisdom is made explicit: "I am about to re-broach my cask . . . of Pantagrueline sentences. You have license from me to call them Diogenical" (pp. 284–85). Diogenes represents wisdom within the apparent absurdity of the "canine" exterior, and he may be added to the list of container-contents metaphors: the wine in the bottle, Rabelais's (Socratic) wisdom in his (barrel) books, precious spices in the (Socrates) Silenus box, the marrow in the bone, etc. As the philosopher with the lantern, Diogenes might stand for a paragon of all true seekers who see through worldly distractions. His self-sufficiency, his uncomplicated mode of life, and his indifference to luxury led Alexander, of all men the most immersed in worldly concerns, to envy him. His simplicity may have led Rabelais to associate Diogenes with the Evangelical ideal of *simplicitas*.

As a cynic, a "dog," Diogenes seeks out the marrow, which proves to be a complex symbol for spiritual, as well as bodily, food. The equation of marrow with substance or essence undoubtedly hearkens back to Plato's explanation of the creation of mankind:

> The bones . . . were made as follows. The first principle . . . was the generation of the marrow. For the bonds of life which unite the soul with the body are made fast there, and they are the root and foundation of the human race. . . . God [the Demiurge] . . . made the marrow . . . to be a universal seed of the whole race of mankind; and in this seed he then planted and enclosed the souls. . . .[14]

The ancient Greeks considered the brain to be a large reservoir of semen, the spine a conduit through which this "grey matter" flowed to the reproductive organs. Through this conduit, too, the souls or animal spirits pass on to the future fetus in the act of generation.[15] This is the original marrow implanted by the Demiurge which is passed on "to be a universal seed of the whole race of mankind." This "aliment elaboure a perfection de nature," "food refined to the peak of natural perfection," "first principle" and habitation of the soul, may be eaten, and thereby may transfer its properties to the consumer. As nutriment, Galen compares marrow (which feeds and sustains the bones which enclose it) to the blood which feeds the organs, and to the wine, which he believes is transformed almost instantly into blood.[16]

A close study of the Rabelaisian metaphors of the tippler, a participant in the symposium, and the dog has revealed his constant reliance on Plato. In the Prologue to *Gargantua,* he refers overtly to the *Symposium,* while he covertly relies on the *Republic* and *Timaeus.* The Socratic metaphor with which Rabelais introduces his writings is continued throughout; he displays sustained Socratic irony in the very way in which he uses Plato's texts with apparent flippancy, but with a genuinely serious purpose, and with a consistency which lends additional coherence to his work.

The Hermetic Metaphor of the Outer and the Inner: The Contents

Laughter

Rabelais compares his own offering to Diogenes' "war effort." [17] As Diogenes rolled his barrel in order not to appear idle, so Rabelais broaches his winecask to offer the content to us, his readers. The content is joy, a gift of God's grace depicted in ideal form in Thélème and elsewhere in simpler, more earthy ways. It is presented to the reader as a cure for body and soul alike. As scholar-physician-priest, Rabelais offers *salut,* "health, wealth, and eternal life," to all his patients, his reading public. Wolfgang Raible emphasizes the literal aspect of Rabelais's "cure," since laughter was considered "good medicine" by many Renaissance writers. The *topos,* he avers, may be found in Boccaccio's *Decamerone,* in Marguerite de Navarre's *Heptaméron,* and in Bonaventure des Périers's *Nouvelles recréations et joyeux devis.* Raible quotes Gabriello Fallope (1526–62), a student of Vesalius, on therapy for syphilitics, of whom Rabelais also frequently speaks: "those who are joyful and laugh at illness, who are never downhearted, get well twice as fast." Raible also notes a spiritual application of the *topos:* the patients whom Rabelais addresses are ill in soul as well as in body.[18] But a Renaissance physician, believing in the fourfold soul of man, would go further. Laughter, a mental phenomenon, would influence bodily welfare, because the higher dominates the lower. The higher souls (rational and intellective), being more nearly perfect and less terrestrial, would of course "pass on" to the animal and vegetative souls any benefit they might receive. For Rabelais, the joy which springs from the spirit is the greatest, most nearly divine gift to the entire man. According to a Christian tradition assimilated from the Stoics and Philo Judaeus, true wisdom, far from being somber and gloomy or heavy with care, is joyous and friendly. The source of the soul's wisdom, the Good News, is joyful news, enough to make a man drunk with happiness. For Philo, the true philosopher is a laughing, self-intoxicating man, who like a wine barrel is filled with divine wisdom.[19] Philo adapts earthy Old Testament scenes to express the same idea: he interprets Isaac sporting with his wife Rebecca, in Genesis 26:8, as a figure of the playful soul filled with divine wisdom.[20] Rabelais's mentor Erasmus also champions joyous Christianity: "Spiritum, optimam nostri partem, a quo ceu fonte felicitas omnis nostra proficiscitur, quoque Deo copulamur . . . ," "the spirit is the highest of our parts. From it, as from a fountain, all our happiness springs, and through it we are joined to God." [21] Laughter, generally considered lowly or crude, "opens up" to reveal divine truth. In this way, Rabelais's cure bears close resemblance to contemporary Franciscan sermons, where the preacher attempted to gain and to hold the attention of his audience by bawdy stories, and then to convey the most sacred Christian truths through ribald similes.[22] Likewise, Renaissance artists like Giovanni da Udine, having rediscovered the ancient stucco technique, exploited the symbolic value of the laughter-provoking grotesque. Luca Signorelli, as early as 1499–1504, had painted the Cathedral of Orvieto with grotesques; Pinturicchio was commissioned in 1502 to paint the cathedral library in Siena in this style. Raphael, in 1515, painted grotesques in the papal *loggia* of the Castello Sant'Angelo.[23] It is interesting to note the occasional obscenity of these paintings which decorate cathedral sanctuaries and other holy places. Michelangelo planned to use grotesques to decorate the upper part of the Medici chapel. Intended to communicate truths in ludicrous guise to the devout, they were visually to represent Pico's definition of the Orphic hymn. Divine secrets were to be imparted disguised as fables so that none but the initiates might perceive anything but trite and amusing stories.[24] Thus Rabelais's Franciscan, as well as his humanistic, heritage would have taught him that laughter through ribald joking is a most effective means of making plain, by a flash of intuition, a truth beneath the droll covering. Rabelais plays a game of hide-and-seek with the reader, revealing his message by his very means of concealment.

The power of laughter as a means of immediate communication to the soul closely parallels the contemporary notion of the Neoplatonic and hermetic *Nous* as something that all knowing creatures share. Rabelais, who read Macrobius (4.xxv–xxviii), may have kept his *Commentary* in the back of his mind as he speculated on the divine source of merriment. *Mens* or *Nous,* says Macrobius, taken from the eternal stellar fires, allows man to participate in pure divinity. Mind is the great chain which binds everything together (Plotinus 1.1.8). Macrobius also describes the soul by the image of a spring, ever-renewed source of great rivers (2.16). The wine, living font, is also a spring which feeds the great river of healing laughter. Just as *Nous* raises man above the rest of nature, his ability to laugh sets man off from all other creatures: "Mieux est de ris que de larmes escripre,/Pour ce que rire est le propre de l'homme," "It is better to write of laughter than tears, since laughter is proper to man" (G, "Aux Lecteurs," p. 2). The spontaneity of communion in laughter, which like the great chain of *Nous* binds men together, might well have led Rabelais to speculate on its divine origin. It has the immediacy of divine revelation, and is likewise irresistible. Laughter is the immediate effect of the gift of Grace. But at the end of book five, Rabelais acknowledges that the wine, as spirit and cause of laughter, is more important than its effect: "Et icy mainctenons que non rire, ains boyre est le propre de l'homme: je ne dis boyre simplement et absoluement, car aussi bien beuvent les bestes; je dis boyre vin bon et fraiz. Notez, amys, que de vin divin on devient," "And we here maintain that not laughter but drinking is proper to man. I don't mean simple, unadorned drinking because the beasts drink as well. I mean drinking good cool wine. Note well, my friends, that through wine one becomes divine" (CL. xlv.883; my trans.).[25] Through wine we become divine, puns Rabelais; wine, then, resembles *Nous,* the holy spirits in which we all may share.[26]

33

Wine

The theme of the wine, which, along with its effects, may at first lack grandeur and even appear vile and ridiculous, becomes increasingly admirable the longer it is contemplated. It fits to perfection Erasmus's definition of a Silenus as "a thing which in appearance (at first blush . . .) seems ridiculous and contemptible, but on closer and deeper examination proves to be admirable." [27] An obvious leitmotiv, it binds the ostensibly scattered elements of Rabelais's five books into a closer unity than has ever been suspected. For although his metaphorical use of wine and *Pantagruelisme* evolves in some particulars, the underlying concepts are the same from *Gargantua* through the *Dive Bouteille*. Rabelais's insistence on food and drink has led the popular imagination, prone to confuse the author with his characters and with the always fictitious narrator, to picture him as a drunken, ribald *bon vivant*. The image of a depraved Rabelais is oddly similar to the Silenus-Socrates of the Prologue to G, but any wary reader notices the superhuman wisdom behind the comic mask. The relation of Silenus to Socrates corresponds exactly to that of wine to wisdom: Silenus, god of wine, conceals Socrates, wisdom incarnate. The wine reveals a multitude of Christian and classical symbols that tell us what the Good Life really is, how we must live it, and why. Wine is literally a part of the Good Life, since wine drinking contributes to joy and physical pleasure; wine stands for Rabelais's books (cf. his books as wine casks in the Prologue to TL), which also give pleasure to the reader; wine symbolizes the holy spirit(s), which inspire the poet and gladden his heart. Wine benefits the drinker on three levels, which correspond to tripartite man: body (physical pleasure), soul (mental enjoyment), and spirit (divine inspiration).

Food and Wine as Sources of Inspiration

Food and wine metaphorically represent the true essence which Rabelais's seekers may find if they search diligently and with good will. Armed with this knowledge, we can return to Rabelais's synthesis at the end of the Prologue to G and understand it more fully. Crack the bone like the philosophical dog, but, Rabelais had warned, beware of absurd interpretations! Do not, by burning much oil in your lamps, "scab over" the text with allegories. Rather, without really thinking about it, read while drinking and its meaning will come to you in a flash of insight. For, says Rabelais, I only write while eating and drinking, "A la composition de ce livre seigneurial, je ne perdiz ne emploiay oncques plus, ny aultre temps que celluy qui estoit estably à prendre ma réfection corporelle, sçavoir est beuvant et mangeant" (Prologue to G. 5). Here, Jacques Boulenger incredulously comments, "Ainsi Rabelais aurait dicté son merveilleux livre tout en prenant ses repas. C'est difficile à croire," "So Rabelais is supposed to have dictated his marvelous book while taking his meals. It's hard to believe!"[28] Difficult indeed if this passage is taken at face value. But Rabelais names ancient authority for his strange writing habits: "Homer, paragon of all philologers" and "Ennius, father of the Latin poets."[29] This reference leads the reader to seek a solution to the riddle in the ancient belief that intellectual and sexual power were both directly connected with the "life fluid" in the body. A fat, sleek young man would therefore enjoy greater vigor than a "dried out," thin one. From Plautus' time at least, taking nourishment, feasting, was synonymous with benefitting the genius, "genio meo multa bona faciam" (*Pers.* 263). In Petronius' *Satyricon,* wine in particular was identified with life fluid, as even Trimalchio knows: "vita vinum est" (347).[30] Ovid identifies wine and genius (*Fasti,* etc.). By eating and drinking, he would automatically benefit his creative powers, which would naturally be at their height at meal time.

"Philologer" provides another key to the hidden content of the passage. As an enthusiastic student of Greek, Rabelais probably meant the word literally: Homer, paragon of those who love the word, i.e., paragon of poets and of writers in general.[31] Rabelais's biblical training would automatically bring to his mind other connotations: "In the beginning was the Word, [*logos*] . . ." (John 1:1). The Word, the Creative Principle, the essence or spirit of the world, all are stoic and Neoplatonic ideas with which Rabelais could have been familiar through both Christian and classical readings. Homer, philologer like all true poets, was inspired, filled with the creative spirit, with the wine of divine wisdom. Likewise, the nourishment on which Rabelais feeds constantly while writing his books is metaphorically poetic inspiration both by the Muses and by the Holy Spirit.

By contrast to the brilliant flash of inspiration that reaches the poet from a divine, vinous source, lamp oil symbolizes the faint glow, a partial illumination at best, afforded by study and unaided reason. A time of repose is the proper time to write of exalted matters. Horace confirms this, too, although his verse has been suspected of smelling more of wine than oil. The same has been said about Rabelais's books, but he justifies himself by reminding us of the delicious, celestial odor of wine compared to the stench of oil.

Alongside the classical poetic tradition, which values inspiration as much as *techne,* runs the tradition of Jewish wisdom literature that presents the wise man as recipient of sudden insight, not as one who has gained knowledge by long and painful development. The perfect nature is exemplified in the Old Testament by Isaac, who from his birth was graced by divine wisdom, and who therefore was able to skip the stages of mental growth which the ordinary mortal must struggle through.[32]

If wine and food are symbols for the divine inspiration which feeds the genius, and through which one may "savor" wisdom (*sçavoir*), then lamp oil, also a traditional symbol for "busy-ness" (*negotium*), is positively repulsive.[33] "L'odeur du vin, o combien plus est friant, riant, priant, plus céleste et délicieux que d'huille" (Prologue to G. 6). Rabelais's list of adjectives may be taken literally. The odor of wine is *friant,* exciting us to thirst, *riant, joyeux* — the quality closest to Rabelais's heart, which characterizes his style and distinguishes the personalities of Gargantua and his son. Wine is *céleste* since it is a divine draft and it must be *délicieux* if it is to be worthy of the gods. This description closely matches that of "le piot" in *Pantagruel*: "Celle nectaricque, délicieuse, précieuse, céleste, joyeuse et déificque liqueur qu'on nomme le piot" (P.i.172). The oil, human industry and unrevealed knowledge gained by plodding reason, is, by comparison to wine, "ord et sale." Wine and oil oppose divine wisdom to human logic, a theme that dominates the *Tiers Livre* and crops up occasionally in the first two books as well. True insight, as the word itself implies, comes only through a flash of inspiration.[34] This is how Rabelais composes while eating and how he hopes that we, his readers, will understand him.

When he asks himself just what his books will accomplish, he confesses ignorance: "Wait a little, till I've swallowed a draft from this bottle. It is my [one true Helicon, it is my caballine spring,] my sole enthusiasm" (Prologueto TL.284; party my trans.). The *Dive Bouteille* chapters of the fifth book elaborate this passage: Rabelais, like Panurge, awaits a revelation from the bottle, a divine revelation in answer to his questions. Besides evoking the Mount of the Muses, "caballine spring" contains a deliberate ambiguity, like most of Rabelais's references, for he uses it to recall the idea of his work as a "religious cabala" (Prologue to P). Inspiration gushes forth not only from Rabelais's bottle, a Pegasus spring, but from a hidden, divine source as well, since *enthusiasme* refers both to the Muses, and to possession by, communion with, God.

The Word Is the Wine in Rabelais's Barrel
(The Parable of the "parolles gelées")

Directly from his "caballine boozing" Rabelais receives the words which entertain, inform, and, he hopes, inspire the reader, "As I drink I here deliberate, discourse, resolve, and conclude. After the epilogue I laugh, write, compose, and drink again" (Prologue to TL.284). His words proceed from drinking and lead back to it in a perpetual circle of inspiration. The words are in themselves drink for the reader, a heady draft, whether taken at face value or not.

Every reader of Rabelais realizes how exuberantly and almost independently alive is his universe of words. His nouns and adjectives are heaped up to transform what they describe or sometimes even to create their object. In many episodes, the word alone is protagonist.[35] The word is the wine in Rabelais's barrel, it is obviously also the wisdom that the boozer, the dog, and Panurge seek;[36] it is *logos* which already in the dawn of Christianity had become identified as Christ.

The "parolles gelées" (QL.lv–lvi), one of the best known instances where words considered in themselves hold the spotlight, allegorizes certain abstract problems of language. At the same time, the parable conveys a concrete meaning. On the abstract plane, Rabelais plays with the distinction between the beauty of a word per se and its meaning; between aesthetic and metaphysical values. *Parolle* also, consistent with its etymology, means a parable, a story presented in a beautiful crystalline form with wonderfully colorful imagery, but which remains unintelligible until "warmed into life," melted down to its essential meaning. The *parolle gelée* also represents the visual versus the audible word, written versus spoken. Lifeless in unspoken (unread) form, it becomes alive and meaningful only to melt away instantly. Words are like hard candies: as they are "eaten" (understood), they melt into nothingness, leaving only a fleeting taste behind.[37] Through the use of taste, touch, and sight to describe language, Rabelais approaches the synesthesia of late nineteenth-century poetry. Jean Guiton recognizes a close kinship between Rabelais's *dragée* "perlée de diverses couleurs," "multicolored, candied words" and Rimbaud's "Confiture exquise aux 'bons' poètes," "exquisite confections of the so-called good poets" from the *Bateau ivre*.[38] As frozen word, it could stand not only for any written text but for the Scriptures in particular, especially since these are known as the *Parole de Dieu*. The *sacres bibles* contain the word of God in suspended animation, meaningless until a reader appears to reawaken the message. The *parolles* stand for Rabelais's own work as well: both the Bible and Rabelais's writings overflow with the sounds described in the parable: the noise of battle, whinnies of horses, cries of women and children, swear words and more "unmentionable" sounds. Like the breviary stuff, the words remain unspoiled, "bottled up" in their frozen form, waiting to be "drunk in."

If the reader wishes to drink in the *parolles,* he must first thaw them by determining the concrete meaning of the text. The parable begins, as so many Rabelaisian episodes do, with a banquet. The resulting state of physical well-being, of psychic harmony, of *communion,* like that of Plato's revelers at the symposium, seems to presage the revelation of a new truth, just as did the Last Supper before Jesus began to speak. Pantagruel interrupts the convivial conversation; he is first to hear people talking in the air. When, after great effort, the remainder of the company begins to hear the noises, Panurge bursts into a characteristic chant of fear, a long comic monologue alternating between the urgent request "Let's flee!" and elaborations on how and why flight is advisable. But Pantagruel, shaming him into silence, has the "last word," as did Jesus and Socrates. He "sermonizes" to the end of the chapter, furnishing a series of classical similes as possible explanations for the disembodied words. The passage merits closer analysis:

"I have read that a philosopher named Petron was of the opinion that there were several worlds touching each other in the figure of an equilateral triangle. In the marrow and center of them, he said, was the abode of Truth and the habitation of the Words, the Ideas, the Exemplars, and portraits of all things past and future; and around them was our world of time. In certain years, at long intervals, part of these falls on humans like distillations, and as the dew fell on the fleece of Gideon, remaining there reserved for the future, awaiting the consummation of the millennium" (QL.lv; my trans.).

Pantagruel's stature and wisdom make him a hero in the Greek sense, larger than life, intermediate between man and the gods (cf. QL.xxvi–xxviii). As a more nearly perfect being, he is privileged to hear the Words first, to see the Platonic Ideas that are too quintessential to be perceived by the common herd. Rabelais's passage is drawn almost literally from Plutarch, who speaks of *logoi,* variously translated as accounts or reports, on the Plain of Truth.[39] As good boozers, Pantagruel and his company have merited a revelation of eternal truths. These, however, are "but a dream of that highest rite and initiation," the "mot de la Dive Bouteille," for which Panurge sighs at the end of the parable. Rabelais "Christianizes" Plutarch by introducing the fleece of Gideon (Judg. 6:36–40), where God communicates to Gideon through a visible "word" (i.e., dew) rather than by direct speech.[40] Through this allusion, Rabelais implies that God is the actual source of the Words, Forms, and Patterns on the Plain of Truth. Only a few of these Words fall like dew on the fortunate and virtuous listeners, since most words remain fixed "until the consummation of the millennium." Here Rabelais, the Christian, interpolates somewhat, for Plutarch nowhere mentions a millennium. To Rabelais, the opposition of time and eternity, and the "highest rite and initiation," of which the earthly one is but a dreamy foreshadowing, cannot fail to have an apocalyptic ring. Obviously, all divine truth cannot be revealed to any mortal at any time. Even the revelation of the Scripture is at best partial, fragmentary, a mere preview. St. Paul's "Now we see in a mirror dimly, but then face to face" (1 Cor. 13:12) seems appropriate here: the confused noises we now hear will become clear at "the consummation of the millennium." Pantagruel continues: "Besides, Antiphanes said Plato's doctrine was like words in some distant country that, when spoken in the depths of winter, freeze and congeal in the frigid air and are not heard. Similarly, what Plato taught the young children was scarcely understood (*entendu*) by them until they had become old" (QL.lv; my trans.). Here again, Rabelais follows Plutarch very closely but, oddly enough, the humorous quality of Plutarch's text contrasts sharply with Pantagruel's seriousness.[41] For him, the profundity of Plato's discourse, the poetic and metaphorical veil he uses, operates like the Silenus box to hide, perhaps forever, in a beautiful shell, the true meaning within. Rabelais's own words, like Plato's, may become clear to the initiate when he has become old. But, for most readers, the words will never melt.

Rabelais also quotes Aristotle (*Rhet.* 3.2), who refers to Homer's winged words that, since they move, must be animated or ensouled. "I remember, too, that Aristotle maintains Homer's words to be bounding, flying, and moving, and consequently alive [*animées* = ensouled]" (QL.lv.568). What Aristotle says of Homer can be applied to poets in general, whose words are ensouled because they communicate a divine essence. Pantagruel's suggestion that the words come from the severed head of Orpheus ("Nous serions bien esbahiz si c'estoient les teste et lyre de Orpheus.") strengthens the link between Rabelais's parable and hermetic literature, since Orpheus is often invoked in the Middle Ages and Renaissance as a master magician, holder of the keys to the secrets of the universe. The link with classical poetry in its most spiritual, divine form is implicit, too, in the reference to Homer (paragon of all philologers, cf. Prologue to G) and to Orpheus.[42] Through his song, Orpheus raised himself to the status of demigod, for until his voice was drowned out by the shouts of the Bacchic revelers, he overcame the world, the underworld, and even death itself. But the divine element is not the poet but his poetry, for, though the poet dies, his song remains behind long after his soul has fled. The word preexists and remains, it is immortal, it creates, it is more real than the outer world, it is *logos*.

The end of the parable (QL.lvi) resumes a much lighter tone, alternating between descriptions of how the frozen words look and how they sound as they thaw, and lively puns on *parolle*. The reader begins to wonder if the *parolles* have divine significance after all, or if they are merely the frozen record of last year's battle between the

Arismapiens and the Nephelibates. Pliny (7.22) and Herodotus (4.27) both list Arimaspians in their account of fabulous tribes of the far North, whose strange appearance and habits are only known by hearsay.[43] Nephelibates, Greek for cloud walkers or cloud wanderers, are still more fabulous and have remained unknown to the source hunters. They could be thought of as the gods, the angels, or the heavenly hosts.[44] The handful of *parolles,* cast upon the deck, thaw and, as they do, a series of confusing sounds become audible: "hin, hin, hin, hin, his, ticque, torche, lorgne, brededin, brededac, frr, frrrr . . . goth, magoth" (QL.lvi.693).[45] In this medley of "motz barbares," only two stand out immediately as meaningful: *goth* and *magoth.* In two other passages, Rabelais uses Goth as invective against his hypocritical enemies.[46] In the first of these texts he uses both *Gotz* and *magotz:*

> Cy n'entrez pas, hypocrites, bigotz,
> Vieux matagotz, marmiteux, borsoufléz,
> Torcoulx, badaux, plus que n'estoient les Gotz
> Ny Ostrogotz, précurseurs des magotz
> Haires, cagotz. . . . (G. liv. 151)

> Enter not here, vile hypocrites and bigots,
> Pious old apes, and puffed-up snivellers,
> Wry-necked creatures sawnier than the Goths,
> Or Ostrogoths, precursors of Gog and Magog
> Woebegone scoundrels . . . (G. liv. 153).

In the second passage *Gothz* is used as symbol of the Dark Ages when they snuffed out the light of learning: "Le temps estoit encores ténébreux et sentant l'infélicité et calamité des Gothz, qui avoient mis à destruction toute bonne litérature" (P.viii.204). The Goth is the enemy of enlightenment and of poetry, he is a northern barbarian (an *Arismapien*) through whose native waters Pantagruel and his company are sailing. The combination "goth, magoth," together with the words which remain "until the consummation of the millennium," confirm the lurking apocalyptic character of the entire parable. This battle, partly preserved in frozen form, will also remain until the millenium. These "Gotz . . . précurseurs des magotz" who may not enter Thélème are not only enemies of evangelism and humanistic learning, they are, by acoustic assimilation, Gog and Magog, the final Enemy of the Apocalypse:

And when the thousand years are ended, Satan will be loosed from his prison and will come out to deceive the nations which are at the four corners of the earth, that is, Gog and Magog, to gather them for battle; their number is like the sand of the sea. And they marched up over the broad earth and surrounded the camp of the saints and the beloved city; but fire came down from heaven and consumed them, and the devil who had deceived them was thrown into the lake of fire and brimstone where the beast and the false prophet were and they will be tormented day and night for ever and ever.

(Rev. 20:7–10)

Gog, covering the earth like a cloud, descends from the north to clash with Israel in Ezekiel 38:15–16, a passage which could either predict the invasion of Rome by Germanic hordes or prefigure the final battle:

You will . . . come from your place out of the uttermost parts of the north, you and many peoples with you, all of them riding on horses, a great host, a mighty army; you will come up against my people Israel, like a cloud covering the land. In the latter days I will bring you against my land.

The frozen record of battle, even though it took place "last year," has reached the Plain of Truth where there is no time. Our Rabelaisian heroes "glimpse" (given the warlike character of the noises they hear) the actual final battel of the millennium, which takes place "out of time," since the struggle between the dark and the light is eternal.

The end of the world is not yet come, however. The solemnity of the parabolic message is balanced by play with puns on *parolle:* words being given, words being sold, and on "motz de gueule," [47] which the author would like to preserve in frozen form because of their intrinsic beauty, but Pantagruel refuses, since there is no use hoarding something as plentiful as are "motz de gueule" among hearty Pantagruelistes. Rabelais pokes fun at his own delight in using meaningless words for the sheer pleasure of the word in itself, which remains "frozen" since it is unintelligible. They are "motz de gueule" because they are the drunken sounds made by Pantagruelistes in their cups (cf. "Les Propos des bien yvres"). By their red color, these words represent the wine, which Pantagruel rejects in frozen form, since there is no shortage of the liquid. Rabelais cannot resist further puns which are suggested by word association: Panurge angers Frère Jean by taking him at his word (il le vous print au mot sus l'instant qu'il ne s'en doubtoit mie"); Frère Jean threatens to take Panurge, future cuckold, by the horns "comme un veau." The final word is serious, though: they have received revelations of the far-distant future, yet the travelers have not received the specific revelation they seek: the "mot de la Dive Bouteille."

Rabelais's preoccupation with the word in itself, the word as autonomous creative force, and with the word as *logos,* evokes other Christian associations as well. His contemporary Cornelius Agrippa, particularly interested in demonstrating the orthodoxy of Neoplatonists, attributes trinitarian notions to them, and cites Augustine, Porphyry, Plotinus, and Philo as his authorities. God is divided into three persons: the Father of the universe, the Son and highest Understanding, and the Spirit or world Soul. The Son, also called the First Spirit or Divine Understanding, proceeds from the Father like a word which materializes without a speaker, or like a light emanating from another light. This is why the Son has been called *logos,* the Word.[48] Similarly, in Rabelais, Christ is *logos,* Gospel is *logos, logos* is the divine wine of the *Dive Bouteille* (CL.xlv.883). Rabelais's words, frozen or otherwise, participate on many levels in the divine *logos;* they vibrate in tune with celestial harmony. The virtue of a thing is hidden within the sound which represents it, independent of any meaning and before the sound is formed into spoken or written word: "The intrinsic 'names' of things are certain rays that are everywhere present, and that retain their force as long as the essence of the thing remains dominant in them . . . Any word . . . has meaning — first through the influence of celestial harmony, then through man's imposition . . . ; when the two meanings coincide . . . the word then becomes very potent in action since it has double virtue . . . natural and voluntary." [49]

Continuous discourse is naturally more powerful than are single words because of the cumulative effect of individual meaning and harmony, plus the complex truth the words convey.[50] Rabelais inebriates his boozers through accumulations of heady sounds. The occult energy which communicates itself to the reader is inspiration and laughter, a divine, stellar spark.

It is evident that Rabelais occupies an important place in the long and respectable line of hermetic writers in the Christian and Neoplatonic tradition, since he fully exploits the cryptic commonplace of the container and its contents in a wealth of protean transformations. The grotesque box which contains precious drugs becomes the bottle containing the wine = the bone with its marrow = the barrel and its contents (Diogenes and his wisdom, good hope, wine, Rabelais's wisdom) = the book and its words = the word and its meaning = the *logos* and *Evangelion* (the Good News).

A container with unknown contents presupposes a seeker whose curiosity will lead him to discover the hidden divinity within. This seeker is Rabelais's boozer whose thirst may be slaked, or the poxy whose disease may be cured by precious drugs.

As to the reader, provided he be a persistent seeker, almost any passage in Rabelais will prove to have multiple hidden associations that form a coherent message. The cumulative evidence tends to indicate that Rabelais meant literally what he promised in the thesis of the Prologue to G, and that his disclaimer in the antithesis proposed to throw his enemies off the track.

The effect of Rabelais's drollery upon the seeker — be he boozer, poxy, or philologer (a lover of letters, i.e., the careful reader) — is laughter, just as the effect of wine and good companionship is heady gaiety. On a more esoteric level, the effect of the Good News, of his Evangelical message is unearthly joy.

Chapter 2

The Wine Incarnate

Bacchus and Silenus take their first bow in the Prologue to *Gargantua* and their last one in the final chapters of the fifth book. Numerous overt references to them are scattered throughout the text as well, but Rabelais intends his tutelary deities to exercise their most decisive influence on a more subterranean level. Just as God is said to manifest Himself in the world indirectly, so Rabelais's Bacchus reveals himself to the reader through his effects: the excitement, joy, and heat of the wine with which he is often identified. Dionysus or Bacchus, god of the *Dive Bouteille,* arises from the complex Greco-Christian tradition, from which Erasmus's Silenus also derives. Rabelais's Silenus-Bacchus owes a considerable debt to Erasmus's bold, playfully serious identification of Silenus with Diogenes, Socrates, the Scriptures, the Sacraments, Christ, and even God Himself.[1] These equations, which startle the modern reader, depend upon *topoi* which were current in the Renaissance, and which must be reestablished before a balanced view of Rabelais's Bacchus may be presented.

Bacchus = Christ

Despite the ostensible return to "pure" classical learning, the treatment of the myth of Bacchus in the Renaissance continues a gradual assimilation of pagan and Christian symbolism which began when Christianity spread beyond the borders of Palestine into other parts of the Roman Empire. The impulse to use Bacchus as a Christian symbol was strengthened by the similarity of the Christian mysteries to the ancient myths of Dionysus. In the Greek theaters of Dionysus, the *Agon,* part of the complex ceremonies in honor of the god, represented the conflict between good and evil forces, between summer and winter, life and death. The good force is killed, torn apart, and eaten in a communal feast only to rise again.[2] The language of John the gospel writer evokes the violence of the Dionysian frenzy with which he was undoubtedly familiar: "Unless you eat the flesh of the Son of Man and drink His blood, you shall have no life in you; he who eats My flesh and drinks My blood has eternal life, and I will raise him up at the last day" (John 6:54-55). The cult of Orpheus offers another close parallel to Christianity, for Orpheus, too, voyaged through the underworld and rose again; he, too, died a death of martyrdom, torn apart by the Maenads.[3]

The survival of the Dionysian and orphic cults in St. Augustine's lifetime caused him to write diatribes against them, vilifying them as obscene.[4] Although these cults may have become corrupt by the fourth century A.D., it is more likely that Augustine feared the rivalry of the mystery cults because of their similarity to his newly adopted religion, and used the entire gamut of classical rhetorical exaggeration in an effort to discredit them. He magnifies the license of the phallic rites, omitting any mention of their *raison d'être* as symbols of the eternal renewal of life.

Many biblical commonplaces, e.g., the "song of the vine" which goes through the Old and New Testaments, also prepare the ground for identifying Christ as Bacchus. The "vine" in the Old Testament stands for Israel;[5] in the New Testament parable, the vineyard is the faith or service of God, the vinedressers are Israel, and the son of the owner is Christ.[6] The "song" goes through yet another transformation in the patristic period, e.g., in a sermon of St. Zeno, where the vine becomes the Synagogue in the Old Testament and the Church in the Christian era.[7] This "vine" is grafted onto the stock of Jesus Christ, the true vine, with which Bacchus is also identified.[8]

Certain Greek Church Fathers, who realized that the old, well-known myths would make more of an impact on their audience than the relatively unfamiliar Judeo-Christian scriptures, often used ancient Greek texts as a basis for their sermons. There is a constant ambiguity in their attitude toward Bacchus, whom they at times see as a prefiguration of Christ.[9] Christ, in turn, is depicted on the Damascene chalice as a holier Bacchus, enthroned among trailing grapevines. Yet Bacchus epitomizes debasement and rejection of grace. Clement of Alexandria, using the *Bacchae* of Euripides as a text for a sermon, contrasts the *sophrosyne*, "moderation," of the blessed state with the deplorable behavior of the "drunken" Pentheus, who, falling under the sway of Bacchus, dresses in feminine attire to spy out the secrets of the Maenads. The Maenads symbolize for Clement the disorders of paganism which must be supplanted by the chorus of the just.[10] Ironically, this same chorus of the just, as it follows the triumphal chariot of Faith in Renaissance paintings and bas-reliefs, or as it contorts itself in grief at the foot of the cross, is depicted in poses copied directly from Greek and Roman paintings representing Maenads in Dionysiac processions.[11]

The Renaissance humanists used Bacchus as both a concrete and an abstract symbol to represent Christian and pagan mysteries. Nicholas of Cusa's *coincidentia oppositorum,* "coincidence of opposites," summarizes in an oxymoron the same concept which Bacchus or the Graces allegorize: the ultimate unity of contradictions. Just as the Three Graces show three aspects of the one goddess of love, Venus (*voluptas, castitas, pulchritudo,* "sensuality, chastity, beauty"), which do not per se harmonize with each other, so Bacchus symbolizes brutalizing drunkenness and, at the same time, the inspiration and increased strength which wine can provide the moderate drinker. Bacchus symbolizes nature and the lower realm, and yet furnishes the key to heaven.

Both Pico della Mirandola and Cornelius Agrippa make use of Bacchus as a divine symbol. Pico's Dionysus plays a major role in artistic creation and religious experience:

> Thereupon Bacchus, the leader of the Muses, by showing in his mysteries, that is, in the visible signs of nature, the invisible things of God to us who study philosophy, will intoxicate us with the fullness of God's house, in which, if we prove faithful, like Moses, hallowed theology shall come and inspire us with a double frenzy.[12]

For Pico, nature itself is divine and worthy of study, but in the same way that Egyptian hieroglyphics were believed to point toward and to participate in eternal truth, nature corresponds to a higher set of truths which the seeker can only grasp through a revelation accorded after long and patient contemplation of the lower realm. As leader of the Muses, Bacchus provides the key to nature's hieroglyphics: he is at once nature god, and god of artistic creation. Thanks to him, the worshiper may become "drunk" on the fullness of God's house: Pico's metaphors echo the pronouncements of Philo and such Greek Fathers of the Church as Origen.

Where Pico uses Bacchus as a nature god, Agrippa uses him in a highly abstract way to represent the intellective part of celestial or stellar souls, each of whom is divided into two parts: the intellective or knowing, and that part which governs the life of the body. Orpheus called the first part Bacchus, the other Muse. No one can be intoxicated by some Bacchus without first having joined himself to the corresponding Muse. There are nine persons in Bacchus, one for each Muse.[13] Agrippa goes on to list the heavens or spheres (*le ciel des étoiles, la sphère de Saturne, le ciel de Juppiter,* etc.), and for each heaven he names a Bacchus, representing the conscious aspect of the celestial soul, and a Muse. Bacchus, identified with knowing, appears in nine different ways (nine for the planets, nine for the Muses), in a form to guide any suppliant no matter which temperament he has: saturnine, solarian, mercurial, etc.

Initiates into the Eleusinian mysteries knew Bacchus primarily as a god of purification. The lion skin that Michelangelo's statue of Bacchus holds recalls that the god brutally purges brutish and ferocious instincts. Flaying, a symbol of renewal through a variety of torture and death, approximates the fate of Bacchus himself and is reminiscent of the fate of Pentheus, taken for a "lion's whelp" in Euripides' *Bacchae*.[14] Bacchus is said to purify and console through the mad raging he produces;[15] one of his symbols is the sieve by which grain is rid of chaff and impurities.[16] The initiate into the mysteries is purged in like manner. Drunkenness itself has, in its aftereffects, a purgative power and is supposed to renew and cleanse the mind.[17] Besides inebriation, several other means of purgation are depicted in the woodcut *Men's Bath* by Dürer, which Wind interprets as a Dionysian mystery.[18] One figure is shown holding a razor (purification by bloodletting or flaying) while another drinks (purification by inebriation). Another stands beside a water tap, while a fourth sniffs a flower. Two

Figure 1. Albrecht Dürer, *Men's Bath* (c. 1498). The Smith, Kline and French Laboratories Collection, '58–150–15. Philadelphia Museum of Art.

musicians play for the benefit of all. The mysteries involve purification of the senses and the humors. Dürer pictures a choleric man gripping the razor, a dry, melancholy person standing beside the water tap, a heavy phlegmatic drinker raises his cup, while the sanguine man sniffs a flower.

Dionysian Furor

The chief method of bacchic purgation involves furor or frenzy. All traditions about furor depend heavily on certain ideas of how a human being may invoke the divine presence.[19] Divinity enters the body of the worshiper through the vapor inhaled from the cliff crevasse at Delphi (Apollo's breath); through the wine and the raw flesh of the sacrificial beast torn apart still living during bacchic frenzy; through chewing the bayberries sacred to Dionysus and Apollo, or drinking milk, honey, or the waters of a holy fountain.

The Alexandrian Church Fathers who first sought to reconcile the Old and New Testaments were imbued with the classical notion of furor which they incorporated into their biblical exegesis. To explain Hannah's apparent drunkenness in the temple (1 Samuel 1:12–14), Noah's drunkenness, or the line "introduxit me in cellam vinariam," "he led me into the wine tavern," of the Song of Solomon 2:4, they applied their idea of furor, a state in which, though perfectly sober, the ecstatic person reels in an apparently drunken frenzy. Philo Judaeus' concise oxymoron, *methē nēphalios* (*sobria ebrietas,* "sober inebriation"), describes this state which he also at times calls "unearthly joy," for God alone is truly happy, he alone enjoys unmixed gladness. Man can only glimpse this gladness if he shakes off some of the shackles of matter; if he ceases for a moment his striving and allows God's grace to fill him, he will then be carried away, raised to the highest point of experience possible for mortals to attain.[20] A few, chosen by God, remain permanently in such an ecstatic state: these are the blessed, the saints. A saint may even be chosen against his will for a joyous experience of such intensity that it will change the entire course of his life. The conversion of Saul is often taken as the paradigm of all such experiences: his vision on the road to Damascus is expressed in the language of the mystery cult as an ecstasy or furor.[21]

Renaissance humanists, fascinated by inspired creativity or ecstatic prophecy, sought to explain it in "natural" terms, the better to utilize it at will. Ficino believed furor to be derived from the spirits of a melancholy humor that, being highly combustible like aqua vitae, can produce mania and exaltation, followed by extreme depression and lethargy. He proposes a regime to achieve a better balance, for if melancholy is tempered with the other humors, phlegm, bile, and blood, the spirits will glow steadily and make possible the highest quality of thought and study. Melancholics, subject to furor, are likewise subject to the ambivalent sway of the planet Saturn. Ficino's program would attract the influence of more benign planets: the Sun, Jupiter, Venus, and Mercury. He proposes an all-around "diet" for the melancholy genius: wine and aromatic foods, sweet odors, pure, sunny air, and music.[22] Agrippa explains waking divination in terms of furor, and, alleging Aristotle as his authority, he explains that divination or furor arises from the melancholy humor. The Sibyls and followers of Bacchus became seers and poets through this humor, which is also called "natural" or "white." When this humor is excited or set alight by some celestial influence like that of Saturn, furor results.[23] Agrippa's doctrines of furor, which coincide largely with those of Ficino, depend upon the classical authorities Plato and Democritus, as well as Aristotle.

Although Agrippa carefully skirts the pitfalls of magic in his acknowledged works, his disciples, like Pierre d'Aban, readily attribute to him writings in which the Magus gives recipes not only for foretelling future events but for controlling them as well.[24] The evidence is strong that Renaissance humanists knew about the classical chants and mystic ceremonies which preceded possession by the god, and which were meant to force revelation of the future and to control subsequent events through the use of hypnotic rhythms.[25] Panurge, who cannot make up his mind whether to marry until he knows that the future will be kind to him, also seeks to bind the future to his desires by magical means.

Renaissance figures made a casual assimilation of classical notions of divination or furor with the inspiration of the Holy Spirit. Agrippa does this in an offhand manner, as though the Christian connotations had been understood from the beginning. He avers that Cicero, fol-

lowing the Stoic opinion, believed that prediction was a divine pre-
rogative. Ptolemy affirmed that no one uninspired by divinity could
prophesy. St. Peter agreed with Ptolemy, saying that a man never
prophesies when he wishes but only when inspired by the Holy Spirit.
The Holy Spirit may descend in three ways: in furor, ravishment, or
dream.[26] Agrippa compares Socrates' daemon with the power which
inspired the Old Testament prophets; both he and Ficino assume that
their readers accept a casual and somewhat naive syncretism which
was certainly not unfamiliar to Rabelais. In another passage on faith
and divine ecstasy, Agrippa identifies inspiration with nectar and
wine, as well as with Christ and Bacchus. He tells us that, after pre-
paring ourselves through a good life, we should devote ourselves, in
total stillness of the senses and tranquility of spirit, to love of God and
religion. In this quiet state we should await the divine ambrosia (that
nectar called by Zaccharia the wine which causes virgins to conceive),
praising and adoring Bacchus who is raised above the heavens, Sover-
eign of the gods, Priest of priests, author of the rebirth foretold by the
ancient prophets, the twice-born, from whom we receive divine gifts.[27]

Characterizing inspiration as "that divine nectar, a wine which
causes virgins to conceive," Agrippa parallels Rabelais's "ambrosial
(*nectaricque*), delicious, precious, celestial, joyous, and deific liquor
which is called wine (*piot*)" (P.i.171). The "divine ambrosia" of course
represents the Holy Spirit by which Mary conceived Jesus, and by
which all creative efforts are inspired. This new wisdom that the
artist experiences would be, according to Agrippa a Bacchus (which
would have a corresponding Muse); Bacchus, the nectar or wine, becomes interchangeable with the Holy Spirit as well as with Christ.

Rabelais's Bacchus

Agrippa's Bacchus and Erasmus's Silenus are two striking examples of exploitation of pagan mysteries for Christian purposes, a
practice which was the rule rather than the exception. In his Prologues,
as elsewhere, Rabelais employs many pagan as well as Christian associations with the wine, assuming that a good reader, a learned one,
would be able to follow him. Throughout his books, the Dionysian
revel — the symposium — recurs (G.v; xxxix–xl; P.xx; xxvi–xxvii; TL.

xxix–xxxvi; QL.i; lxv; etc.) where Bacchus is present in liquid form.[28] The effect of the Rabelaisian drinking bout is not, as it appears on the surface, vulgar drunkenness, but a type of inspiration, or ecstasy, modeled closely upon the classical ideas of furor. The literal entry of the god into the body of the worshiper is of the greatest importance: in a true state of furor the normal faculties of the intellect and senses are in a state of suspension, while the god speaks through the person possessed.

In the *Timaeus* (71–72), Plato clearly expresses the notion that divine wisdom, divination, cannot come from human wisdom, but from human madness or foolishness in the suspension of reason. This is the device Erasmus exploits, too: since Folly herself speaks, surely what she says (if we only know how to listen) is wise.

A False Furor: The Praise of Debtors

In his praise of debtors, Panurge becomes ecstatic in defense of a personal vice to such an extent that he adapts for his improper purpose material which could be used in a panegyric to, say, Christian charity, or to the great chain of being. Panurge achieves a highly sophisticated level of rhetoric, not to say propaganda, in his lyrical presentation of generally acceptable truths to further his very questionable purposes. "Imagine . . . another world in which . . . all are debtors and all are lenders. Oh, what a harmony there will be in the regular motions of the heavens! . . . What sympathy there will be between the elements! . . . God's my life, I drown, I perish, I lose my way when I begin to consider the profound abyss of this world of lenders and owers" (TL.iv.299,301).[29] Pure rhetoric has borne the speaker to great heights of enthusiasm, but Panurge, never losing sight of his purpose, comes back constantly to "this world of lenders and owers"; his claim to be lost in the abyss of the world he has evoked is a rhetorical trick. His furor is a sham Dionysiac fever which Pantagruel deflates calmly and precisely: "You provide me with fine illustrations and figures, which please me greatly. But . . . I don't think the Persians were wrong either when they reckoned lying to be the second vice; to owe being the first. For debts and lies are generally involved together" (TL.v.302). Panurge may be "possessed" during his panegyric, but it is by his own expanded ego. Not until he "loses his mind" at least momentarily can Panurge glimpse the truth, for he is too corrupted by self-will and self-interest to be open to any voice but his own.[30]

The Divine Fool Triboullet

Of all the authorities to whom Panurge appeals in order to determine whether or not he should marry, the fool Triboullet is the last to be consulted. He is the last resort before the trip to India is undertaken; he is the most important Rabelaisian oracle before turning to direct consultation with God. Triboullet promises more wisdom than the combination of sages at the symposium — Hippothadée, Rondibilis, and Trouillogan — since "a fool may well give lessons to a wise man. Now since you're not fully satisfied by the answers of the wise, take counsel of some fool" (TL.xxxvii.390).

The true fool, as Pantagruel describes him, is a perfect empty vessel who awaits divine inspiration. Plato clearly states that divine wisdom is given only to human madness or folly, never to human wisdom:

> For the authors of our being, remembering the command of their father when he bade them create the human race as good as they could, that they might correct our inferior parts and make them to attain a measure of truth, placed in the liver the seat of divination. And herein is a proof that God has given the art of divination not to the wisdom, but to the foolishness of man. No man, when in his wits, attains prophetic truth and inspiration; but when he receives the inspired word, either his intelligence is enthralled in sleep, or he is demented by some distemper or possession.[31]

Having no intelligence himself, he can be depended upon to transmit to his bearers in undistorted form what he receives from above. Counselor of princes, he is born under the same zodiacal signs as royalty. According to Pantagruel, the fool is a perfect Christian, since he cares nothing for earthly wealth and fame. One must be unmindful of self, in order to appear wise enough before the celestial intelligences to receive the gift of divination. Everything which appears important here on earth must be set aside, in a quiescent state which is commonly imputed to madness.[32]

The disciples of Jesus could, according to this list of requirements, be considered mad, as indeed they were considered by the vulgar crowd around them. The "fool" is filled with divine wisdom like

Fatuel (Fatuus), son of Picus, king of the Latins, whose name means at the same time idiot and seer. Pantagruel continues, "Hence it is that when the strolling players distribute their parts, the role of fool and jester is always played by the most skilful and perfect actor in the company" (TL.xxxvii.391).[33] Pantagruel repeats the paradox that only the wise can playact the fool because only the foolish can be truly wise.

Pantagruel and Panurge cast about for someone who can fit their requirements for foolishness; they remember Triboullet, court fool of Francis I, and immediately launch into a paean of praise:

'Triboullet' (dist Pantagruel) 'me semble compétentement fol.'
Panurge respond: 'Proprement et totalement fol.'

" 'Triboullet,' said Pantagruel, 'seems competently foolish.' Panurge replied, 'Properly and totally foolish.' "

Panurge and Pantagruel continue:

Pantagruel	*Panurge*
Fol fatal,	F. de haulte game,
F. de nature,	F. de *b* quarre et de *b* mol,
F. céleste,	F. terrien,
F. Jovial,	F. joyeulx et folastrant,
F. Mercurial,	F. jolly et folliant,
F. lunaticque,	F. à pompettes,
F. erraticque,	F. à pilettes,
F. eccentricque,	F. à sonnettes,
F. aeteré et Junonien	F. riant et vénérien
	(TL. xxxviii.464)

Panurge and Pantagruel vie with each other in characterizing Triboullet, each from his own point of view and yet with reference to Pantagruel's "objective criteria" of what an ideal fool should be. Pantagruel's list is designed to illustrate and complete his stated criteria: "Fol fatal" refers to Triboullet's predestined foolishness; he is later said to be inspired by "the fateful spirit" (*l'esprit fatidicque*) (TL.xlv. 488), in the sense of the spirit "which reveals the dictates of destiny," according to Godefroy. He is "F. de nature" since he is born a fool, not made one; "F. céleste" since, as Pantagruel has already said, he is judged wise by the celestial intelligences"; "F. Jovial" since he is merry, and because the "house of Jupiter," as the horoscope tells us, is a source of madness; "F. Mercurial" because of his eloquence, his variability, his quickness; "F. lunaticque" because in the sway of Hecate, he is mad; "erraticque" and "eccentricque" because his mind wanders; "aeteré et Junonien" because his head, being empty, is filled with inspiration.[34] Pantagruel's list also shows how closely bound up are Rabelais's ideas of personality with the notions of astrological influence which were current in his day. The influence of the stars was considered synonymous with the influence of "celestial intelligence."

On the other side, Panurge first brings out the harmonic qualities of Triboullet who is "de haulte game," "de *b* quarre et de *b* mol," "in upper register, in *b* flat and *b* sharp," because he is in harmony with the "celestial intelligences," the spheres, and because Panurge hopes Triboullet's prediction will harmonize with his own innermost desires. "De haulte game" also means that he is a "high class" fool. However, Panurge quickly brings Triboullet back down to earth, calling him "F. terrien," which forms a direct antithesis with what he has just said and with Pantagruel's simultaneous "F. céleste," but which proves that the jester is equally foolish everywhere. "F. joyeulx et folastrant" begins a series of rhymes which illustrate in sound the harmonic qualities of Triboullet. Panurge also begins a physical description ("F. jolly et folliant"), continuing to describe items of the fool's clothing, and with "à sonnettes" returns to the harmonic theme. "F. riant et vénérien" reflects Panurge's deepest preoccupations of the moment. Pantagruel's epithets for Triboullet remain on the divine, predestined, celestial level, or on that of innate forces of nature (*erraticque, eccentricque*), while Panurge's epithets are on a profane, earthly, libertine scale.

Panurge's high hopes for a solution to his problem are dashed by Triboullet's brief prophecy: "By God, God, mad fool, beware of the monk! The hornpipe of Buzançais!" (TL.xlv.412). Panurge angrily rejects the prophecy: "We've been nicely caught . . . That's a fine answer. He's a fool all right. There's no denying that. But the man who brought him to me is even more of a fool, and I am a perfect fool for explaining my thoughts to him" (TL.xlv.412). But Pantagruel, analyzing Triboullet's behavior, demonstrates how he has exhibited every sign of divine furor: "Did you notice how his head shook and waggled before he opened his mouth to speak? By the teaching of the ancient philosophers . . . you may consider this movement to have been caused by the invasion and inspiration of the prophetic spirit (*l'esprit fatidicque*) . . ." (TL.xlv.412–13). He lists several examples of similar possession, among them the Maenads: "Catullus also tells, in *Berecynthia and Atys,* of a place where the Maenads, Bacchic women, priestesses of Dionysus, and frenzied prophetesses who carried ivy boughs, used to shake their heads" (TL.xlv.413). The prediction makes perfect sense to Pantagruel: Panurge will be cuckolded by a monk; he will become horned (cuckold) like the hornpipe of Buzançais; his wife will be empty of prudence, noisy, and filled with the winds of presumption like a bagpipe. Triboullet's possession, compared explicitly with the "distemper" caused by drink, is very similar to that of the illustrious boozers when they are in their cups: a company to which Rabelais himself — of course — belongs.

The "Propos des bien yvres"

Readers of the magnificent tour de force, the "Propos des bien yvres," "the Drunkard's Conversation," are always amused by the souvenirs of Rabelais's monastic training (bits of biblical quotations, puns involving Church or Scripture), that alternate with wanton humor. This chapter has traditionally been interpreted, like Frère Jean's breviary stuff, as proof of Rabelais's depravity and irreligion.[35] Far from trivial, the "Propos" provide an instance of immediate, divine (bacchic) inspiration. As direct communion with God, they are here treated out of chronological order in an ascending "order of divinity": the Praise of Debtors, Triboullet, the "Propos."

Though in none of Rabelais's many banquet scenes and drinking bouts is the casual conversation so carefully and extensively developed, at least two of the other symposia,[36] "Thaumaste Speaks of the Virtues and Knowledge of Panurge" (P.xx) and "Pantagruel Passes the Time Gaily with His Retainers" (QL.lxv), might shed light on the "Propos" and reveal certain new facets. Both these chapters contain phrases reminiscent of the "Propos," bacchic exclamations which may be used as a gloss. The "Pantagruel" chapter, in part, almost duplicates the beginning of G. v.

Saincte Dame, comment ilz tiroyent au chevrotin, et flaccons d'aller et eulx de corner: "Tyre!"

"Baille!"

"Paige, vin!"

"Boutte, de par le diable, boutte!"

Il n'y eut celluy qui ne beust vingt cinq ou trente muys et sçavez comment? *Sicut terra sine aqua,* car il faisoit chault, et dadvantaige se estoyent altéréz (P.xx.259).

Lors flaccons d'aller, jambons de troter, goubeletz de voler, breusses de tinter: "Tire!"

"Baille!"

"Tourne!"

"Brouille!"

"Boutte à moy sans eau . . . Ainsi, mon amy."

. . . .

"Je ne boy en plus q'une esponge."

. . . .

"Et moy sicut terra sine aqua." (G.v.16,18)

"Blessed Mother, how they pulled at the goat's skin! How the flagons went round, and how they called for them!

'Give it here!'

'Page, some wine!'

'Reach it here, in the devil's name, reach it here!'

There was not anyone who did not drink twenty-five or thirty pipes, and you know how! *Sicut terra sine aqua* [Like a land without water], for the weather was warm, and what is more, they were thirsty" (P.xx.239).

"Then flagons went round, hams started trotting, goblets flying, glasses clinking.

'Give it here!'

'Pour!'

'A mixture!'

'Give it to me without water, like that, my friend.'

. . . .

'I drink no more than a sponge.'

. . . .

'And I *sicut terra sine aqua.'* " (G.v; my trans.)

Thaumaste, illustrious boozer, lover of wisdom, has come across the sea to debate with Pantagruel. The night before the debate, he suffers in a particularly poignant way from his thirst. "Ne pensez que jamais gens plus feussent eslevéz et transportéz en pensée que furent . . .

58

tant Thaumaste que Pantagruel; car ledict Thaumaste dist au con-
cierge . . . Donnez ordre que beuvons . . . De l'aultre cousté, Pantagruel entra en la haulte game,[37] et toute la nuict ne faisoit que
ravasser après: Le livre de Beda, *De Numeris et Signis*" (P.xviii.250–
51). "Do not think that ever any two men were more elevated and
transported than were . . . Thaumaste and Pantagruel as well; for
the said Thaumaste told the hotelkeeper . . . 'Order us some drink.'
. . . On the other side, Pantagruel got into high gear, and did nothing
all night but brood on Bede's book, *On Numbers and Signs*" (P.xviii;
my trans.). The important phrase "tant Thaumaste que Pantagruel"
places Thaumaste's thirst on a par with Pantagruel's scholarly investi-
gations. Both men seek the same thing. Panurge, who sees that his
master has taken the debate too seriously, sends him to bed, telling
him to drink twenty-five or thirty good draughts (P.xviii.232). This
will prepare him just as well for the morrow as would his research, since drinking feeds the *genius* and, literally, raises the spirits.
Panurge, confident that his unaided daemon will win tomorrow's
battle, feeds it exclusively with wine: "So Panurge spent the night
tippling with the pages and played away all the points of his breeches
at *Primus Secundus* and push-pin" (P.xviii.233). When the debating
parties arrive, the audience mutters, "This devil of a Pantagruel who
has got the better of all these tricksy, callow sophists will be paid out
this time (*aura son vin*). For this Englishman is another Devil of
Vauvert" (P.xviii.233). "Aura son vin" means both "he will get his
comeuppance" and he will be taught a lesson through the debate. But
it is "this Englishman" who learns instead — or *thinks* he does — from
Panurge's gestures, which Panurge *thinks* are merely obscene mockery.
The debate illustrates Pantagruel's observation: "I've often heard the
vulgar proverb quoted, that a fool may well give lessons to a wise
man" (TL.xxxvii, 390).

After verbal thanksgiving, Thaumaste and Pantagruel dine together. Their conversation at the symposium could only be heady; they
drink in one another's wisdom, exalting themselves to such realms,
raising their spirits so high, that they are no longer in contact with
reality ("Dont venez vous?"). They imbibe the spirit(s) of wisdom
sicut terra sine aqua, a biblical reference, which, when replaced in its

context, "Anima mea sicut terra sine aqua tibi" (Ps. 143:6), reflects its gravity back upon Rabelais's use of it: the soul without God is like waterless soil, its capacity to absorb liquid appears endless.

The other banquet scene (QL.lxv) recalls the "Propos" by its context and by several characteristic expressions:

QL.lxv	G.v
"J'ay maintenant . . . mon estomach sabourré à profict de mesnaige."	"J'ay bien saburré mon stomach."
"I've got my stomach pretty properly ballasted."	"I've got my stomach well ballasted."
"Trefves de soif, trefves de faim."	"Trèves de soif!"
"Hunger, farewell. Thirst, you're dead."	"Thirst, you're dead!"
"J'ay ouy . . . que Tirelupin . . . espargne par chascun an plus de dix-huyct cens pippes de vin, par faire les survenens et domesticques boyre avant qu'ilz aient soif."	"Nous aultres innocens ne beuvons que trop sans soif."
"I have heard . . . that . . . Tirelupin saves more than eighteen hundred pipes a year by making the visitors and servants drink before they're thirsty."	"We poor innocents drink only too much without thirst."
"Car" (dist Pantagruel, continuant) "comme les chameaulx et dromadaires en la caravane boyvent pour la soif passée, pour la soif présente et pour la soif future, ainsi feist Hercules."	"Non, moy pécheur, sans soif, et sinon présente, pour le moins future, la prévenent comme entendez. Je boy pour la soif advenir. Je boy éternellement. Ce m'est éternité de beuverye et beuverye de éternité."
"For," continued Pantagruel, "just as camels and dromedaries in the caravans drink for the thirst that is past, the thirst that is present, and for the thirst that is to come, even so did Hercules." (Pp. 590–91)	"Sinner that I am, I never drink without thirst: if not present thirst, at least future, for I forestall it, you understand. I drink for the thirst to come. I drink eternally. It's an eternity of drinking and drinking for eternity." [My trans.]

The title "Comment Pantagruel haulse le temps . . ." provides the key to the chapter. The idiom "hausser le coude," "to lift the elbow" = "drink heavily," is common enough in modern French; "hausser le temps," according to Littré, means "rendre le temps beau, gai en buvant," "to brighten the weather by drinking" and simultaneously "to have a good time while drinking," [38] and is roughly equivalent to English "to have a high time." This is, of course, what Pantagruel and his companions are doing. Saulnier notes that Rabelais *seems* to contradict himself: he has thoroughly examined and roundly condemned "gastrolatry" in the preceding chapters, but here, the Pantagrueline heroes seem to solve their problems by committing that very sin. The contradiction is merely apparent, for their "meal" stands for an affirmation of faith in a communal meal rather than for indulgence of physical appetites.[39]

> "I've thrown off my melancholy," said Panurge, "thanks to God and to you . . . Your excellent Euripides wrote the truth when he made that famous boozer Silenus say:
> 'He's out of his mind, he's raving mad,
> The man who drinks and still feels sad.'
> We ought [without fail] to give great praise to the good God, our Creator, Savior, and Preserver [who cures us through] this excellent bread, . . . this [good cool] wine, and . . . these splendid meats, . . . of certain disorders, both [of body and soul]."
> (QL.lxv.590; partly my trans.)

The bread and the wine, symbols of the Eucharist, provide a means of God-given *salut,* "health and salvation," of body and soul. Raising the spirits means communion with God; Rabelais here, as in many other cases, symbolizes prayer and inspiration by eating and drinking. Atlas and Hercules "haulsèrent le temps" quite literally, as Pantagruel points out: they both lifted the whole world into the air. Hercules (like Bacchus, frequently a Christ symbol) drank for future (and eternal) thirst, an eternal communion.

Since in eating and drinking one feeds the spirit and the life-fluid, the body actually becomes lighter: "For just as a dead body is heavier than a living one, so a man fasting is heavier and more earthy (*terrestre*) than when he has eaten and drunk" (QL.lxv.591). A final passage translated from Pausanias (3 *Laconia* 19.6) reports that Bacchus has also been called *Psila,* "wings," since "with the aid of Bacchus — of good, tasty, and delicious wine, that is to say — the spirits of humankind are raised on high, their bodies manifestly made nimbler, and what was earthy in them becomes pliant" (QL.lxv.592). Everything becomes lighter — bodies, spirits, ship, and weather — everyone becomes more spiritual, higher in the chain of being, more angelic.[40]

The "Propos des bien yvres" conveys a similar message. The enumeration and staccato series of commands which begins the chapter communicate the frenzied movements of a bacchanal:

> Lors flaccons d'aller, jambons de troter, goubeletz de voler, breusses de tinter:
> "Tire!"
> "Baille!"
> "Tourne!
> "Brouille!"

Wine is presented as a universal cure both for fever (heat) and for cold:

> Ha, faulse fièvre, ne t'en iras-tu pas?
> "False fever, will you not begone?"
>
> Par ma fy, ma commère, je ne peuz entrer en bette.
> "[By my faith], my dear, I can't get my gullet working."
>
> Vous estez morfondue m'amie?
> "You've caught a chill, old girl."
>
> Voire.
> "You're right."
>
> Je ne boy que à mes heures, comme la mulle du pape.
> "I only drink at [my hours] like the Pope's mule."
> (G.5.48; partly my trans.)

Various ecclesiastical puns are used to compare modes of "communing." The possible meanings are multiple, not counting the puns on "mulle du pape" (simultaneously the pope's mule and slipper, kissed by the faithful): (1) I only drink when thirsty; (2) I only drink at the canonical hours; (3) I only communicate with God (i.e., pray) at the canonical hours; (4) I only pray when I have to.

The rejoinder is just as complex:

> Je ne boy que en mon bréviaire, comme un beau père guardian.

(1) I only drink on the sly, from my breviary-bottle; (2) I receive

sçavoir divin (*sapience, savourement divin*) only from my breviary (where the *vin divin,* divine wisdom, is kept). A scholastic note is introduced:

> Qui feut premier, soif ou beuverye?
> "What was first, thirst or drinking?"

This could be generalized to read, "Qui fut premier, besoin ou grâce," need or fulfillment? Thirst! cries one reveler, for who would have drunk without thirst while still in a state of innocence? Drink, answers his adversary, for *privatio praesupponit habitum,* "privation presupposes habit." To justify his pedantry, he explains, "je suis clerc": lawyer, or, perhaps Churchman, since *clerc* could designate either. Fulfillment or grace must precede need, since no one misses something he never had to begin with. And in the Garden, grace obviously preceded the lack of it.

A boozer quotes an excerpt from Horace: "Faecundi calices quem non fecere disertum?" "Brimming cups impart eloquence to all" (*Epist.* 1.5.19). The quotation could stand as motto for the entire celebration — cups of eloquence brim with *logos; in vino veritas.*[41] But, objects the second speaker, even though we are innocent, we still drink only too willingly without thirst. Another boozer provides the solution to the miniature scholastic argument: Though I am a sinner, says he, I never drink without thirst, if not present thirst, at least future thirst — I look ahead:

> "Je boy éternellement. Ce m'est éternité de beuverye et beuverye de éternité."

Although I may have no present need of grace, I commune with the divine in view of future need — an eternity of mutual communion. Let us rejoice, then, intoning a motet while we drink:

> "Chantons, beuvons, un motet entonnons." [42]

The choice of *motet* rather than *chanson* or *ballade* indicates that praises will be sung to God; divine, not profane things will be celebrated. An immediate pun follows on "entonnons": "Où est mon entonnoir?", "Where is my funnel?" (*Entonnoir,* "funnel, musical instrument or glass"; in any case, a means of pouring forth the joyful spirit.)

Je mouille, je humecte, je boy, et tout de peur de mourir.
"I moisten, I sprinkle, I drink, and all for fear of dying."

Beuvez tousjours, vous ne mourrez jamais.
"Drink all the time and you'll never die."

Si je ne boy, je suys à sec: me voilà mort. Mon âme s'enfuyra en
quelque grenoillère. En sec jamais l'âme ne habite.
"If I don't drink, I dry out: I'm as good as dead. My soul will take
refuge in some frog pond [slang for tavern]. The soul can't live in
the dry!"

"Je mouille, je humecte" suggests baptism, just as "je boy" refers to the
Eucharist. Both sacraments are taken "de peur de mourir," for without them the soul could be damned, and, according to the ancients,
the soul can only exist in a moist place. This idea, traced by the *Ed.
cr.* and by Gilson to St. Augustine,[43] goes much farther back into
antiquity, since the lungs (*praecordia* or *phrenes*) were believed to be
the seat of the *animus,* the conscious mind. Drink was believed to go
where the *animus* was.[44]

It is the wine which determines the essence of the boozer:

> Somelliers, ô créateurs de nouvelles formes,
> rendez-moy de non beuvant beuvant!
> "Waiters, o you creators of new forms, turn
> me from a non-drinker to a drinker."

The editorial commentary in the *Ed. cr.* (1.55; my trans.) merits
quotation for its accuracy: "A scholastic pun on the forms or substantial forms. Here the distinct principle which gives the bodies their
mode of existence is that of the wine." The meaning of "rendez-moy
de non beuvant beuvant" takes on Christian, even sacramental significance: the *somelliers* serve as a synonym for ministrants or priests, or
even for *logos* or for Christ Himself.[45] The *nouvelles formes* symbolize spiritual rebirth, regeneration, reformation. "Sommelier éternel,
guarde-nous de somme," "Eternal waiter, keep us from sleep," is a
prayer: Keep us from (eternal) sleep, *O Dieu Servateur* — Savior-
Ministrant!

> Je ne boy en plus q'une esponge.
> "I drink no more than a sponge."
>
> Je boy comme un templier.
> "I drink like a templar."

Et je *tanquam sponsus.*
"And I *tanquam sponsus* [like a bridegroom]."

Et moy *sicut terra sine aqua.*
"And I *sicut terra sine aqua* [like a land without water]."

In this list of comparisons, two are biblical and one refers to a *templier:* not only a thirsty crusader (which evokes multiple associations, some serious, some comic) but also, literally, a temple dweller, i.e., a priest.[46] "I drink like a priest" not only calls to mind standard medieval jokes at the expense of the clergy but also the fact that a priest drinks the blood of Christ. The *sponsus* of the first biblical reference may also refer to Christ, the bridegroom of the Church, the Faithful. Christ, too, imbibes the wine of the Holy Spirit. *Sicut terra sine aqua* (as we have seen above) occurs in Ps. 143:6, where the seeker of righteousness stretches out his hand to God. A boozer from Basoche cries out piteously: "Respice personam, pone pro duos" "(Waiter) have pity! Pour a double portion!" Another sinner comments wryly,

Si je montois aussi bien comme j'avalle, je feusse pieçà haulte en l'aer.

Beside the obscene pun with *monter* and the surface word-play on *avaller/tomber,* the boozer tells us, "If I climbed as well as I sin (fall), I would already be on my way to heaven." Bacchus, patron of the celebration, is remembered as having conquered India while drunk: the citizens of Malindi philosophize while boozing, like Homer, Ennius, Æschylus, Cato, Rabelais, and, it is to be hoped, the reader.[47]

The "Propos" continue at a dizzying pace: obscenities alternate with comments on food and drink along with ostensibly blasphemous references to New Testament scenes, including the Crucifixion: "J'ai la parolle de Dieu en bouche: *Sitio,*" "I speak the word of God: 'I thirst' " and *"O lachryma Christi."* [48] The priest at the symposium shouts, "La pierre dicte *asbestos* n'est plus inextinguible que la soif de ma Paternité," "Even the asbestos stone is not more inextinguishable than the thirst of my Paternity." Rabelais may here refer to his own burning thirst: Lefranc indicates that *Paternité,* which began as a reference to the Pope, came to mean any priest or confessor. Rabelais gives himself the title in the Prologue to QL.

The "Propos," joyful and frivolous in themselves, present a masterful example of Rabelaisian *serio ludere.* Absurd on the surface, they lead up to the birth of the king. The events surrounding chapter 5, so much larger than life, are supernatural on this ground alone. Gargantua is born amid signs and portents: his genealogy is first discovered (*découverte*) in a mysterious and symbolic book buried in the grave of a superhuman monarch; the unusual pregnancy of Gargamelle is compared to pregnancies of various goddesses; and, after the symposium, the miraculous birth occurs. Within this complex of preternatural events, the feast which precedes the miraculous birth, like Gargamelle, is pregnant with meaning. The bacchic celebrants, the *bien yvres,* so far along in their frenzy, are possessed by the Holy Spirits; their pronouncements, which seem unintelligible gibberish at first, are inspired utterances. There is little rational continuity in the "Propos," since each boozer speaks according to his inspiration, as the spirits move him:

> And they were all filled with the Holy Spirit and began to speak in other tongues, as the Spirit gave them utterance.
>
> . . . .
>
> And all were amazed and perplexed, saying to one another, "What does this mean?" But others mocking said, "They are filled with new wine."
>
> (Acts 2:4–13)

Chapter 3

The Temple of Bacchus

On Rabelais's *Dive Bouteille*

Although the ravings of the drunken revelers, the *bien yvres,* may be considered a Silenic disguise for pentecostal utterances, Rabelais goes still further in portraying the divinely inspired furor. The *Dive Bouteille* chapters (34–47) of the *Cinquiesme Livre* lead up to a furor which represents direct, divine revelation to Panurge. Every ritual, every description which precedes that final rite and highest initiation merits examination in order to understand the "mot de la Dive Bouteille."

For this development I assume that the last fourteen chapters of the fifth book are authentic; the remainder will not come under discussion in the present work. Unfortunately, the very suggestion that one intends seriously to examine any selection from the *Cinquiesme Livre* will elicit instant rejection by many readers. However, my belief in the authenticity of these final chapters is shared by a number of eminent scholars of Rabelais: Tilley, Sainéan, Lefranc, Marty-Laveaux, Spitzer, and Masters. Of course, since there are no purely "scientific" proofs available on either side, those who cannot believe in the authenticity of the last book will remain unconvinced, no matter what arguments are proffered.

Spitzer states forcefully that the last scenes of book five are "among the most beautiful selections of French prose, which could only have been written by Rabelais."[1] The vocabulary of these chapters as well as the use of enumeration as an end in itself differ very little from the previous books. A few examples will serve to illustrate: On their way to the temple, the Pantagrueline company passes under an arch incised with "flagons, leather-bottles, bottles . . . garlics, onions, shallots, hams . . . smoked ox tongues, old cheeses . . . intertwined with vine leaves . . . glasses on feet and glasses on horseback . . . goblets and other such Bacchic artillery" (CL.xxxiv.683). This list echoes a number of other descriptions of feasts. "Then flagons went round, hams started trotting, goblets flying, glasses clinking . . ." (G.v; my trans.), or the spurs to wine at the birth of Pantagruel: "hams and smoked ox tongues, seven camels loaded with salted eels; then twenty-four cartloads of leeks, garlics and onions . . ." (P.ii.176). The first enumeration, from the *Cinquiesme Livre,* not only contains variations on a favorite Rabelaisian theme, it also includes a pun, "glasses on feet and glasses on horseback" ("verres à pied, verres à cheval"), brought about in a way typical of Rabelais's pure, exuberant word association.

Still other texts show stylistic and structural parallels which are remarkable in their fidelity to theme and motive, without being repetitive or clumsy imitations. Panurge cries out in fear at several stages in the journey to the Bottle. One of these terrified chants occurs during the adventure of the frozen words, another during the descent into the cave: "God's my life, is this a trick? We are lost. Let's get away. We've fallen into an ambush. Brother John, are you there, my friend? Keep close to me, I beg of you. Have you got your cutlass? . . . Let's run away, I won't say with our feet and hands as Brutus did at the battle of Pharsalia, but with sail and oar. Let's get away. I've no courage on the sea. In a cellar [*cave*] or elsewhere I've more than enough. . . . Let's run away . . . I would to God I were at Les Quinquenais at this moment, even if it meant never marrying! Let's fly" (QL.lv.567). But in a cave, Panurge scarcely shows more courage, as he implores the Lantern who guides the company: "Most wondrous lady, I beg of you with a contrite heart, let us turn back. For, by God's truth, I'm dying from sheer fright. I agree never to marry . . . I shan't be ungrateful either, when I get out of this Troglodytes' cave. Let's turn back, if you please. I'm very much afraid that this is Taenarus, which is the way down to hell. I think I can hear Cerberus barking. Listen, that's he, or I have a singing in my ears . . . Are you there Friar John? I beg of you, old paunch, keep close to me. I'm dying of fear. Have you got your cutlass? . . . Let's turn back" (CL. xxxvi.686).

The two passages are structured in the same general way. The introductory sentence, or series of outcries, is followed by "Let's get away" ("Fuyons!") and "Let's turn back" ("Retournons!") in passage B, and both excerpts are punctuated by repetitions of the same plea; both close with "Let's fly" ("Fuyons!") and "Let's turn back" ("Retournons!"), respectively. Panurge calls upon Frère Jean in almost the same words in both examples; he is willing to forfeit his dream of marriage in order to escape present danger; his display of erudition in both passages is drawn from Erasmus. The reference to Brutus in the first passage comes from *Apothegme* V.2 and the contrast between "feet and hands" versus "sail and oar" refers to *Adage* I.iv.19. The references to St. Patrick's Hole in Ireland and the cavern of Trophonius in Boeotia which precede the second passage, are drawn from *Adage* VII.57. Passage A is preceded in Rabelais's text by the phrase, "Either we could hear them too, or else there was a ringing in our ears" ("les aureilles nous cornoient"). An echo of this sentence clearly occurs in passage B: "That's he, or I have a singing in my ears" ("les aureilles me cornent"). Beyond showing a panic-stricken Panurge, both situations are parallel in other ways. The company is favored in both by a glimpse of something beyond ordinary human experience. The frozen words rain down on the deck from the Plane of Truth, from eternity; the black cave and its terrors precede the revelation which the companions had come so far to hear. The long journey over the sea has been considered an image of the journey of life: a pilgrimage, a sort of purgatory which the seeker must undergo before he is worthy to understand the truth. In like manner, the cave is explicitly compared to St. Patrick's Hole in Ireland, which was supposed to be an entrance to Purgatory, and to the cavern of Trophonius in Boeotia, an oracle of Apollo. The anal imagery of this hole (from which emerges eternal truth) is typically Rabelaisian (cf. "Les Fanfreluches Antidotées" [G.ii.105]). The number of steps within the cave, which corresponds to Plato's psychogeny, recalls a similar use of number symbolism in QL.xxvii (on heroes and good daemons). Besides the consistency in using classical and traditional Christian comparisons, and in exploiting Erasmus, Rabelais uses Colonna's *Hypnerotomachia Poliphili* extensively whenever he describes architecture: in Thélème, in the Isle of the Macraeons (QL.xxv), and in the Temple of the Bottle. Like Colonna, Rabelais consistently describes architecture for its symbolic significance. A thematic element can also be advanced to support stylistic considerations. The bacchic imagery, continued in these chapters very much as it has been used throughout, is brought to a culmination: the serious aspects of Rabelais's play are closer to the surface here than elsewhere.

Key to Bacchic Iconography

Bacchic symbolism reaches its climax in book five, where the mysteries (according to Rabelais) are revealed and all secrets made known. The knowledge necessary to decipher these final chapters is the same that Rabelais had assumed from the outset, for the remarks of the *bien yvres* — " 'This is how Bacchus conquered India.' 'This is how they philosophize in Malindi' " — anticipate the Dionysian conquest of India which forms such an important part of the decoration of the Temple walls.

Rabelais's Bacchus is taken largely from Lucian with some additional borrowings from secondary sources: from Euripides, Ovid, Vergil; possibly from surviving Roman paintings which he may have seen in Italy; and from contemporary copies of ancient allegorical paintings. The Bacchus of the Rabelaisian mosaic is seated on a magnificent chariot drawn by three yokes of young leopards. His face is like that of a young child, ruddy and beardless, to show that good boozers do not age. He has sharp horns on his head and a crown of grapes and vine leaves, a scarlet miter, and golden buskins on his feet. Most of Rabelais's bacchic symbols admit of simultaneously opposite interpretations. The young leopards represent fury and cruelty, forces which the god can, and often does, release, but which he holds under restraint if his followers only drink moderately.[2] Bacchus' youthful face, ruddy with wine, signifies the ever renewed life and vigor of the *bon beuveur,* but he is beardless to signify the loss of virility produced by heavy drinking (cf. TL.xxxi.439–40). The sharp horns he wears could signify cuckoldry, according to the normally unfavorable French interpretation; they also symbolize power, courage, and godliness, like the "horns" of Moses. In ancient Egypt, the horn also signified elevation, glory, and the path upward.[3] His crown of grapes and vines needs no interpretation; the red and gold, colors which signify royalty, also represent the colors of the wine and of the fertilizing, fructifying rays of the sun.

His followers, the Maenads, Bacchides, Satyrs, and the like, represent the forces of nature, those bestial impulses within man that Bacchus can either control or unleash. In their fury they prove completely irresistible; their opponents fall victim to them without a struggle. After their victory, Bacchus and his army deck themselves with ivy, and Bacchus exchanges his leopards for elephants (CL.xl.869). The ivy, another ambiguous symbol, is believed to produce furor and to have aphrodisiac qualities,[4] while it symbolizes glory as well because it is evergreen regardless of the season.[5] The elephant represents strength, piety, and chastity, and hence is also an appropriate symbol of victory over the world.[6]

In these murals, Rabelais's *serio ludere* presents a serious portrait of deity in the Renaissance mode of *trionfi*. Bacchus' ambiguity is the same as that of the Christian or the Old Testament God: his strength can bring all the glory of man down to overwhelming destruction; it can force man back into a bestial condition just as when Nebuchadnezzar was forced to eat grass, or it can exalt man above the skies.

Purification, a Bacchic Mystery

The timeworn *topos* of the voyage of life takes yet another bow in Rabelais's work. A voyage in self-knowledge, as Masters points out,[7] it is also a voyage in purification, for the lands and peoples which the heroes visit along the way represent the perils and temptations which the world of the flesh, the domains of philosophy and of religion present to the pilgrim: so many stages in a long inner development.

Their perilous journey done, the Pantagrueline company arrive "at the island of [their] desire, in which was the Oracle of the Bottle." And though the entire voyage has been a sort of purgatory, the suppliant voyagers must go through a final series of ritual purifications before they can be admitted to the Holy of Holies. The Lantern leads them to the temple, through the magnificent vineyard which surrounds it, where all kinds of wine are represented (Rabelais lists fifteen varieties). The vineyard, planted and blessed by Bacchus, simultaneously bears leaf, flower, and fruit, like the orange groves of Saint Remo. The Lantern tells each of the companions to eat three grapes, fill his shoes with grape leaves, cover his head with ivy leaves, and take a green branch in his left hand. The good Bacchus, Shepherd of the Vine and holy Wine Steward, who has blessed the temple of the Bottle (his own temple), has made of its grounds a paradise. Rabelais's text also recalls the "song of the vine" in Isa. 5:1-7, but, unlike the biblical vineyard, Bacchus' paradise yields abundantly according to his expectations. The Lantern explains the significance of the Albanian hat of ivy leaves and the grape leaves in the shoes. In the tunnel leading to the temple, they will walk beneath "the wine (that is to say, grapes)," no doubt represented on the roof. They would thus be symbolically overcome by wine, if they were not also protected from it by their hats of ivy. The *Dive Bouteille* would not receive them unless their shoes were filled with vine leaves, indicating dominion over worldly or common drunkenness by means of Bacchus: they defeat the "false" with the "true" Bacchus. Frère Jean correctly understands the Lantern's explanation of the leafy hat and the shoe padding. Although he, as always, denies being a scholar, he remembers a passage in his breviary drawn from Revelation, where a woman is depicted treading the moon underfoot. A strange and admirable sight, he comments, since for most women the moon floats overhead, thus signifying their lunacy (CL.xxxiv.856-57). Eating three grapes demonstrates that the voyagers can ingest and benefit from the wine ("that is to say, grapes") without suffering drunkenness; the number three, according to the Pythagoreans, represents intellect, good counsel, and knowledge.[8] Drunkenness is overcome by wisdom. At the same time, in typically ambiguous fashion, the "communicants" receive within them the Trinity, source of the *vin divin,* while rejecting all that is false and worldly in wine.

Acceptance of the true Bacchus is symbolized by passing through the arch and by the green branch each man carries, a Dionysian *thyrsos.* The branch, which apparently comes off some of the grape vines in the temple vineyard, signifies also that the Pantagruelistes belong to the true faith, they are members of the body of Christ/Bacchus: "I am the vine, you the branches" (John 15:5). The arch is incised with all the paraphernalia of the bacchic symposium named each time Rabelais describes a feast (e.g., in the "Propos," "Thaumaste," and "Chaneph"), which will appear once more in the Agapē feast served by Bacbuc's ministrants beside the holy fountain.[9]

The company descends into the "abyss of Truth," or, as G. M. Masters believes, into the subterranean center of the universe, by the Platonic staircase of one hundred steps which ends before a vast jasper portal inscribed *"Hen Hoinō Halētheia . . . In wine lies Truth"* (CL. xxxvii.688).[10] Here they must leave behind their good Lantern, for its light can no longer guide them: it is surpassed by the light of the inner sanctum.[11] Like Dante's Vergil, the faithful guide can lead the pilgrim to, but not through the Christian mysteries, which are illuminated by an admirable lamp whose light outshines the sun, and whose flanks are embossed with Dionysian reliefs.

As the group passes through the doors, they see two inscribed tablets, one in Latin, the other in Greek:

DUCUNT VOLENTEM FATA, NOLENTEM TRAHUNT:
"Fate leads the willing, but the unwilling drags."

PROS TELOS AUTON PANTA KINEITAI
"All things move to their end."

(CL.xxxvii.689)

Both inscriptions remind us of the inevitable character of the voyage of life, and they also underscore the finality of what the heroes are about to witness: the ultimate mysteries, the Truth, the goal of their spiritual development.

The Allegory of the Temple Walls

Bacchus Conquers India

Pantagruel and his followers cross the temple floor which is so cunningly paved with reproductions of grape vines that it gives the sensation of actual depth. Bacchus is beneath their feet, his image is embossed on the lamp above them which lights the scene, the allegory of his conquest of India moves on the wall before their eyes in a colorful mosaic to which Rabelais devotes two full chapters. Unlike Lucian, Rabelais opens his account by telling the reader that Bacchus conquered India by fire and blood. Though he later dwells on the comic aspects of the bacchic hordes, he introduces them as a serious destructive force, stressing the violence and brutality of the attack by an army which the Indians had chosen to ignore:

> At the beginning various towns, villages, castles, fortresses, fields, and forests were shown all fiery and ablaze. In this same picture some frantic and depraved women were seen furiously tearing to pieces live calves, sheep, and ewes, and consuming their raw flesh. This picture was meant to convey how, in his invasion of India, Bacchus put everything to fire and sword (*à feu et à sang*). (CL.xxxix.691)

By contrast, Lucian had emphasized the apparent absurdity of the Dionysian army: "When Dionysus lead his host against the men of Ind (surely there is nothing to prevent my telling you a tale of Bacchus!) he was held at first in such contempt . . . that they laughed at his advance" (Dion.7.49). Why does Rabelais pick this particular Dionysian episode to illuminate the temple walls? What could India mean to him? Land of mystery, of untold wealth, of fabulous sights, of spices, brocades, precious jewels; the El Dorado which the explorers sought; India, confused with the unexplored, unexploited New World, stands for the complexity, riches, pride, and abuses of this world. Its pomp and wealth display worldly, not divine, treasure and wisdom; it betrays pride and self-satisfaction. It must therefore be put to fire and to the sword by Bacchus, brought low by an "army" which, like the early Christian "army" of slaves, women, freedmen, and fishermen, appeared so ridiculous as to be despised. Once conquered, India becomes the center of the Dionysian universe. The sanctuary of the *Dive Bouteille* is located at the heart of the land in upper India near Cathay (QL.i.541); here the waters of the *Ur*-fountain take on the flavor of any wine one could possibly imagine; here, too, Rabelais hints, is the home of the philosopher's stone (P.xxxiv.311). India, like Egypt, Israel, and later Greece, is a storehouse of the wisdom of the early sages (P.xviii.249), whence Bacchus carries on his further world conquest.[12] From India, Bacchus bestows upon the rest of the world his gift of viticulture and the art of winemaking. As a world conqueror, Bacchus, like Alexander the Great who is said to have conquered India in imitation of the god, becomes a figure for Christ who also overcomes the world. The images of violence, which open Rabelais's description of the symbolic mosaic, are reminiscent of the descriptions of Christ and the end of the world which are repeated in various books of the Old and New Testaments. They also represent Christ's first coming since that was not at all a peaceful occurrence, but one of bloody violence: "Do not think that I have come to send peace upon the earth; I have come to bring a sword, not peace. For I have come to set a man at variance with his father, and a daughter with her mother . . . and a man's enemies will be those of his own household" (Matt. 10:34–36). Peter, explaining to the gaping multitude what the disciples meant when they spoke in tongues, predicts the increased violence of the second coming:

> And in the last days it shall be, God declares, that I will pour out my Spirit upon all flesh . . . and on my menservants and my maidservants in those days I will pour out my Spirit; and they shall prophesy. And I will show wonders in the heaven above and signs on the earth beneath, blood and fire and vapor of smoke.
>
> (Acts 2:17–19)[13]

St. Paul unites the Old Testament apocalyptic tradition with his new faith, exhorting the faithful to believe in Christ or be burnt by the final fire:

> For no other foundation can anyone lay than that which is laid, which is Jesus Christ. Now if any one builds on the foundation with gold, silver, precious stones, wood, hay, stubble — each man's work will become manifest; for the Day will disclose it, because it will be revealed with fire, and the fire will test what sort of work each one has done. If the work which any man has built on the foundation survives, he will receive a reward. If any man's work is burned up, he will suffer loss, though he himself will be saved, but only as through fire.
>
> (1 Cor. 3:11–15)

That fiery day is depicted allegorically by Bacchus' flaming conquest of India. Despite his bloody successes in battle, the Indians continue to scorn the god, his absurd captains, Pan the goat man, and aged, potbellied Silenus and his comic hordes. They resolve to let them pass, as though it would be a disgrace to fight such an army. Thus Bacchus continues to gain territory unopposed, and puts everything to the torch, "because fire and lightning are the paternal weapons of Bacchus . . ." (CL.xxxix; my trans.).

Jupiter, like the avenging Yahveh of the Old Testament in whom St. Paul also believes, is a god of fire and of lightning: "Our God is a consuming fire" (Heb. 12:29). According to the theory of the four elements, fire is the most celestial of the four, and a sign within nature of a higher, parallel phenomenon: divine love, which can manifest itself simultaneously as its opposite, divine vengeance and destruction. Bacchus, son of Jupiter, wields lightning and fire by hereditary right. His identity as Christ becomes even more apparent, since Rabelais also uses Jupiter as a synonym for God.[14] The Indian rulers, who scorn the coming of Jupiter's son, resemble the Roman emperors. They, too, at first scorned Christianity as an obscene cult, but were soon forced to take it seriously enough to slaughter Christians at the circus, and were at last overwhelmed by the "slaves and drunken women" whom they had despised.

Rabelais's Pantheon

Although Rabelais models his temple on Colonna's Temple of Venus, the goddess of love does not appear in the Rabelaisian version. Instead, the trinity on the temple walls includes Bacchus, Pan, and Silenus. Bacchus commands the attacking army, while the other two act as his captains.

Pan had been identified by Rabelais earlier as a Christ figure. After recounting the legend of the death of Pan, Pantagruel explains that Pan was that Savior of the faithful, ignominiously killed in Judea by the envy and iniquity of pontiffs, doctors, priests, and monks of the Mosaic law. Such an interpretation is not repugnant, he continues, since this Pan is our all, all that we are, have, or hope. The Pan who appears on the temple walls in his usual mythical guise as horned and goat-legged could be similarly interpreted. However, "seeing that he is our All, all that we are, all that we live by . . ." (QL. xxviii; my trans.), he is, even in the *Quart Livre* sequence, a symbol for the One, i.e., for God the Father. Pan is one of the most important humanistic symbols, as Pico attests in one of his Orphic *Conclusiones*: "He who cannot attract Pan approaches Proteus in vain."[15]

In Bacchus, we have already discovered a Christ figure, giver of the breviary stuff, the wine of *logos;* in Pan we detect the unity behind the multiple phenomena of this world, the coincidence of all contraries. But what of Silenus, the third member of the trinity? So far, Silenus has been considered roughly equivalent to his pupil Bacchus. But he appears first of all quite independently: in the Prologue to G, Silenus has just as much right to the serious attention of the reader as does Socrates, for the equation Silenus = Socrates could just as easily be read Socrates = Silenus. If Socrates is a Christ figure for Renaissance humanists (and for Rabelais as well), then so is Silenus. Thus Rabelais's trio forms a very unusual trinity, consisting of three Christ figures. But each member may assume the role of the other Persons: Pan is also the One (the Father), and Bacchus, the Holy Spirit. Proteus-like they blend into each other. Silenus, too, can be a figure for God the Father, as he appears in Erasmus:

> In the universe, the greatest things are those not seen, like substances which are called separate. And at the highest point of these there stands what is furthest removed from the senses, namely God, further than our understanding or our knowing, the single source of all things.[16]

Potentially, Silenus is any god of the Pantheon, and hence he can assume the role of the Many, opposed to and yet identical to the One: he, too, is a key to the Orphic mysteries.

Among Silenus's many incarnations is one of his most ancient disguises: the ithyphallic god Priapus, delight of all Rabelaisian women. Priapus was often confused with, or identified as, the son of Bacchus. This is how Rondibilis describes him in his advice to Panurge: "It was the opinion of the ancients according to Diodorus Siculus's account, and particularly of the Lampsacenes, as Pausanias affirms, that Master Priapus was the son of Bacchus and Venus" (TL.xxxi.373). Rabelais refers to a whole complex of ancient traditions involving the worship of the procreative powers of nature. Lampsakos, as Rabelais implies, was the center of Priapic worship. Priapus was the chief god of procreation, a full member in the Olympian circle, identified as founder of the city and protector of the vineyards. His cult spread outside the borders of Lampsakos and intermingled with the cults of Hermes and Dionysus. The "St. Ithyphalle" was an image sacred to Dionysus and carried in bacchic processions. In the satyr plays, Silenus, Priapus, and Bacchus seem to have been barely distinguishable.[17]

Plotinus interprets the ithyphallic Hermes as the mystical representation of the Ideal Principle of the universe, opposing him to sterile and passive Matter:

> This is . . . why the doctors of old, teaching through symbols and mystic representations, exhibit the ancient Hermes with the generative organ always in active posture; this is to convey that the generator of all things of sense [sense objects] is the Intellectual Reason Principle: the sterility of Matter, eternally unmoved, is indicated by the eunuchs surrounding it in its representation as the All-Mother. (*Enn.* 3.6.19)

Thus, gross Priapus, "raising his red, flaming, cocksure head" (Prologue QL.442) also came into the Neoplatonic tradition as the purest disembodied Power, the One. Lovers are listed among those who seek this Unity, since the soul's longing for the One resembles the lover's yearning for his mate; the beatific vision is likened to the sight and possession of the beloved.[18]

Priapus seldom appears in person in Rabelais's work; his most spectacular role is that of adviser to Jupiter in the Prologue to QL. More important to Rabelais, at any level of interpretation, are the effects of Priapus upon his followers. These rank in importance with the boozers, for the Prologue to G is dedicated both to the illustrious boozers and to the precious poxy. These poxy, who have sometimes been interpreted as the syphilitic patients whom Rabelais wishes to cure with his gallic humor, are certainly more than that. Rabelais does not love syphilitics any more than he loves drunkards, for elsewhere in his writings, he vilifies his enemies as syphilitic: "You with your sores, gnawed to the bone by pox,/Take your ulcers elsewhere and show them to others,/Scabby from head to toe and brimful of dishonour" (G.liv.154), or "Don't speak to me of high-hatted academicians . . . and of hypocritical scoundrels even less, although they all may be outrageous drinkers, all poxy and scabby . . . (Prologue TL; my trans.). The ambiguity is the same one incarnate in Bacchus and his drinkers: there are the bad and the good, the base and the sublime. The scabby are those who follow the seven fickle ladies who wait behind the portal of Venus in the *Hypnerotomachia Poliphili* to entrap the unwary pleasure-seeker. From the front they present the most alluring appearance, but when you view them from behind, "You would be constrained to vomit: you would recognize treason, and would smell dead flesh stinking beyond endurance."[19] The precious poxy are those who do not tarry with the seven ladies but travel onward to seek out the eternal truth hidden behind the priapic symbolism: *caritas* and divine love.

The Final Furor

While the group contemplates in ecstasy the marvelous temple and its lamp, the Venerable Pontiff Bacbuc and her train arrive to extend a joyful welcome, and to show the companions the miraculous fountain which occupies the center of this Dionysian splendor. *Bacbuc* means "bottle" in the sacred Hebrew language; *bac* means a tub or container in French (cf. TL.li.506); the name resembles the noise a bottle makes as wine is poured from it and, in addition, evokes the name *Bac-chus*. The high priestess offers her guests a drink of the harmonious water from the fountain which appeals to all five senses, being melodious, crystalline, and "so beautiful, so limpid and cold in the heart of summer. . ." (CL.xlii; my trans.). But, though the company admires the coolness and limpidity of the water, Bacbuc perceives that their sense of taste is still too coarse to appreciate its true virtues. She provides a feast of "scourers . . . so that we can rake, clear, and clean their palates" (CL.xlii.700), which prove to be the "bacchic artillery" of the archetypal Rabelaisian feast: hams, sausages, pressed eggs, caviar, and the like. Having finished their meal, the Pantagruelistes, now properly athirst, can distinguish in the liquid crystal of the fountain the flavor of any favorite wine they wish to imagine.[20] After this reenactment of the miracle of the wedding of Cana, Bacbuc reminds them all of the wonder of God's works: "After this you must confess that to God nothing is impossible." Rabelais himself replies: "We never said that anything was . . . We maintain that he is all-powerful" (CL.xlii.701).

Bacbuc prepares Panurge for the revelation he has sought so long. The preliminary purificatory ceremonies, which were necessary in order to enter the temple, are not sufficient for entry into the Holy of Holies: Panurge is put through a mysterious ceremony which includes both mock and serious elements, and which provides another instance of Rabelaisian *serio ludere*. Bacbuc addresses Panurge, telling him that she has only one important instruction: that he listen to the word of the oracle with one ear only. Friar Jean interposes: that is because it is "du vin à une aureille," one-eared wine. Panurge is dressed in a green smock, a white nun's snood on his head, a "chausse d'ipocras" (Hippocratic sock) with three wafers ("oblies") dangling from it, two old codpieces for gloves, and three bagpipes for a belt. His forehead is bathed in the fountain three times, a handful of flour is thrown in his face, three cock feathers are added to the right side of the "Hippocratic sock." He takes nine turns around the fountain, makes three little leaps, bumps his bottom seven times against the floor, all the while reciting a ritual (CL.xliv.701–02). "Vin à une oreille" according to Littré, is the *good* wine (spiritual wine). Panurge is clothed completely in mystical raiment: his head is covered with a white hood (white signifies "gladness, pleasure, delights, and rejoicing" [G.ix.57]), and his body cloaked in a green smock (green signifies strength, hope, and sexual vigor). He also wears a "chausse d'ipocras," which is a conical, woolen "sock" meant for straining mulled wine (Masters seems to think that Panurge's nose is wrapped with this "sock" [?]).[21] On the end of the sock, instead of a tassel (somehow, the description reminds the reader of Panurge's *braguette* in the Thaumaste episode), Bacbuc affixes three *oblies* (thin pastries or host wafers [!!] according to Hatzfeld). The colors symbolize Panurge's character and desires, while the sock and wafers are meant to purify the very "heart" of his desire. He is given two old codpieces as gloves and three bagpipes are tied around his waist. Both symbolize sensuality: the bagpipe is synonymous with stomach in the proverb cited by Littré: When the bagpipe is full, one sings better. The triad of bagpipes suggests a Pythagorean solution: intellect and good counsel overcome or purify the appetites. The ritual continues with Panurge's triple baptism. Water from the fountain is sprinkled on his forehead, the seat of his higher nature; a handful of flour is thrown into his face which both whitens (purifies) him and evokes the image of the "amourabaquin" (cf. CL. xlvii.886), Harlequin, the love fool of the *soties* and the *commedia dell'arte,* whose face is always whitened. The cock feathers indicate lascivity,[22] a fault which is again mitigated by the power of the number three. Triads multiply themselves in this ceremony: Panurge takes nine turns around the fountain — nine is thrice three; the intellectual power of three is raised to the second power; it has significance as an intensified trinity,[23] and also Cornelius Agrippa reminds us that Christ died in the ninth hour.[24] According to the Pythagoreans, nine flows around the other numbers within the decade like the ocean; it also is called the horizon. It is the most exalted point that can be reached before a retrogression takes place.[25] An end and a beginning, it symbolizes Panurge's situation: he is ending a crassly physical stage to enter a more spiritual one, but always, of course, within the limitations imposed by his essential nature. He performs three leaps, a striving toward heaven and higher things; Bacbuc then "had him bump his bottom seven times against the floor." Seven is "a number beloved of Nature" (CL.xlii); since it is the number of the seven stars which guide and govern the universe, it represents Panurge's lower nature dominated by the upper: in Pythagorean terms, seven represents tetrad (symbol of earth) surmounted by the triad (symbol of heaven). Clearly, Panurge is ritually purifying himself of worldly dross and lascivity throughout this comic ceremony.

The rites ended, Panurge is led, not by his left (*gauche,* "sinister") hand but by his right, into a round chapel built of transparent stone and abundantly lit in fluorescent fashion by the rays of the distant sun refracted from the cliff walls high above. The form of the chapel of the Bottle is itself the shape of a bottle, and it is transparent like glass. The round chapel is as high as it is wide, it is spherical and thus assumes the shape of the transparent orb that Christ is often shown holding: *urbi et orbi* — a symbol for the world as well as for "this intellectual sphere, the center of which is at all points and the circumference at none, and which we call God" (CL.xlviii.709). The Holy of Holies is a fountain heptagonal in shape, made of alabaster. The heptagon which allegorizes the union of earth and heaven is also the shape of the carbuncle or philosopher's stone surmounting the lifegiving fountain in the outer temple. The water which fills the basins appears to be "an element in its purest form" (CL.xliv; my trans.); perhaps the quintessence which ensouls the universe.[26] In its midst reclines the ovoid sacred Bottle. The sphere, here modified into an egg shape, emphatically suggests the *source* of all. Panurge must kiss the margin of the fountain, then perform three bacchic dances around it. The *épilénie* (grape harvest song) which he sings has, since the 1565 edition of the fifth book, been printed in the form of a bottle:

O Bouteille
Pleine toute
De mistères,
D'une oreille
Je t'escoute:
Ne différez
Et le mot profères
Auquel pend mon cueur!
En la tant divine licqueur,
Qui est dedans tes flans reclose,
Bachus, que fut d'Inde vaincqueur,
Tient toute vérité enclose.
Vin tant divin, loing de toy est forclose
Toute mensonge et toute tromperye,
En joye soit l'ame de Noé close,
Lequel de toy nous fist la tempérye.
Sonne le beau mot, je t'en prye,
Qui me doibt oster de misère.
Ainsi ne se perde une goutte
De toy, soit blanche, ou soit vermeille,
O Bouteille
Pleine toute
De mistères,
D'une oreille
Je t'escoute:
Ne différez
Et le mot profères
Auquel pend mon cueur!

(CL.xliv.881)[27]

O Bottle
Quite full
Of mysteries,
With one ear
I hark to thee:
Do not delay
And speak to me
The word on which my heart depends!
In the very holy licquor
Enclosed within thy sides,
Bacchus, conqueror of India,
Encloses all truth.
O very holy Wine, far from you is kept
All lying and all trickery.
May Noah's soul be immersed in joy
Who first taught us temperate use of thee.
Sound the good word, I beg of thee,
That will save me from misery.
Thus not a drop will be lost
of thee, be it white or be it red,
O Bottle
Quite full
Of mysteries,
With one ear
I hark to thee:
Do not delay
And speak to me
The word on which my heart depends!

(My trans.)

In the poem, Bacchus is identified with the divine draft, the nectar of *sobria ebrietas* which Noah drank: Bacchus contains all truth. "Thus not a drop will be lost" reminds the reader of another sacred ceremony, the mass, where the chalice is emptied with the greatest care lest any drop be spilled. Rabelais's fountain provides a link in the chain of archetypal fountain symbolism which has had universal meaning as an image of the soul, as the source of inner life and spiritual energy, as a symbol of the life-force of man and of all living things besides, i.e., as the very center of life.[28] In this as in other Rabelaisian fountains, its basic significance as the source of all things animated is coupled with numerous learned associations from the Western tradition. Like the bacchic Hippocrène of the Prologue to TL, this fountain also provides enthusiastic inspiration. All Rabelaisian fountains, including the fountain of the Graces of Thélème, flow from Judeo-Christian springs.

The combined *topoi* of Greek and Old Testament fountains produced a typically lyrical response in Philo Judaeus: "Wisdom pours forth in extravagant fullness the spring water of its purest teachings, and persuades the thirsty seeker to give himself up to a sober drunkenness." [29] This traditional symbolism of the holy water which produces divine furor was by no means lost to churchmen of the Renaissance: Nicholas of Cusa distinguishes between one type of thirst and another, just as there are different qualities of water. Thirst may be bodily or spiritual, for sensible or intellectual "water." [30] Further refining his distinctions, Cusa adds a third level. There are three wellsprings: the sensible fountain, "From the first, which I consider to be of animal nature and which is deep, drink father, sons, and the flock"; the rational fountain, "from the second, which lies at a deeper level of nature, drink the 'sons of men,' those who have vigorous minds and who are called philosophers"; and the fountain of wisdom, "of the third, which is deepest, we sing: 'Thou alone are most profound, Jesus Christ.' In this deepest well, I believe, is the font of wisdom which lends joy and immortality." [31]

Cusa's three fountains find a somewhat modified parallel in Rabelais's imagery: the bodily, sensible wine, which must be trodden underfoot, and from which the seeker must shield his head if he wishes to discover deeper truth — this is the first and most superficial fountain.

The second fountain, the one from which the "sons of men" may drink, produces the exquisite water-wine which refreshes the entire Pantagrueline company. This water is not to be despised, for it represents the loftiest aspirations of mankind: the seven pillars of the fountain which support the philosopher's stone not only represent the seven pillars which guard (and support) the firmament but they are also the seven pillars of wisdom; their symbolism unites the Neoplatonic with the Judeo-Christian tradition.[32] The deepest wellspring is not merely a font of wisdom; its pure element represents the Word of God itself.

The illumination of the inner temple by the wonderful lamp and of the round chapel by the sun itself also parallels Cusa's symbolism. In the same commentary, he equates the spiritual water with divine fire, a typical *coincidentia oppositorum*: "He who drinks of the spirit, drinks from a gushing fountain. For the spirit is like a spark of God's fire, of whom it is said, 'He is a consuming fire,' which, when it is sent into the earth, causes a fountain to flow with fire. . . ."[33] But Rabelais goes further; he introduces Cusa-like distinctions in his gradations of fire (or light): the inner temple, though brilliantly lit, is still artificially illuminated, while the chapel is brightened by the great source of all light, the sun, God, who is likewise the water and the very cliff face into which the holy temple is sunk. The apotheosis of Rabelais's work reveals that God inhabits the center of the "rock" (the world), and that tireless searching can bring the seeker to the deepest truth: "Christ is called 'the rock of the desert' . . . the Word in the rock was the open treasure-hoard of God which yielded living waters. That water which flowed so abundantly had its origin in the Word or in the power of His omnipotence."[34] The command of God to Panurge is *Trinch*, but before he can understand, Panurge must *drink in* the interpretation from the gloss, for, as Plato tells us, divine wisdom can never be grasped by mere human means; only in his madness or foolishness can man know the truth. Panurge drinks in the contents of the gloss and becomes "clerc jusques au foye," "learned to the teeth [liver]": his "knowledge" and subsequent power of prophecy are given to his liver while his intellect slumbers in the confusion of bacchic enthusiasm (Christian ecstasy). Pantagruel asks his protégé,

"What does your heart tell you, raised by bacchic enthusiasm?" (CL. xlv.883). "Heart" is used here by Rabelais in the sense of *estomac* (or liver) ;[35] and Panurge, speaking from the heart, replies:

> Trinchons, dist Panurge,
> Trinchons, de par le bon Bacchus!
> Ho, ho , ho, je voiray bas culz
> De brief bien en poinct sabourréz
> Par couilles, et bien embourréz
> De ma petite humanité.
>
> .   .   .   .
>
> Io Péan, Io Péan!
> Io Mariage troys foys!
> Czà, czà, frère Jehan, je te fais
> Serment vray et intelligible
> Que cest oracle est infalible;
> Il est seur, il est fatidicque!

(CL.xlv.884)

> " 'Let us drink,' said Panurge,
> 'Come, *trink,* by Bacchus, let us tope!
> Ho, ho, for now I truly hope
> To see some round and juicy rump
> Well tickled by my carnal stump
> And stuffed with my humanity.'
>
> .   .   .   .
>
> 'Io Paean, Io Paean!
> Io marriage, three times dear.
> Listen, Brother John, I swear
> My true and intellectual oath
> That this oracle speaks truth
> It's certain, and it's fateful — both.' "

(CL.xliv.705–06)

His Dionysian and Priapic poem shows that he at last has been given the grace to solve his dilemma. His sober drunkenness on holy water releases him to follow his natural drives. *Trinch* means "fulfill thyself," and in Panurge's case, fulfillment means marriage regardless of risk, even though all the negative prophecies will no doubt come true.

Frère Jean ridicules Panurge's behavior, but Pantagruel rebukes the monk and contributes his own hymn:

Croyés que c'est la fureur poëticque
Du bon Bachus: ce bon vin ecliticque
Ainsi ses sens et le fait canticqueur.
Car, sans mespris,
A ses espritz
Du tout espris
Par sa liqueur,
De cris en ris,
De ris en pris,
En ce pourpris,
Faict son gent cueur
Rhétoricqueur,
Roy et vaincqueur
De nos soubriz;
Et, veu qu'il est de cerveau phanaticque,
Ce ne seroit acte de topicqueur
Penser moucquer un si noble trinqueur.

Believe me, it's the [poetic furor
Of good Bacchus: this fine wine eclipses
Thus his sense and makes of him a songster.]
For [without] doubt
[His spirit
Quite overcome
By liquor, turns
From cries to laughter,
From laughter to drink,
And in this circle
His noble heart becomes
Rhetorical,
King and conqueror
Of our scoffing smiles;]
And since his brain's inspired by wine,
'Twould be the act of a mean thinker
To mock at such a noble drinker.

(CL.xlvii.706; partly my trans.)

This poem, a sort of calligram like Panurge's poem of supplication but in the shape of a chalice, offers to Frère Jean an argument in favor of Panurge's genuine possession: the wine of Bacchus conquers his senses and makes of his heart a Rhetorical Poet; it would be "acte de topicqueur" (a petty act) to make light of his "cerveau phanaticque" (a state of mind in which one believes himself divinely inspired).[36] Frère Jean is convinced in spite of himself, and, in his short, inspired prayer, he simultaneously evokes for the reader the miracle of Christ, who changed water into wine at the wedding of Cana, and the bacchic transformation Frère Jean has just experienced:

> O Dieu, Père paterne,
> Qui muas l'eaue en vin,
> Fais de mon cul lanterne,
> Pour luyre à mon voisin.

Oh God, paternal Father divine,
Who turned water into wine,
Make a lantern of my bum,
That I may light my neighbor home.

Since Frère Jean has been guided in the right path, he generously wishes to guide his fellow man. What more appropriate request than that his bum be made a lantern to light the steps of those who come behind?

Panurge continues rhyming, and explains what has happened to all those oracles which had become "struck dumber than fish by the coming of our king and savior" (TL.xxiv.355): they have all been transported to the Temple of the Bottle, "If Plutarch had drunk here like us, he would never have wondered why the Delphic oracles are dumber than mackerels since they no longer make any replies. The reason is rather plain; the oracle is no longer in Delphi, it is here . . . full of one-eared wine, I mean, the wine of truth" (CL.xlvi; my trans.).[37]

Panurge urges Frère Jean to ask whether he too should marry (whether the clergy should cease to be celibate), but Jean furiously rejects the idea, seeing marriage as a trap in which his freedom would be forfeit. Panurge, *advocatus Priapi*, makes a stinging rejoinder, but the question of freedom versus paternity cannot be so easily resolved; it raises one of the basic difficulties of Christianity: whether purity (which St. Paul tended to equate with chastity) should be sacrificed to propagation of the race with all the woes attendant upon marriage. Bacbuc cuts short the debate, assuring Panurge and Jean that each one will be satisfied, since down here, in these circumcentral regions, supreme good consists in increasing and giving, not in taking and receiving (CL.xlvii.887–88). Grace does not receive; it gives unstintingly and need never be replenished. And it would be the same with any Christian as with Panurge or Frère Jean, Rabelais tells us, should he give in like manner.

A Recapitulation of Christian Symbolism:
Eucharistia — Evangelium — Ecclesia

In representing the Christian mysteries as he does, Rabelais is neither original nor blasphemous, for his basic metaphors had been in general use for centuries. His Temple of the Bottle, which houses the Fountain of Wisdom, has been shown to combine elements drawn from the hermetic, Pythagorean sources with those traditional Christian elements which hearken back to the early Alexandrian Church Fathers. Origen ties all the biblical passages describing drinking bouts to Proverbs 9:1–6, and designates the pupils of Wisdom as *societas componantium vinum,* "a society for sharing wine." Wine functions for Origen as Wisdom's drink, the mystical union of *Nous,* and the Godhead is presented as a banquet where the saints, prophets, and angels drink the *potus laetitiae,* "liquor of joy" from the *fons bonorum,* "font of the good" and nourish themselves with *cibus sapientiae,* "food of wisdom." [38] Perhaps the best example of Origen's procedure may be seen in his explanation of the Song of Solomon, 2:4, "Introduxit me in cellam vinariam," "he led me into the wine tavern." The tavern becomes Wisdom's house which is also the house of God or the Church, where Wisdom mixes the wine and invites the multitude to come inside. Origen weaves a number of vinous verses from the Bible into his explanation, noting that the table of Abraham, Isaac, and Jacob in heaven (Matt. 8:11) is in this same tavern and that Psalms 8, 80, and 83 celebrate the pressing of this same wine, which comes from the true vine which is Christ (John 15:1). It is a wine on which the righteous, like Noah, become drunk. But there is always another wine, that of the evil ones who eat the bread of impiety and drink the wine of iniquity (Prov. 4:17).[39] This commentary has close analogues in Philo, in the Church Fathers, in Duns Scotus, and, later still, in Nicholas of Cusa. It expresses in very compact form those mysteries which Rabelais weaves into so many different patterns.[40] The "Propos des bien yvres," which combines so many semi-autonomous parts into a harmonic unity, presents themes which reappear again and again, to culminate in the *Dive Bouteille* chapters. All the "bien yvres," whether protagonists of Rabelais's books or readers of them, drink the "one-eared wine," the wine of truth, which has only beneficial effects ("Avalez, ce sont herbes!"), and which represents a "cure" (salvation) for body and soul alike.

The participation in the *logos* which the *Dive Bouteille* episode describes is probably the most striking version of the Eucharist. The mystery of the mass is celebrated there in its most vital form: direct communication with the Godhead. Although the high priestess is present to keep the sanctuary and explain the ritual, the actual communication between *logos* and listener, gloss and boozer is direct and need not (indeed cannot) be interpreted by an intermediary. In representing the Eucharistic mystery as he does, Rabelais may well have had recourse not only to hermetic and Christian writings but also to contemporary and near-contemporary Church art. The symbolism of the wine had become increasingly important in the Church of the fourteenth through the sixteenth centuries, a preoccupation which expressed itself in particularly bloody representations of Christ on the Cross. Christian art became obsessed with the implications inherent in the shedding of divine blood; the crucified Christ was painted in gory detail, covered with wounds.[41] Eventually, this preoccupation with divine blood led to the mystical theme of the Fountain of Life, which depicts the cross rising in the center of a large chalice, filled to the brim with the blood which spurts from the wounds of Christ. Around the chalice press crowds of sinners who remove their clothing in preparation for a cleansing baptism of blood. The blood was called a "bath for souls," a "pool for the sick," a "fountain of purity" ("an element in its purest form": CL.xliv; my trans.). But this bloody imagery still did not satisfy the Christian imagination in late medieval and Renaissance France. In order better to express the horror of the crucifixion

Figure 2. *Le Pressoir Mystique.* Engraving from the Cabinet des Estampes, Bibliothèque Nationale, Paris.

91

and to illustrate more graphically that Christ gave his last drop of blood for the sinner, artists began to picture him in the grip of an enormous cruciform wine press; his blood jets out like the juice of a grape, and flows into the waiting vat[42] (see figure 2).

Rabelais, Franciscan preacher, Benedictine healer, Evangelical believer, distributes the wine through his new Gospel. The good companions of the "Propos," who remain the same throughout the work, form a part of the complex and mystical tradition, representing the Faithful in all stages on the ladder of perfection. They form a church which is independent of, but not opposed to, the established one. Their church is reduced to its bare essentials: a communion in prayer, in thanksgiving, and in the commemoration of eating and drinking the Eucharistic bread and wine in which God is really present. They partake of the Word, the breviary stuff, and the "motz de geule" which are always on hand. The sharing of joys and sorrows among the Pantagruelistes is a communion also in the sense of *koinōnia* (a word from which we derive "communion," and which is related to *chairein* "to rejoice"), which originally signified having something in common that had first been equally divided among all participants.[43] The three mysteries of the Christian religion, *Eucharistia, Ecclesia, Evangelium,* blend into one, since all are aspects of the mystery of Christ, the *logos;* all are parts of the "good news," *potus laetitiae.*

The archetypal Rabelaisian parable resembles a series of Silenus boxes, one inside the other. The "letter" outside leads the boozer, if he is sufficiently inspired, to find the spirit within. But this task must be performed by understanding rather than reason. In a state of holy furor, during the suspension of reason, the spiritual eye may become well enough focused to perceive the swarming, protean metamorphoses of Christian symbolism that lie "inside" the parables: these are the spirit of the letter, Pan within Proteus, the wine within the bottle, for which Gargantua thirsts from the moment of his birth, when, instead of "mies! mies!" he cries, "drink! drink!"

PART II

Will and Nature:
Rabelais's
Neoplatonic-
Christian
Ladder

Chapter 4

The Giants

Body, the Language of the Soul

Every man is a Silenus box to every other man, for each is made up of body and soul, an outer appearance and an inner reality. The ideal state of man is the joyful harmony of body and soul with the divine plan: man should "drink in" God's grace, "Pantagruelizing, that is to say, drinking to your heart's content" (G.i; my trans.), but many circumstances may stand in the way of total harmony with the will of God. Man's will is free: he may choose discord or, because of his place in nature's hierarchy, he may find it more difficult to discover the right path, even though he seeks it earnestly.

Educated men of the sixteenth century, whatever their persuasion, conceived of the universe as a hierarchical construction. Virtually all the ontological systems invented up to that period involved a graded scale of values applied to the structure of the world that could be conceived as a ladder, ranging from base matter through the vegetable and animal world to man, and, above man, through the various levels of spiritual beings to God. Rabelais invariably refers to this hierarchy and shows particular interest in the means of communication between levels.[1] The giants, highest in Rabelais's hierarchy, representatives of Bacchus as their names imply, always conform to the divine will. Friar Jean, too, though certainly not superhuman, remains in constant touch with the divine through his breviary stuff. Panurge is "out of tune" but his problem has a beneficial effect, acting as a catalyst. Panurge leads the other Rabelaisian heroes to seek out the *Dive Bouteille*.

Rabelais accepts the doctrine of the Platonists that much of life takes place on an unseen, spiritual level. A constant interchange operates between the invisible world and everyday reality, since all things are "shot through" with soul ("l'âme de l'univers": TL.iii.341). Rabelais furnishes several examples of the "normal" influences of spirit on body through the various levels of the hierarchy. Although man may be in constant touch with the rest of creation, he only becomes aware of it under certain conditions. Superior beings watch over him at all times, but they do not communicate with him until he nears death. Similarly, when a ship comes into harbor, the spectators on the dock wait in silence, praying for the safe arrival of all on board, until it comes within hailing distance. In the same way the angels, heroes, and good daemons (according to the Platonists), seeing human beings approaching the safe haven of death, salute them, console them, and begin teaching them the art of divination (TL.xxi.402). A dying poet would of all men be most apt to prophesy since he is not only helped by the daemons and heroes but he is also under the protection of Apollo: "The poets who are under Apollo's protection, on approaching their deaths, generally become prophets and sing by Apolline inspiration, foretelling future events" (TL.xxi; my trans.).

On the human level, communication may take place between men in ways that have no connection with the senses. One man's "animal spirits" may influence directly those of his fellow, as when a gloomy, ill-humored physician saddens his patients or when a serene, joyous doctor produces the opposite effect by making his patients feel better. All this is obvious and needs no proof, but Rabelais wonders whether these effects are caused by apprehension or joy as the sick man watches his doctor's expression, or if there is an actual "transfusion of serene or of gloomy spirits" (*Anc. Prol.* to QL; my trans.).

Rabelais prescribes a special regime for the education of Gargantua, so that he might avoid the influence of noxious humors from the atmosphere and from matter. On rainy days he eats lighter, drier foods, "so that the intemperate humidity of the air, communicated to the body by necessary proximity, would be corrected in this way . . ." (G.xxiv; my trans.). If a man indulges his base appetites too liberally, he may render himself unfit to receive communications from the higher realms. Like a mirror whose surface may become dulled by steam or fog, so the spirit cannot receive "the forms of divination by dreams" if the body is troubled by the vapors and fumes of heavy food (TL.xiii.374). These ideas make clearer Rabelais's notion of the structure of the universe. A man must become aware of his place in the hierarchy, and must live his life accordingly. In order to know what regime to adopt, Rabelais believes that a man should know himself, body and spirit, as completely as possible: not only through reading ancient authority but through direct observation as well. Grandgousier advises his son to read with care the Greek, Arabic, and Roman physicians without scorning the Talmudists and Cabalists, and to perform frequent anatomical dissections in order to become perfectly acquainted with that other world which is man (P.viii.195). Man, the microcosm, exists in two modes, body and soul, just as does the universe. These two modes inevitably parallel each other, even though the outer, visible shell may caricature the inner self. Insofar as the body "shadows forth" the soul, as the flickering light in Plato's cave bears a distant resemblance to the true light, the body mirrors the moods and passions of the soul, and thus, in some sense, is the soul's creation. The body is the language of the soul.

Gargantua and Pantagruel, Heroes and Good Daemons

The chief obstacle to achieving perfect microcosmic harmony is man's free will. When his appetites draw him downward, his reason will be caught in a ceaseless pro and con, unless he chooses a definite course of action. The giants are paragons of harmony with the divine plan: they successfully maintain the delicate balance between natural inclination (determined by blind destiny) and free choice. In conformity with the idea that the body is the language of the soul, Rabelais describes the huge bodies of his heroes, telling the reader that they are, in Platonic terms, "great-souled men" as well. He often appears to forget the unusual size of his heroes, an inconsistency puzzling to most readers. But since size stands as a metaphor for spiritual greatness, Rabelais hopes that the reader will apply to the soul what he says of the body.

Thaumaste, frightened at first by Pantagruel's size, "sees through" his physical enormity to the Pantagrueline essence, just as we are expected to do. He is as astonishing and wonderful to see as the image of Platonic wisdom and knowledge made flesh (P.xviii.248).

The giants, incarnations of wisdom, occupy the topmost rung of the Rabelaisian ladder. What this position entails may be deduced from the accounts of their births. Rabelais pretends that his stories of the giants were discovered in the vast grave of a hitherto unknown monarch. The supernatural note is struck from the outset, and, coupled with the antiquity of the "little . . . book which smelt more strongly but not more sweetly than roses" (G.i.42), the contents are identified with the hallowed wisdom of the ancients. The gravemarker is engraved with the shape of a goblet over the inscription *hic bibitur,* "this is to be drunk," an echo of — although it does not coincide with — the words of Jesus as he handed his disciples the commemorative cup of wine at the Last Supper. Upon excavation, nine flasks lined up in three rows of three were uncovered; the *hic bibitur* becomes an invitation to the seeker to drink from these symbols of triple trinity.[2]

The Birth of Gargantua

Beneath these very solemn markers lies the giants' family history, including the account of the pregnancy of Gargamelle. She is reported to have carried Gargantua for eleven months, which gives rise to comparisons with Neptune and Hercules. Both these superhuman beings, in order to reach perfection, required long periods for their conception or for their incubation. Thus Gargantua, even before his birth, belongs to an exalted company.[3] The birth, which occurs through his mother's left ear, has been considered by Lefranc a blasphemous parody of the birth of Christ. Febvre contests this, pointing out that Christ's birth was normal enough, except that Mary — a very different case from Gargamelle — was a virgin. The point of the episode, according to Febvre, was to recommend that Christians be circumspect in what they believe; that one cannot believe everything he hears.[4] Rabelais contests the Pauline injunction, "Charity believes all things" (1 Cor. 13); the story of Gargantua's miraculous birth should be believed just as little as the Golden Legend for which Rabelais shows such contempt. No doubt this is one of Rabelais's aims in writing the episode, but since, in later editions, as a result of Church censure, he drops all reference to the Bible, it is likely that his other purposes were at least as important to him. By his grotesque and comic account, he underscores the supernatural origin of the child. (He names Bacchus, Minerva, Adonis, Castor and Pollux, not to mention his own inventions, Rocquetaillade and Crocquemouche — all of whom were born in similarly miraculous ways.)

The child's father, "a good jester in his time with [a] great . . . love of tossing off a glass . . . [and] a liking for salt meat" (G.iii.46), exemplifies Rabelais's ideal from the outset. His spiritual affinities as an illustrious boozer described here covertly are detailed at length as Rabelais describes his role during the Picrocholine war. The old gentleman does nothing without first consulting God and his own good counsel. Like Grandgousier, Gargantua arrives in this world with a thirst for the spirit perhaps even greater than his father's, and "cried out . . . Drink! Drink! Drink! as if inviting the whole world to drink, and so loud that he was heard through all the lands of Booze and Bibulous" (G.vi.52). But Rabelais makes clear that this is no selfish request; he wishes everyone to share his joy. His father names him, according to the ancient Hebrew tradition, after the first exclamation that he utters when his son is born: "Que grand tu as!" "What a big one you've got! — [the gullet being understood]" (G.vii.53). What a great capacity for absorbing the spirit(s)!

Gargantua's childhood behavior confirms his divine inheritance. A genuinely bacchic child, the mere sound of pints and flagons clinking together suffices to send him into ecstasy, "as if tasting the joys of paradise. Taking this divine disposition into account, therefore, in order to cheer him up in the mornings, they would have glasses clinked for him . . ." (G.vii.54).

In his account of how Gargantua was dressed (G.viii), Rabelais alternates between hyperbolic insistence on the baby's size and references to his divine or superhuman qualities. His cape, replete with bacchic symbolism, is embroidered with grapevines, pints, and vine stocks, thus denoting that he would be a good boozer in his day:

> As his hat-medallion, he had a fine piece of enamelled work . . . on which was displayed a human body with two heads turned towards one another, four arms, four feet and two rumps — the form, accord-

ing to Plato in his *Symposium,* of Man's nature in its mystical beginnings; and around it was written in Ionian script:

AGAPÉ OU ZÉTEI TA HEAUTÉS.

"Charity seeketh not her own profit."

(1 Cor. 13:5)

The comic obscenity of Gargantua's emblem strikes the reader first:
Rabelais is describing the "two-backed beast" and *not* Aristophanes'
androgyne:

> The primeval man was round, his back and sides forming a circle;
> and he had four hands and four feet, one head with two faces, looking
> opposite ways, set on a round neck and precisely alike; also four ears,
> two privy members, and the remainder to correspond.[5]

Rabelais obviously does not see why *his* androgyne should not enjoy
himself more than Aristophanes', in a continual giving and receiving
of love. Ignoring Rabelais's travesty, Masters solemnly, and no doubt
correctly, assures us that Rabelais's androgyne symbolizes *caritas,* not
physical love, a supposition which the Pauline motto would bear out.
He also attests that the androgyne was a favorite symbol of prelap-
sarian man.[6] Gargantua's neckchain, made of gold and green jasper, is
engraved with the magical and astrological signs worn by the Egyptian
pharaoh Necepsos: dragons surrounded by sparks and rays of light.
These Gargantuan dragons are guardians of light rather than devilish
harbingers of obscurity and destruction. Pliny (H.N.8.12) and Galen
attribute positive characteristics to the dragon: because of its strength,
vigilance, and keen vision, it is given the function of guardian of tem-
ples and treasures. Its name derives from the Greek *derkesthai,* "to
see"; it becomes an allegory of prophecy and wisdom.[7] It is in this
sense that Rabelais uses it as a symbol for the young giant. One of
Gargantua's rings is made of "or de seraph" (meaning pure gold but
also referring to divine origin); another is a combination of four
metals, gold, silver, steel, and copper, joined in such a way that no
metal actually touches any other ("This was all the work of Captain
Chappuis and his good assistant, Alcofribas" [G.viii.57]). The reader
must not forget that Alcofribas, Rabelais himself, is a consummate
magician, "Abstractor of the Quintessence." In alchemy, each metal
symbolizes a planet and a celestial influence. Gold denotes the sun,
Apollo, supreme masculine beauty and beneficence; silver denotes the

moon, Diana and chastity; steel is Mars' metal, symbolizing the art of war; copper reflects the beauty of Venus, love and sensuality. The bacchic child thus wears a ring in which "masculine" and "feminine" influences, as well as the personality traits dominant in all mankind, are equally balanced.

Another ring is made in the form of a spiral, "in which were set a perfect "balay" ruby, a pointed diamond, and a physon emerald. . . ." The emerald comes from Physon, one of the four rivers of Paradise. This ring is estimated by Hans Carvel to the worth "sixty-nine million, eight hundred and ninety-four thousand *moutons à la grande laine*" (gold coins imprinted with the image of the *Agnus Dei*). The child's colors, Rabelais tells us, are white and blue. White, the opposite of black which signifies sadness and mourning, means joy, and blue, a heavenly color, means "celestial things." Thus the child wears the colors appropriate to the good boozer, since "humer la purée septembrale," "slurping the septembral soup," the wine, brings celestial joy. His image pictures the dual modes of physical enjoyment and divine love, the dragons on his neckchain indicate that the vigilant and farseeing spirit of wisdom and prophecy will act as his guardian; his remaining insignia elaborate still other aspects of his divine calling.

One item of his clothing most elaborately described is the baby's opulent codpiece. Somewhere between two and three meters long, it is made of blue damask and decorated with lace, diamonds, rubies, turquoises, emeralds, and pearls in such profusion that it resembles a beautiful horn of plenty, filled with all delights (G.viii.27–28). The codpiece, "pinked out" in blue, is a celestial object, decorated accordingly in a way which reminds Rabelais of a cornucopia, symbol of abundant nature and divine liberality or grace. Rabelais evidently wants us to conjure up divine as well as natural associations for this cornucopia, since he likens it to the one Rhea gave to Jupiter's nurses. Gargantua will pass on with his seed the blessing and grace of God, for the first product of his codpiece-cornucopia is Pantagruel, a son worthy of such a father, as great of soul as of body.

The Birth of Pantagruel

Pantagruel's birth is deliberately described in a manner reminiscent of the great chronicles of antiquity, not only the "Arabs, Barbarians, and Romans but also the noble Greeks who were eternal boozers" (P.i; my trans.). The first edition of *Pantagruel* reads more significantly: "not only the Greeks, the Arabs, and the Gentiles but also the authors of the holy scripture like St. Luke and St. Matthew." Rabelais's first version more explicitly links his comic hero with the savior of mankind.

The opening statement on Pantagruel's lineage gives the condition of the earth: "At the beginning of the world . . . shortly after Abel was killed by his brother Cain, the earth, soaked with the blood of the righteous, was one year so very fertile in all the fruits which are born from her loins for us, and especially in medlars [*mesles*], that from time immemorial it was called the year of the great medlars, for three of them filled a bushel."

"In that year the kalends were determined by the breviaries of the Greeks" (P.i; my trans.). In Rabelais's account, the "blood of the righteous" causes the earth to produce abundantly, but in Genesis 4: 11–12, we learn that the opposite was the case: "And now you are cursed from the ground, which has opened its mouth to receive your brother's blood from your hand. When you till the ground, it shall no longer yield to you its strength; you shall be a fugitive and a wanderer on the earth." The fruit which Rabelais's "fertile soil" produces is "mesles" (*nèfles,* "medlar," a fruit resembling the crab apple and worthless until it is dried). The French expression "Des nèfles!" means, according to Larousse, "Rien, pas du tout," "nothing, not at all." [8] The Greeks did not count their months by kalends as the Romans did; and naturally, they had no breviaries. Rabelais's reference to time is a redoubled way of saying "never," hence the conditions which were to give rise to Pantagruel's line were never met.

Because they ate the plentiful *nèfles* produced by the fertile soil (blasted by the blood of the righteous), the peoples were tricked like Noah, who drank too much of a good thing. Several monstrous races (never) arose, among them, the giants. Rabelais lists their names and the deeds of the most noteworthy in an imitation of the "begats" in Genesis; then he describes the birth of Pantagruel.

Gargantua, having achieved the biblical age of "four hundred, four score, and forty-four years," engenders a son by his wife Badebec (she dies in childbirth). The year is a marvelously dry one: "in that

year there was so great a drought throughout the land of Africa, that
. . . not a tree in the land . . . had either leaf or flower" (P.ii.175).
Even the earth itself becomes so overheated it sweats great drops of
water. The people begin to rejoice, but they are soon undeceived: the
water is like brine, saltier than sea water. Because he is born that very
day, Gargantua names the baby Panta (all) Gruel (athirst), "by this
meaning to infer that at the hour of the child's nativity the world was
all thirsty, and also seeing, in a spirit of prophecy, that one day his son
would be ruler over the thirsty . . ." (P.ii.176). It is prophesied that he
shall lead those who thirst. The circumstances of his birth, his name,
the fact that he is preceded from his mother's womb by sixty-eight
mules loaded with salt, nine dromedaries bearing hams and smoked
beef tongues, seven camels carrying salted baby eels, etc. (P.ii.180) —
everything indicates that Pantagruel is a messenger of God, full of the
Spirits, and never out of tune with the divine will. He will be a spur
to the thirst of the boozer for righteousness, inciting the guzzlers to seek
the right path.

Later, after his education has been completed, Pantagruel assumes
the duties of his father and grandfather: protector of his land against
invaders. His character and training, like that of Grandgousier and
Gargantua, fit the archetype of the Platonic guardian of the Republic,
from whose ranks the philosopher-king is to be chosen. Socrates summarizes the required characteristics of the warrior in the opening passages of the *Timaeus,* describing him as merciful to his subjects but
fierce to his enemies, both passionate and philosophical by temperament, and well educated in gymnastics, music, and all other branches
of learning suited to his calling.

In the war against the Dipsodes, Pantagruel captures one of the
enemy who fears that his captor will hold him for ransom, but Pantagruel replies that his purpose is not to rob or ransom men but to en-
rich and reform them in total freedom (P.xxviii,285). This same total
liberty will prevail in Thélème, where men will live subject only to the
divine plan, to the grace of God.

Pantagruel Conquers India

Rabelais's account of Bacchus conquering India in book five is
prefigured by a burlesque antecedent at the end of *Pantagruel,* written

roughly twenty years earlier. Pantagruel is a "vicar of Bacchus on earth," for, though he is evidently not a god, he incarnates many of the god's most important attributes.

Shortly after his father is "translated into Fairyland by Morgan" (P.xxiii.245), Pantagruel receives news that the Dipsodes have invaded his homeland. From Paris he rides in haste to Rouen and thence to the port of *Hommefleur* (Honfleur) where he embarks with his trusty lieutenants Panurge, Epistémon, Eusthenes, and Carpalim. Their route: "passing Porto Santo and Madeira, they landed on the Canary Islands. Leaving there, they passed by . . . Senegal . . . and the Cape of Good Hope, and disembarked in the kingdom of Melinda" (P.xxiv. 247). This is precisely the itinerary, made famous by Vasco da Gama, that the Portuguese and Spaniards followed to India. Our hero's homeland, in book two at least, is the same as that of Bacchus: the land where grape culture and winemaking are supposed to have originated. After landing, Pantagruel and company withstand the first enemy attack; they kill all the Dipsodic knights except one, whom they send back to his king with a rather dubious gift. The lone messenger arrives before his monarch and presents the gift box of preserves. As soon as the king has swallowed a spoonful, his throat and tongue begin to burn and pain him so much that he can only find relief in continuous drinking. The servants, no doubt tired of filling the king's goblet, invent a better expedient: they pour wine into him through a funnel. Meanwhile, his captains, whose curiosity about the preserves has been aroused, try a spoonful for themselves, and each is affected like the king. The whole army begins to guzzle until at last everyone in the camp drops down asleep pell-mell, like so many hogs. Having thus overcome his enemies with drink, Pantagruel orders his trusty Carpalim to burn the enemy camp. After setting fire to tents and pavilions, he passes over them without even disturbing their heavy slumbers. A typically Rabelaisian touch is added to this scene of bacchic destruction: "Suddenly, because of the drugs that Panurge had given him, Pantagruel felt a desire to piss; and he pissed over the camp so well and copiously that he drowned them all, and there was a special flood for thirty miles round. . . . When the enemy had awoken, seeing on one side the fire in their camp, on the other the inundation and deluge of urine, they did not know what to say or think. Some said it was the end of the world and the last judgment, which is to be consummated by fire . . ." (P.xxviii.259–60). Pantagruel ends the battle with a flood which, when viewed from the nearby city by firelight, appears to be a sea of blood. Rabelais has rewritten, in his highly original style, the Dionysian (re)conquest of India: "This picture was meant to convey how, in his invasion of India, Bacchus put everything to fire and sword (*à feu et à sang*)" (CL.xxxix.691).

Pantagruel, whose Dionysian lineage is revealed in the family names Grandgousier, Gargamelle, etc., excites men to thirst for knowledge, truth, and righteousness; he is a representative of the *logos* on earth. In this capacity, he does his best to guide Panurge in his dilemma, telling him that every man must make his own choice, that external circumstances are neither good nor bad, and that to the pure, all things are pure (TL.vii.352).[9] As Screech points out, Pantagruel is pure and wise; Panurge impure and a fool, seduced by the evil spirit. Additional reasons for Pantagruel's superiority to Panurge may be discovered in the theory of the fourfold soul. Lower on the ladder of being, Panurge can only "see" with the eyes of the sensitive and rational souls; he cannot find the solution to a problem which demands more insight than he possesses. Pantagruel knows instantly what must be done in all matters which appear insoluble to reason. He resolves the litigation between Messieurs Baisecul and Humesvesne to the great satisfaction of both parties; he rejects Panurge's clever rhetoric in praise of debtors; he sees how Panurge may resolve the question of his marriage. All these miraculous insights are achieved by the intellective soul (*qui voit d'une vue*), affording instant access to Truth.

The giants, who bear witness to the *logos,* also may be considered good daemons and heroes. Rabelais equates heroes and daemons in the Raminagrobis episode (TL.xxi.402); Pantagruel's role, in the *parolles gelées* episode, bears out his heroic superiority over all the others (cf. also the elaboration on heroes in QL.xxvii.615–17). Masters points out that Gargantua (and Pantagruel, who inherits his characteristics) is an allegory of *caritas,* divine love.[10] Cornelius Agrippa's chapter "De l'ordre animasticque, et des héros," furnishes a striking example of the same variety of syncretism which Rabelais practices: Directly after the choirs of angels comes the "animastic" order called Issim by the Hebrew theologians who are powerful men, called heroes, demigods, or daemonic gods by the Magi. Fulgentius thought they were so-called because they were not quite worthy of heaven but merited more than earth, as did Priapus, Hippo, and Vertumnus. The power of our own heroes, the saints, is given them by God. Among these, the twelve Apostles are the most important.[11]

Saints, heroes, and daemons, the giants are greater still. Gargantua's miraculous birth is reminiscent in part of biblical accounts; Pantagruel's own birth is linked explicitly with the Gospels. Gargantua also appears to be immortal, for, like a dying-rising savior figure, he is translated "into Fairyland" only to reappear at Panurge's symposium in the *Tiers Livre*. An abyss of knowledge as his father hoped he would be, Pantagruel represents a compendium of all the wisdom accessible to mortal man. As a *logos* figure, he becomes a Christ figure as well. In the Thaumaste episode, the English scholar describes Pantagruel in words which Christ used to refer to Himself, "Et ecce plus quam Salomon hic" (P.xx.258).[12] In Luke 11:31, Jesus explains that if the Queen of Sheba had come from the ends of the earth to hear Solomon, how much farther would she have traveled to hear one who is greater than Solomon? For "behold here is one greater than Solomon." Thaumaste also explains that his praise goes to Pantagruel and not to Panurge because "non est discipulus super magistrum," "a disciple is not greater than the master [teacher]" (P.xx.259), words from Jesus' Sermon on the Mount that also refer to Himself (Luke 6:40). Both passages, adapting Christ's words to apply to Rabelais's hero, make of him a link between Creator and man, between the macro- and the microcosm.

Chapter 5

Man: The Abbot of Thélème and His Abbey

Frère Jean, Servant of Bacchus

Rabelais's evaluation of human nature remains "realistic" throughout his work. Frère Jean becomes abbot of Thélème not because he is without fault (he is indeed far from perfection), but because he compensates for his many vices with more important virtues. Jean lives healthily on all levels of his being: on the bodily level, he participates heartily in vegetative and animal functions; on the level of reason, he uses his common sense to good effect in the battle of the abbey close; but it is his spiritual goodness which earns him Thélème. He is a perfect microcosm, exactly in the middle between the animal and the divine. The reader may cease to puzzle over his hearty base appetites, since his appetite for the divine is still more voracious. He needs no learning, since he knows the very essence of his breviary stuff. The comic errors he makes in quoting its Latin version merely serve to demonstrate once again one of Rabelais's major points: external form and ritual are irrelevant, only "simple" Christianity and direct communication with God are important.

Although Frère Jean plays roughly the same role throughout the four books in which he figures, he still remains in some ways puzzling to the reader. What, precisely, is the function of the intensely corporeal and bawdy Benedictine in the Evangelical circle around the giants? How can his incredible feats of mayhem and mass slaughter harmonize with the Rabelaisian motto, implicit in the *Tiers Livre,* explicit in the *Quart,* "médiocrité en tout?" Finally, why does Rabelais award the Abbeye de Thélème to Jean, who has so little of the polish and elegance which characterize the noble inhabitants?

The first clues to these problems are furnished in the description of Frère Jean, savior of the abbey close of Seuilly. Jean is "jeune, guallant, frisque, de hayt, bien à dextre, hardy, adventureux, délibéré . . ." (G.xxvii.83). Physically, Jean's clean-cut appearance contrasts sharply with Rabelais's usual portrayal of degenerate and sloppy monks. His youth and gaiety, particularly the latter, are typical of Rabelais's heroes, as is gallantry, although this seems an odd quality in a monk. Jean is "bien à dextre," adroit as well as bold, adventurous, and prudent. "A dextre" implies more than merely skillful or graceful. It means, literally, right-handed as well as right-thinking, fortunate, and lively, by contrast to the gauche, sinister, unlucky left-handed unfortunate. "Tall and thin," Jean also has "a great gaping mouth": In certain ways he is unique among monks; in other ways, he typifies monkery, since, as we all know, monks stick close to the kitchen. He has a "fine outstanding nose," a mark of true beauty in a French male, later to be seen in other great men such as Louis XIV and de Gaulle.

After the physical description comes what might be called Jean's "professional competence": "beau despescheur d'heures, beau desbrideur de messes, beau descroteur de vigiles . . ." (G.xxvii.83). The three Rabelaisian nouns, *despescheur, desbrideur, descroteur* all mean roughly the same thing: Jean is a record-breaking dispatcher of his offices. Rabelais sums up: "Pour tout dire . . . vray moyne si oncques en feut depuys que le monde moynant moyna de moynerie; au reste clerc jusques ès dents en matière de bréviaire" (G.xxvii.83–84). We may translate, in part, "A true monk, *if* there ever was one since monkery began," for we soon discover, in the course of Jean's second appearance, that *all* the rest of monkery is harshly and summarily rejected, while Jean alone is accorded full approval. In other words, except for Jean, there are no *true* monks. Besides, he is *un clerc* to the teeth in breviary stuff: he knows by heart the Scripture on which the breviary is based. The phrase "jusques ès dents en matière de bréviaire," expresses a typically Rabelaisian ambiguity, since the breviary also stands for a leather-covered hip-flask, and the *matière* that fills it is the wine, the holy spirit(s), which fill Jean to the very teeth.

So far, we know that Jean is young, strong, joyful, skilled, handsome, and a man who does not take the rituals of the hours, the mass, or the vigils very seriously, and yet who knows the breviary by heart.

He combines the characteristics of the chivalresque hero and certain telling traits of the Evangelical: he performs Church rites in a most perfunctory way, while his true concerns lie elsewhere, closer to the heart of Christianity, as we are shown during the first major battle of the Picrocholine war.

The war, initiated by a quarrel between the shepherds (*bergiers*) who were tending the vines of La Devinière and the cake or wafer bakers (*fouaciers*) of Lerné, begins over a disagreement about bread and wine. To most of us in the twentieth century, a quarrel about bread and wine still brings to mind the violent controversies of Rabelais's day over the meaning of the Eucharist. Corroboration of such an interpretation comes from a source much closer to Rabelais, Pierre-Antoine Le Motteux, a seventeenth-century translator of Rabelais and a Protestant, who considered that "most of the adventures, which are mystically represented by Rabelais, relate to the affairs of religion." [1] Taking a fiercely partisan position, he interprets the *bergiers*, Grandgousier's servants, as pastors of the Lutheran or Calvinist faith; the *fouaciers* as the "priests and other ecclesiasticks of Spain" and "the mistificators of the church of Rome." [2] The *fouace*, he believes, represents the host wafer, since both are made in a similar manner. Although undoubtedly correct in his initial assumption of underlying religious meaning, Le Motteux's partisan feelings lead him to read back into the 1530s the Protestant situation as he himself knew it. At the time Rabelais wrote his account of the Picrocholine war, there were very few Protestant pastors who considered themselves separate from the Catholic Mother Church; Calvin himself was just making up his mind whether he would be ordained a priest in the ordinary way or not.

The battle of the abbey close does confirm the religious interpretation of the war. As in all conflicts, a relatively trivial clash sets off a chain reaction of ever-increasing violence, until thousands of people lie massacred. Early events of the war appear to illustrate the maxim that "God helps those who help themselves." Rabelais emphasizes the puzzling phenomenon that the wicked attackers seem to lead "charmed lives," for they enter in safety to sack homes where the plague is rampant, while the doctors and priests, who come to help the sufferers, all die of the disease. "Dont vient cela, Messieurs? Pensez-y, je vous pry" (G.xxvii.83). Rabelais slyly challenges the reader to try to solve the traditional problem of evil: the undeserved misfortunes of good people. Most Evangelicals *were* prepared (or believed they were prepared) to suffer misfortune or persecution for their faith, and to endure to the end (almost) with hope of a heavenly reward. But what about the success of the evil forces? As the episode unfolds, it becomes clear that the invaders enjoy complete success only until they confront Rabelais's heroes. Gargantua and Frère Jean not only help themselves as vigorously as do the aggressors but they also act in accord with the divine will. Their victory is therefore assured. The "self-help" idea certainly explains why Frère Jean wins his battle singlehandedly.

Jean's story unfolds against the background of a hyperbolic description of the attacking hordes. Once they have pillaged the town, finding nothing too hot or too heavy to carry off, they move on to the abbey, but since it is thoroughly locked and barred, they split up. The main army proceeds toward the *gué de Vede,* leaving seven "enseignes" of infantry and two hundred lances to break down the abbey walls in order to lay waste the vineyard inside. The monks panic, scarcely knowing to which saint they should commend themselves. In emergency session, they decide that the best course of action would be to have a "splendid procession, backed up by beautiful sermons and litanies *contra hostium insidias,* and lovely responses *pro pace"* (G. xxvii; my trans.). Miraculously the monks' savior, Frère Jean, is already among them. Hearing the noise of the enemy ravaging the vineyard, he bursts in upon his fellows as they chant, "Ini nim, pe, ne, ne, ne, ne, ne, ne, tum," etc. With an acid comment on the beauty of their song, he asks, shouldn't they rather sing, "Farewell baskets, the harvest's finished?" "Seigneur Dieu, *da mihi potum!"* "Lord God, give me a drink!" he cries. In a high dudgeon, the prior consigns Jean to prison for troubling the "service divin." But, puns Jean, "le service du vin, faisons tant qu'il ne soit troublé," "Let's see that the wine service isn't troubled, because even you, my lord Prior, like to drink the best and so does every decent fellow. A noble man never hates good wine, it's a monkish saying" (G.xxvii; my trans.).

"Da mihi potum," which echoes the Vulgate's "Da mihi bibere," "give me to drink," from John 4:7 and 10, exemplifies Rabelais's Silenic jesting. Apparently an irreverent use of a biblical text, it actually means what it did in the original context. John 4 had been used traditionally as one of the most important sources of the theme of *sobria ebrietas* and the *fons sapientiae*. Jesus, having sat down by a well, asks a Samaritan woman for a drink. He tells her, "Every one who drinks of this water will thirst again, but whoever drinks of the water that I shall give him will never thirst; the water that I shall give him will become in him a spring of water welling up to eternal life" (John 4:9–10; 13–14). Living water, *aqua vita,* is readily interchangeable with the wine, Wisdom's drink in Proverbs 9, where she sends out her handmaidens to invite all simple and foolish souls in for a drink of the wine she has mixed. Another biblical transformation of water into wine takes place at the wedding of Cana. Frère Jean's vehement cry, "Seigneur Dieu, *da mihi potum,*" funny and apparently satirical on its literal level, is also a request for the "vin divin" (CL. xliv.881).[3] The pun on *service divin* and *service du vin* juxtaposes the formalized, useless ritual, which *men* consider divine service, epitomized in the monks' unintelligible chant (supposed to be "impetum inimicorum ne timueritis"), with the *service de la vérité,* "service of truth [wine service]," which no *homme de bien,* no noble man can desert. This is the "wine" of essential Christianity, evangelical simplicity which the Church *once* recognized as more important than Latin chants. Jean explains that, in the old days, rituals were considered irrelevant when practical action needed to be taken. That is why the hours sung during harvest time are short but are long in winter, so that the wine can be properly made in fall and drunk in winter. Clearly, once upon a time, the spirit(s) ruled the letter in the Church, and must do so once again. Jean sounds the call to battle: "So listen to me, all you who love wine, and follow me too, in God's name. For I tell you boldly, may St. Anthony's fire burn me if anyone tastes the grape who hasn't saved [*secouru*] the vine!" (G.xxvii.99). Although in inverted form, Jean's outcry reminds us of a Pauline remark: "Who plants a vineyard without eating any of its fruit?" (1 Cor. 9:7).

Jean throws off his heavy monk's habit and seizes the staff of the crucifix, made of the heart of an ash tree, one of the hardest and most lasting of woods. The staff, the vertical pole which supports the crucified Christ, anagogically represents the foundation of the faith and of the Church itself. Sallying forth thus armed, Jean routs the enemy, so busied in ravaging the vineyard that it is entirely unprepared for such an attack. The uproar is so great that the monks run out to see what is happening and begin to confess the wounded and dying. Jean's victims call upon all the saints as well as on the Virgin and, like Panurge later in the *Quart Livre,* they receive no help. After all, they are not calling upon the one true savior. Their wish for confession also avails them very little in this life as they, oddly enough, seem to expect, for Jean slaughters them as they try to slip through the breach in the wall, at the same time consoling them by pointing out that their newly cleansed souls will no doubt fly straight up to heaven. So it is that Jean, by a fearful bloodbath, wins the day, killing "thirteen thousand, six hundred and twenty-two, not counting the women and small children — as is always understood" (G.xxvii.101). Jean's apparently heartless cruelty corresponds to many biblical passages in which the unfaithful or unproductive member is brutally destroyed. The text of John 15 provides a convenient example: "If anyone abide not in me, he shall be cast forth as a branch and shall wither: and they shall gather him up and cast him into the fire: and he burneth." The ravagers of the vineyard represent attackers of the true faith: the *cagotz* of the Sorbonne, the Papimaniacs, or any group who has broken so far away from the true spirit of Christianity as to be completely outside the true, evangelical Church. Rabelais attacks the enemy within *and* without. He indicates that the rituals of the Church do not guarantee salvation: in fact they are quite beside the point. If allowed to take precedence over common sense and lively communication with the divine will, they smother the originally active spirit of Christianity, and actually further the destruction of the vineyard by posing no vigorous opposition to a threat from without. The middle position would be Jean's who returns to the "down-to-earth" simplicity of the early Church, and who, to avoid the abuse of either extreme, is willing to defend his beliefs at the risk of life and limb. Jean's position might be called Evangelical "orthodoxy," he is *cooperateur de Dieu,* "coworker with God"; he guards and defends the abbey close, the vineyard which represents the *true* Church established by Christ. Clearly, Rabelais argues for a brisk defense of the Church, but begs, too, for reason and reform within it. It seems clearer that, despite the hyperbolic description of Jean's warlike prowess (for he will go to any extreme to defend moderation), Jean still, in typically Rabelaisian fashion, represents the middle way.

Jean is suitably rewarded for his bravery by a banquet served him by Gargantua, his prince. The dinner, which typifies the Rabelaisian symposium, also furnishes him an occasion to dot the i's of his criticism of Church practices, particularly of the monasticism with which he is most familiar, and to set up Frère Jean in opposition to other monks.

Despite his apparent lechery	"Talking of trowels — why is it that a young lady's thighs are always cool? . . . in the first place, because the water runs all down it; secondly, because it is shady, obscure, and dark . . . ; and thirdly, because it is continually fanned by winds from the northern hole, the smock, and also the codpiece. And heartily too!" (G.xxxix.124),
ignorance	"For my part, I do no studying. In our abbey we never study, for fear of the mumps" (G. xxxix.124),
profanity	" 'By the power of God! . . . [God's body!]' . . . 'What, do you swear, Friar John?' cried Ponocrates. 'It's only to embellish my language' [said] the monk, 'It's [Ciceronian] rhetorical coloring' " (G.xxxix.125; partly my trans.),
gluttony	"I had supped; but I shan't eat any the less for that. I have a paved stomach as hollow as St. Benedict's tun, and always gaping like a lawyer's purse" (G.xxxix.123),
and filth	" 'Friar John,' said Gymnaste, 'wipe off that drip that's hanging on your nose!' " (G.xl.127),

still, he is accepted as an ideal *bon compagnon*. But why are other monks who display the same faults not equally welcome among the good boozers? Gargantua compares the monks to "machemerdes," who eat the world's turds, that is to say its sins (G.xi.118).[4] Their convents are separated from the Christian "household," isolated like the toilets from the rest of the house. The monks are completely unproductive, since Gargantua will not even admit that they pray for us. Instead, they disturb the countryside with their constant bell ringing, they mumble saints' lives and psalms they do not half understand, they repeat *paternosters* and *Ave Marias* without even thinking, "and that I call not prayer, but mockery of God [*mocquedieu*]" (G.xl.126). Gargantua refers here to the monks in Jean's abbey, whose Latin hymn, "not in the least understood by them," was used as a sort of magic charm against the invader. Jean, lecherous, gluttonous, and blasphemous as he is, still has many virtues which outweigh his vices, and which make him much superior to other monks. Gargantua pauses to make his opinion of Jean explicit: "All true Christians, of all degrees, in all places and at all times, pray to God, and the Holy Spirit prays and intercedes for them, and God receives them into his grace. Now our good Friar John is a true good Christian" (G.xl.126). In his battle, Jean did *not* call upon the saints or the Virgin: his direct prayer is implied in the very weapon he used — the staff of the Cross. He crushes his enemies by using essential Christianity. Jean goes to the heart of the matter; he prays to God and, unlike the Picrocholine invaders, *his* prayer is answered: the Holy Spirit indeed prays and intercedes for him. Everyone wants Jean's company: "He's no bigot, he's no wastrel; he is honest, joyful, resolute, and a good companion; he works, he labours, he defends the oppressed, he comforts the afflicted, he aids the suffering, and he saves the close of his abbey" (G.xl.126). Jean defends and labors in God's vineyard, and those people he succors remind the reader of the "underdog" in the Beatitudes — the poor in spirit, those who mourn, the meek, the persecuted — all those who will, however, inherit the Kingdom.

Jean's rejoinder, on a comic level, introduces Rabelais's third condemnation of Church ritual. On hearing himself so highly praised by Gargantua, Jean hastens to top off the list of his virtues and accomplishments: "'I do a great deal more than that,' said the monk. 'For whilst we're dispatching our Matins and Masses for the dead in the choir I make crossbow strings, I polish bolts and quarrels, I manufacture snares and nets to catch rabbits. I'm never idle'" (G.xl.126). Even while engaged in "mocquedieu," Jean keeps his hands busy for the greater glory of God, and to help feed his brother monks.

Despite his obvious faults, Jean incarnates the Rabelaisian ideal of Christianity in the guise of a knight of the chivalresque novel or of a Bishop Turpin of the *Chanson de Roland*. As Rabelais's custodian of the breviary stuff, the wine, Jean is filled with God's grace, which keeps him safe from all noxious influences from without: "'Friar John . . . wipe off that drip that's hanging on your nose.' 'Ha, ha!' said the monk, 'am I not in danger of drowning, seeing that I'm in water up to the nose? No, no, *quare? Quia.* It goes not in as water, though as water it may come out, for it's properly corrected with grape juice antidote'" (G.xl.127). A simple, even primitive man, Jean is closer to the essence of Christianity by his very lack of sophistication. His will is naturally attuned with the divine: he is God's wine vessel.

Jean continues to function as a soldier in the Evangelical army. The successful campaign against Picrochole is in great part due to his efforts. When the enemy stronghold of La Roche Clermauld is finally taken, Frère Jean obliges the enemy to turn in his arms, and seizes the staffs of all the crosses in town, so that no one can misuse against him so potent a weapon. With the ending of the Picrocholine war, Jean has defeated those who are outside the church and outside reason for a second time.

Jean's function is consistently active and often warlike. The *Tiers Livre* forms a parenthesis in his warlike activity, since he spends his time peacefully at Pantagruel's court. There, he exercises another of the talents which Gargantua had attributed to him: he comforts the afflicted, Panurge, kindly telling his friend to marry if he cannot remain continent, and not to worry too much about being cuckolded, since he can always use the expedient of Hans Carvel's ring. Even while occupied with peacetime pursuits, Jean's healthy physical vitality is emphasized. Jean and Panurge, both very corporeal characters and fast friends, exchange compliments, fondly calling each other "couillon," "ballock." Panurge addresses Jean as, for instance, "Gigantic, oval, cloistral, virile . . . massive, handy, absolute, muscular ballock" (TL.xxvi; my trans.), but Jean has a different list of adjectives for Panurge: "musty, moldy, mildewed . . . broken-backed . . . threadbare . . . exhausted, worm-eaten, wasted, wheezing ballock" (TL. xxviii.366). Rabelais here shows that Jean, living to the full a vigorous physical life, has remained sound, while Panurge abuses his corporality, his entire being becoming concentrated in the sickly venereal functions of the appetitive soul.

In the storm at sea in the *Quart Livre,* the two heroes are again played off against each other. As the storm strikes, Panurge collapses on the deck of the *Thalamège,* weeping, calling on the Virgin, begging Frère Jean to confess him and to record his last will and testament. The other members of the company are properly and usefully employed. Pantagruel makes fervent public prayer to God and then, on the pilot's advice, holds the mast against the savage onslaught of the storm. The mast, a common anagogical symbol for Christendom,[5] here on this Evangelical ship, stands for Rabelais's enlightened Christianity in particular. Frère Jean, like Epistemon and the others, strips down to his doublet to help the sailors. As in the battle of the abbey close, the tempest again shows that God helps those who help themselves, for, if their will is properly attuned to His, they become His co-workers. Working for the common good is much more important than abiding by the empty rituals of confession and last wills and testaments. It is Panurge who now, like the monks of Seuilly, represents Church convention.

Most of the initial questions have by now been answered. We understand Jean's function in the Evangelical circle; a reason has been advanced for his excessive violence in defense of the abbey; we have seen that Jean's role is consistently that of a co-worker with God, on a humble level, of course. The final question still remains: Why does Rabelais award Thélème to rough and ready Jean, primitive and bawdy Jean with the dripping nose? In the beginning, Jean was described as *bien à dextre,* an expression which is translated as adroit or skillful, and lucky. The Christian tradition accepts the pagan notion that a man's right side corresponds to the orient or sunrise side of heaven, and it is thus blessed, or even holy.[6] Jean acts as the "right-hand man" both for Gargantua and Pantagruel in times of stress. Gargantua and, in the later books, Pantagruel are evidently the "brains" of the group, Jean is the right arm. Panurge brings up the rear as the venereal member. Seen in another way, Pantagruel is the intellect, Jean the irascible soul properly attuned to the intellect and therefore its faithful servant, and Panurge the wayward appetitive soul. In the trinity of souls, as long as one soul is out of harmony, the whole group cannot function right. Therefore, the voyage and the search for a means of righting the balance is inevitable. Going further in Platonic investigation, we find in the *Republic* (4. 440) that the philosopher king corresponds to *mens* or intellectual soul, and the guardian, the watchdog of the Republic, to the irascible soul. Jean, who acted so effectively as watchdog for the abbey of Seuilly, will now do the same for Thélème, while the *real* leadership comes from elsewhere. That is why he is given the post of abbot, even though he protests, like Socrates, "How should I be able to govern others . . . when I don't know how to govern myself?" (G.lii.149–50).[7] It is Gargantua, not Jean, who sets the daily round of activities for the Thélémites: "All their life was regulated not by laws, statutes, or rules but according to their free will [*selon leur vouloir et franc arbitre*] . . . So it was that Gargantua had established it" (G.lvii.159). Rabelais rejects the conventional idea that an abbot should *govern* his monks and nuns since, ideally, they are subject to the will of God alone. Rabelais's departure here from the standard organization of an abbey should surprise no one, since Thélème also overturns the vows of poverty, chastity, and obedience as understood and practiced by the Church: poverty is of a technical sort (since all goods are held in common), obedience is to God's will alone (which attunes each individual will to every other one), and chastity is practiced among young people who associate freely with one another, and who may honorably marry if they choose. Thus the final authority to which the "monks and nuns" of Thélème appeal is not Jean or even Gargantua. Each one his own priest, all maintain constant and direct communion with the real "abbot" of Thélème, who is God.

Gargantua ends with the *Enigme en Prophétie,* a poem attributed to Mellin de Saint-Gelais and interpreted by Screech as a comment on the persecution of the Evangelicals around the time of the *Affaire des Placards.*[8] The enigma is quite serious, almost pathetic, as is the attitude of Gargantua, who, afterward, very solemnly and sighing deeply, says, "This is not the first time that men, called to the [Evangelical] faith, are persecuted" (G.lviii.163; partly my trans.). But Rabelais rapidly changes the serious tone, and the book ends on a comic note. Jean interprets the poem merely as a tennis match. In this way Rabelais reminds us that Saint-Gelais apparently intended his original enigma to represent a tennis match and, at the same time, Rabelais returns, after the serious episode of Thélème and the *Enigme,* to the comic spirit of the remainder of *Gargantua.* By implicitly denying any serious meaning in the enigma, he may hope to throw his persecutors off the track, just as he had done in the prologue where he first invites the dog to seek the marrow, and then disclaims any hidden meaning in his work. Since his beginning is comic, Rabelais may have wished to end as he began for aesthetic reasons, or because his fundamental optimism denied gloomy predictions. He had begun his book inviting the bacchic revelers, the illustrious boozers to join his feast; in the end, Jean, perhaps raising his breviary bottle on high, invites us all to share in the heady spirits which fill him: " 'And here's good cheer!' "

The Abbey of Thélème

The abbey, which Frère Jean so reluctantly "governs," is at least as ambiguous as its abbot and merits equally careful study. Among Gargantua's first specifications for Thélème is that it have no clock, "for . . . the greatest waste of time he knew was the counting of hours . . . and the greatest nonsense in the world was to regulate one's life by the sound of a bell, instead of by the promptings of reason and good sense" (G.lii.150). From the beginning, Rabelais suggests that the abbey, being timeless, is an extratemporal allegory of eternity or paradise.

In his "*Quart Livre* Commentaires," Robert Marichal pauses for several pages to puzzle over the location of the chapel in the Abbey of Thélème: "It contained nine thousand, three hundred and thirty-two apartments, each one provided with an inner chamber, a closet, wardrobe, and chapel, and each one giving on a great hall" (G.liii. 152).[9] In order to refute Lucien Febvre's belief in Rabelais's orthodoxy, Marichal decides that Rabelais has enumerated the rooms of each apartment in descending order of merit, ending with the chapel and exit.[10] Without attempting to reconstruct the floor plan of the abbey (a task which Marichal undertakes despite Rabelais's confusing and incomplete description),[11] it would seem more important to remember that, since all good Christians pray to God no matter where they are, a chapel or oratory is actually superfluous, since the tilt-yard, the theater, or the swimming-bath could serve just as well. Wherever they are, "the Holy Spirit prays and intercedes for them, and God receives them into his grace" (G.xl.126).

The Fountain of the Graces

The main symbol for omnipresent divine grace is the fountain in the abbey courtyard. "In the middle of the first court was a magnificent fountain of fine alabaster, on the top of which were the three Graces with horns of abundance, spouting water from their breasts, mouths, ears, eyes, and other physical orifices" (G.lv.155). These rather comic Graces would have brought to the minds of Rabelais's contemporaries a whole flood of associations. The Stoics believed that the Graces symbolized liberality divided into three parts: Men ought to be gracious and bountiful to others, to receive courteously the gifts of others, and to give them adequate thanks.[12] Many Renaissance humanists included the Graces in their Pantheon of Christianized deities as "vestiges of the Trinity." The three naked ladies take their places among the many triads to be found in pagan theology: Mercury-Apollo-Venus; the Fates; the Furies; not to mention Rabelais's own Bacchus-Silenus-Pan. St. Augustine believed the mystery of the Trinity to have been darkly revealed to the pagans, but though these triads pointed in the right direction, they divided the deity into unequal and separable aspects. Only the Christian revelation, of course, explains the actual triune nature of the Deity.[13] Although well aware of the danger of heresy in toying with pagan gods as figures for the Trinity, the humanists fervently exploited all the mythical triads they could discover.

Cristoforo Landino, a member of Ficino's circle, makes the Christian connotations of the Graces quite explicit, emphasizing that all graces proceed from God alone, and that *Laetitia,* "Gladness," is the most precious of them.[14] For Ficino, the Graces symbolized an "unfolding" of Divine Love, which expresses itself toward the creation by an overflowing emanation. When felt by the creature, this divine emanation produces ecstacy (*raptio*), which draws him back heavenward, once again to blend with the One (*remeatio*).[15] Since all communication between God and mortal takes place through love, Venus and Amor play vital roles in the Pantheon of Christianized deities.[16]

Ficino's disciple Pico wore a medal depicting the three Graces bearing the motto *Pulchritudo/Amor/Voluptas,* which Wind believes to have been derived from Ficino's description of the relation of God and man: "It is a circle. . . . Where it begins in God and powerfully attracts, it is beauty; where it travels through the world and ravishes it, it is love; where it returns to the creator and combines with his creation, it is sensuality. Thus love begins in beauty and ends in sensuality."[17] *Pulchritudo/Amor/Voluptas* follows the circular movement of *emanatio, raptio, remeatio,* just as Thalia (*Viriditas*), Aglaia (*Splendor*), and Euphrosyne (*Laetitia Uberrima*) form a circle, a perfect figure of union in joy.

Thélème furnishes Thalia, Aglaia, and Euphrosyne an appropriate abode. The fertile setting beside the Loire, green and flourishing, provides a perfect backdrop for the activities of the talented "monks" and "nuns," in the bloom of youth and beauty. Amusingly enough, every apartment throughout the abbey is carpeted in green, no doubt to imitate the verdant meadows and to provide a contrasting backdrop for the reds, blues, and gold of the opulent costumes. The building and its furnishings rival the Temple of Solomon in magnificence; no royal court ever approached the splendor of the inmates. A mood of joyful and willing cooperation pervades the abbey, for there is no monastic rule, no coercion there.

There is good reason to believe that, in using the Graces as the emblem for Thélème, Rabelais was fully aware of the implications, both Stoico-Christian and Neoplatonic. His fountain has been compared to Francesco Colonna's dream fountain in the *Hypnerotomachia Poliphili,* though Rabelais's gives at the same time a much simpler and more comic version (see figure 3).[18] Where the fountain of Thélème is made of alabaster, Colonna's is amethyst, jasper, chalcedony, ophite, and porphyry. His Graces jet water from their breasts only; they hold a cornucopia in their right hands while they cover their nudity with a modest left hand. The three horns of plenty join above the heads of the Graces to form a single source of bounty. Both fountains combine the Stoic idea of liberality with Neoplatonic *emanatio;* the horns of plenty are figures for both. Colonna's version provides

Figure 3. Francesco Colonna. *Fountain of the Graces*. From *Hypnerotomachia Poliphili* (1499).

a more explicit Trinity symbol; the three horns blend into one above the heads of the Graces: they are at once separate and united.

Of the three cornucopias on Rabelais's fountain, the one which Euphrosyne bears is the most important to him: hers is one of heavenly joy. We are reminded of Rabelais's characterization of his own books in the Prologue to TL: "It's a true cornucopia of joy and mockery. If sometimes it seems to you emptied to the lees, still it will not be dry. Good hope lies at the bottom, as in Pandora's bottle, not despair, as in the Danaids' tub" (my trans.). Rabelais's cornucopia, his wine barrel, stands as a symbol for gladness, for liberality, and, most of all, for God's grace.[19] Even if Pandora's bottle — his books — *seems* empty, good hope, one of the three theological virtues (and Faith/Hope/Charity form yet another trinity of Graces), remains to comfort the thirsty seeker.

Venus

The Graces, although variously "christened" and pictured as Verdure, Splendor, Gladness, or Pulchritudo, Amor, Voluptas — or as Botticelli depicts them in his *Primavera*: Pulchritudo, Castitas, Voluptas — represent aspects of divine love; all move in the same circle of *emanatio, raptio, remeatio;* all "unfold" the attributes of Venus who, herself (along with blind Amor), is among the many aspects of the One. "Amor nodus perpetuus et copula mundi," "Love is the perpetual knot and link of the world," as Ficino summarizes in a succinct motto.[20] Love, Venus, holds the world together; she alone links creature and thing, creature and creature, creature and God. "He that understands profoundly and clearly how the unity of Venus is unfolded in the trinity of the Graces, and the unity of necessity in the trinity of the Fates . . . knows the proper way of proceeding in Orphic theology.[21] The One always remains behind or within the many; the many within the One. Venus, forming a trinity with Mercury and Apollo, could be used as *figura* for the Virgin Mary. Vergil's Venus-Virgo of the *Aeneid* provides the Neoplatonists with a particularly useful image which could be manipulated to portray any gradation from *voluptas* to *castitas,* depending upon the reverence or frivolity of the context.[22] *Voluptas* itself was given an anagogical interpretation by Renaissance Epicureans like Lorenzo Valla, who followed

Plotinus' lead. On the literal level a blind and degrading passion, *voluptas* may stand for the most exalted, heavenly form of pleasure: union with the Divine. This pleasure is set above intellect, since reason limits and circumscribes, while divine *voluptas* flows outward into the infinite. Lorenzo de 'Medici confesses that his being contracts when he tries to comprehend God intellectually, but expands when he approaches him through love.[23]

Rabelais's Thélème evokes Venus not only through the Graces but also through the importance of the number six in the structure of the abbey.

Screech enumerates most of the occurrences of sixes in the architecture of Thélème. Though he is reluctant to admit the relevance of the venereal aspect of the number, he quotes at least one authority, Martianus Capella, who designates six as the Venus number.[24] The abbey is six stories high, has six libraries for books in six languages, the staircases are six *toises* wide, adequate for six men-at-arms abreast; the number of apartments is given in some editions as 932 (Telle analyzes this as an inverted 6 before 3×2); in others there are 9332 apartments (inverted 6; $3 + 3$; 3×2). The abbey is hexagonal with a tower at each corner; the towers are sixty paces in diameter. Screech reports that Philo calls six a terrestrial number (seven is the first heavenly one); it is male and female (a combination of the odd number 3 and the even number 2), and is thus a symbol of mating and fertility. Because of this combination, Martianus Capella attributes this to Venus. Although Iamblicus calls six the marriage number, Screech points out that Rabelais probably did not know this, since the marriage numbers he gives in the *Tiers Livre* are thirty and five. Rabelais could have known Clement of Alexandria, who interprets six as the perfect number from the creation of the world, the mean of the even numbers from two to ten. Francesco Giorgio in his *De harmonia mundi totius* acknowledges that six is attuned to beginnings and marriages; it is especially appropriate that the Creation took six days, a time when all things were coupled together. For Giorgio, the number denotes harmony above all, self-sufficiency, steadfastness in religion, and other forms of perfection.

Screech's authorities do not include St. Augustine or Cornelius Agrippa, whose works Rabelais could have known. Augustine emphasizes that six is the number of days chosen by God in which to create the world and that the number thus signifies the perfection of God's work.[25]

Agrippa paraphrases most of what Augustine says, and adds two more devoutly Christian interpretations of the hexad: "It is also called the number of man because man was created on the sixth day, and it is again called the number of redemption, for on the sixth day Jesus Christ suffered for our redemption."[26] Thomas Taylor, the eighteenth-century numerologist, compiled several opinions on the meaning of the number six, and cites "the Pythagoreans" in general as his authority. He notes in particular that six denotes harmony and the perfection of parts, like Venus herself. It is a soul number, and in music, 6 to 12 forms the symphonic diapson, 6 to 9 the diapente.[27]

In the minds of the Christian commentators, the idea of the perfection and the harmony of the hexad remains uppermost; the pagans, while designating six as a Venus, fertility, or mating number, do so with harmony and the union of the odd and the even in mind. Nowhere is the hexad connected with "easy venereal delights."[28] The perfection symbolized by the number six is most relevant to Thélème. Set in the choicest spot in Utopia, Thélème could easily be seen as a paradise, a habitation approaching the perfection of the Garden of Eden, where man was placed on the sixth day of Creation. It is a place of redemption, for its inhabitants are favored by God, saved from the trials and temptations of the world. It is appropriate that six is a soul number, too, since the Thélémites remain in direct contact with the One, the source of soul itself. Although six was not a marriage number for Rabelais, it undoubtedly *was* a Venus number. Just as the Graces symbolize the grace of God and unfold the attributes of Venus (in her Neoplatonic guise as mediatress of love between God and creature), so the number six repeats the same symbolism. In Rabelais's abbey, the inmates live in complete harmony and in the *voluptas* of direct communion with their creator.

Thélème and Will: Franciscan Thélème

Does "Fay ce que vouldras" Mean "Follow Thy Nature?"

The name *Thélème* has given rise to much speculation, particularly in connection with the puzzling motto of the abbey, *Fay ce que vouldras.* The apparent amorality of this motto sharply contradicts the tone of the book up to this point. Rabelais has gone to great pains, throughout the twenty-five chapters of the Picrocholine war, to contrast the intensely moral and God-fearing behavior of his hero's father, Grandgousier, the ideal feudal ruler, with that of Picrochole, wildly self-willed and impulsive, who turns his back on grace.

Picrochole and Grandgousier appeal to reason in the same words (*la raison le veult*) and yet the two stand in total opposition not only across their battle lines (which symbolize their moral opposition) but also in another important respect: Picrochole, Rabelais's example of a leader who tries to guide himself by human reason alone, fails absurdly in his drive to conquer. As Ulrich Gallet tells the fiery aggressor, he has abandoned himself to devilish fantasies: "If the spirit of slander [*l'esperit calumniateur,* i.e., the devil], striving to induce you to evil, had by deceitful appearances [*phantasmes ludificatoyres*] . . . put it into your head that we had acted towards you in any way unworthy of our ancient friendship, you should first have inquired into the truth of the matter" (G.xxxi.106). These *phantasmes ludificatoyres* lead Picrochole to use "reason" in a way which shows that he can no longer distinguish between reality and fantasy. His "advisers," who play the part of incarnate devils, tempt Picrochole with a bloated dream of world conquest, which they present as a *fait accompli*. Discussing his plans for the world, Picrochole promises to give vast lands to his true servants after slaughtering the Turkish and Mohammedan dogs who now live there. " 'Reason demands it (*la raison le veult*),' said Picrochole. 'It's only just. To you I give Carmania, Syria, and all Palestine' " (G.xxxiii.112). Grandgousier goes to war reluctantly, praying at length before coming to a decision. He decides at last to take mace and lance in his aged and trembling hands in order to guarantee the safety of his subjects, by whose labor he lives. "La raison le veult ainsi . . ." (G.xxviii.89). In his portrayal of Picrochole, Rabelais clearly shows that man without God is feeble indeed, his path uncertain. Left to his own "franc arbitre et propre sens," "free will and common sense," he *cannot but do evil.* But the description of the abbey of Thélème ("Toute leur vie estoit employée . . . selon leur vouloir et franc arbitre," "All their life was regulated . . . according to their free will": [G.lvii.159], with its motto *Fay ce que vouldras,* seems flatly to contradict any orthodox Christian notion of reason and will. From the time the Sorbonne condemned Rabelais's work to our own days, he has been considered either an unbridled hedonist, opening the floodgate to all of man's basest impulses, or a naive precursor of eighteenth-century rationalist humanism.

Jean Plattard summarized an attitude now familiar to thousands of students: "The concept of Thélème . . . rests on principles of that naturalist philosophy which is the expression of Rabelais's temperament and his notion of life (*sens de la vie*). *Fay ce que vouldras* is a rule of conduct which he judges sufficient for honorable people. Left to itself, nature tends to be virtuous" (*Ed. cr.* 1.103; my trans.). If Rabelais in fact intends to exalt the virtue of unaided human nature, then he surely contradicts the sense of Grandgousier's letter to Pantagruel, and blurs the image of the doughty, God-fearing old hero as a model to emulate. Grandgousier had written, "I recognized that God Almighty has abandoned him [Picrochole] to the guidance of his own free will and understanding [*son franc arbitre et propre sens*], which cannot but be evil unless it be continually prompted by divine grace . . ." (G.xxix.103). Grandgousier's strong indictment of human will and reason is echoed by Frère Jean. When Gargantua offers him his choice of abbeys as a reward for his services in the war, Frère Jean exclaims, "How should I be able to govern others . . . when I don't know how to govern myself?" (G.lii.149–50). Frère Jean obviously implies that only God is an adequate governor for errant human nature. But, if the "naturalist" interpretation of the description of Thélème is correct, then Rabelais proceeds at once to contradict himself, for in describing life at the abbey, he tells us how the inmates wake up, drink, eat, work, and sleep when they feel like it. No one forces them to do anything because, "gens libères, bien néz, bain instruictz, conversans en compaignies honnestes, ont par nature un instinct et aguillon, qui tousjours les poulse a faictz vertueux et retire de vice, lequel ilz nommoient honneur" (G.lvii.159), "People who are free, well-born, well-bred, and easy in honest company have a natural spur and instinct which drives them to virtuous deeds and deflects them from vice; and this they call honour" (G.lvii.159).

It would be foolish to deny that Thélème, as an attack on monasticism, goes much farther than Rabelais's critique of monks in chapter 40. Here, he proposes quite a different ideal, a different rule which substitutes the startling *Fay ce que vouldras* for the vows of poverty, chastity, and obedience. There can be no question of poverty within the opulently beautiful walls of Frère Jean's utopian abbey; chastity does not mean total segregation from the opposite sex, since both sexes mingle freely there. But sexual relations in Thélème are not at all libertine. Rabelais tells us that "there one may be honourably married . . ."; Screech points out, "One can: not one must." [29] This idea closely follows St. Paul's recommendations: "To the unmarried and the widows I say that it is well for them to remain single as I do. But if they cannot exercise self-control, they should marry. For it is better to marry than to be aflame with passion" (1 Cor. 7:8–9). It is more blessed to remain in the single state because "I want you to be free from anxieties. The unmarried man is anxious about the affairs of the Lord, but the married man is anxious about worldly affairs, how to please his wife; and his interests are divided" (1 Cor. 7:32–33).

The "monks" and "nuns" of Thélème may mingle freely as long as their relations remain "platonic." If they do not have self-control, they may marry without sin, although they then must leave Thélème. Though not dishonored, they are thenceforth shut out of Rabelais's little Garden of Eden.

Rabelais discards the vow of obedience too: he insists that the Thélémites must be free. They live according to "leur vouloir et franc arbitre;" they arise, drink, eat, and work where and when they please: a situation which may puzzle the reader and recall to his mind Gargantua's abusive "Studies according to the Discipline of his Sophistical Tutors" (G.xxi), before he is introduced to Ponocrate's discipline. But if Rabelais is not again deliberately contradicting himself, how can these apparently opposed ideals of freedom and discipline be reconciled? That he attacks the established monastic system by substituting a utopian dream implies neither an acceptance of "naturalist humanism" nor a rejection of Christian ideals.

Per Nykrog, in an excellent study, devotes himself to the etymology of Thélème and to its significance. Derived from *thelēma* this word appears very rarely in classical Greek, but is often used in New Testament Greek, to mean immediate impulse or desire. It turns up also in Matthew 6:10 in the Lord's prayer: *genēthētō to thelēma sou,* "Thy will be done." The same phrasing is exactly repeated in Jesus' prayer during His agony in Gethsemane: "My Father, if this [cup] cannot pass unless I drink it, Thy will be done" (Matt. 26:42). Nykrog connects *Fiat voluntas tua* with the motto *Fay ce que vouldras* through Erasmus's commentary on the New Testament, where Erasmus suggests that *Fiat voluntas tua,* "Thy will be done [on earth]," should be translated as "Fiat quod vis etiam in terra," "Do thy will on earth," a translation which comes much closer to Rabelais's own construction. With typical playful solemnity (*serio ludere*), Rabelais hides an almost literal translation of *thelēma sou* in his airy motto. If the Greek is read back as *fais ta volonté,* "do thy will," biblical echoes are instantly awakened, and the meaning of the name of Thélème reveals itself as a clear allusion to the Bible and to the Will of God.[30]

Rabelais's optimism lies in his faith that "gens libères, bien néz, bain instruictz" will, because of the circumstances of their birth — *de natura* in the Latin sense — be attuned to the Divine Plan. For Rabelais, "gens bien néz" means the aristocracy (attribution of democratic feelings to Rabelais would be anachronistic indeed!), the "noble gentlemen," the "ladies of high lineage" and those spiritual aristocrats, "you who preach with vigor Christ's Holy Gospel" (G.liv.154–55). The aristocrat forms part of the Neoplatonic ladder which stretches from inanimate objects, animals, and man, through the heavenly hosts to God: a stratification mirrored by Church hierarchy. Placed at the top of the social ladder, he is closer to divinity than other men. Each person must be not only noble but also well-bred or well educated along the lines laid down in the chapters on Gargantua's education. This is the sort of discipline Rabelais favors, even though Gargantua undergoes his instruction at a more advanced age than do the novices who enter Thélème.

The myth of Rabelais's humanist "naturalism" has been fostered by a misinterpretation, according to nineteenth- and twentieth-century connotations, of the meaning of the phrase: "gens libères . . . ont par nature un instinct et aguillon, qui tousjours les poulse à faictz vertueux et retire de vice, lequel ilz nommoient honneur" (G.lvii.159). The words *nature* and *instinct* are particularly dangerous for the contemporary reader and must be stripped, if possible, of their modern connotations. *Natura* in Latin means above all *birth,* secondarily it means *character* and intrinsic qualities. The meaning of Rabelais's *instinct et aguillon* has been succinctly explained by Kurt Weinberg, who derives *instinct* from *instinguere* ("to goad," "to propel"; cf. "stigma" and "sting") and also from *instigare* ("to incite," "to provoke"). *Aguillon* is redundant in his text, a synonym for *instinct.* Both imply an outside force impelling the Thélémites to virtuous behavior, such as divine inspiration.[31] As yet, there is no shadow of the twentieth-century meaning of instinct as given by Webster: "a natural spontaneous impulse or propensity, in the lower animals or in men, moving them without reasoning toward actions essential to their existence, preservation and development."

In order to follow the *instinct et aguillon* of divine inspiration, the Thélémites must be free to overthrow the vow of obedience in its usual sense: "When [they] are depressed and enslaved by vile constraint and subjection, they use this noble quality which once impelled them freely towards virtue, to throw off and break this yoke of slavery. For we always strive after things forbidden and covet what is denied us" (G.lvii.159). They throw off the heavy yoke of obedience to man in order to assume the easy one which is obedience to God. Where there is no restraint, there can be no disagreement and quarreling among the beautiful inmates. "Making use of this liberty, they most laudably rivalled one another in all of them doing what they saw pleased one. If some man or woman said, 'Let us drink,' they all drank . . ." (G.lvii.159). If constraint forces a man to lose God's grace through his revolt against a yoke of servitude, then a group of free men, aristocrats who have been well brought up (born into the grace of God and educated according to his will), most likely will desire the same things. Since each one is attuned to God's will, each individual will therefore agree with the desires of the next man. St. Paul expresses a kindred idea: "For though I am free from all men, I have made myself a slave to all, that I might win the more" (1 Cor. 9:19). In Thélème-Utopia, there is no need for abbey-church or priestly intermediaries; the divine presence is everywhere. Through free, spontaneous prayer, each man may call upon God in his own way and in his own good time, as Gargantua prayed for help after the death of Badebec (P.iii.181–83), and as Grandgousier prayed for guidance in the Picrocholine war (G.xxxii.95).

Nykrog's contribution has made it clear that *thelēma,* by contrast to will in the usual sense, carries the nuance of an immediate appetite or desire. Scotus, Rabelais's Franciscan "ancestor," presents will in precisely this light, for to him will is the form of appetite peculiar to human beings, an immediate impulse which precedes right reason but accords with it, and which moves a man toward a given object.[32] Thélème is the abode of those who practice man's noblest faculty — a *free* appetite; it is the abode and expression of God's will on earth, for *thelēma* describes the divine will too — God's will is an emanation of his being and not the result of reflection.[33] The physical beauty of the Thélémites and their surroundings, their spiritual beauty which expresses itself in the perfect harmony of each individual with every other, indicate that Rabelais does not found his abbey on the single phrase of the Lord's prayer "Thy will be done." To understand the nuances of its utopian character, the reader must refer to the rest of the Lord's prayer. In projecting an abbey which so closely resembles an image of Paradise (Thy kingdom come), he envisions it, "On earth as it is in heaven." The rules of monasticism as *men* understand them have been discarded. The Thélémites *do* practice poverty, chastity, and obedience as *God* understands them: they share selflessly the abundance of the earth; they are modest, honest, and continent; but, above all, they obey God's will. In Thélème, Rabelais envisions a Franciscan paradise, for there, nature and will coincide in complete harmony: they must, if Thélème is to be regarded as *thelēma,* an emanation of divine will.

Thélème and Colonna's Thélémie

The associations in Rabelais's mind, while they include notions which a medieval Franciscan monk could have entertained, range far afield into the Italianate adaptation of pagan allegories to Christian use which we have seen already in the font of the Graces and in the Venus number. Françon, following a lead provided by W. F. Smith in 1906, suggests that Rabelais took the name of his abbey from the nymph Telemia in the *Hypnerotomachia Poliphili.*[34] Since so much of Rabelais's description, both in the Thélème chapters and in the *Cinquiesme Livre,* undeniably derives from Colonna's work, Françon's suggestion deserves further investigation. Why would Rabelais use such an apparently trivial character in the *Typnerotomachia* as namesake for his cherished abbey? [35]

The various lands which Poliphile visits during his dream represent as many stages in his development. The two nymphs Thélémie and Logistique, who are assigned as his guides, represent two faculties of his soul. The first one, reason, is forever reminding him of the grim realities of life and of his duties. When it comes time for him to choose which path of life to follow, she advocates the courses most laborious and repulsive to human nature: ascetic religion or the harsh and Spartan road to glory. As Ficino repeats in *De amore,* reason may raise man above the delusion and debasement of earthly *voluptas,* but it detains him below the experience of the ultimate pleasure, the experience of divine love. Thélémie leads him toward this experience; she (who represents will, the second faculty of the soul) leads him into a lush garden where she sings to him, bestowing upon him the gifts of beauty and harmony. The door to his future which she shows him, the central and therefore dominant door labeled Materamoris (Venus), represents not only those things desired by man's base appetites but also those which his most essentially human appetite (to paraphrase Scotus), his will, desires for him. He is not punished for following Thélémie rather than Logistique, for Colonna, a Renaissance Epicurean, believes in the superiority of pleasure over knowledge: not unlike the mystic's "ecstatic" experience, the final union with God will be a voluptuous, not an intellectual experience. Colonna does not allow his hero to dally with the seven faithless "ladies," the bodily appetites; they, like the door he has passed through, are merely a stage, the earthly disguise of his celestial desire for Polia. When they abandon him, they are replaced by the object of his true *thelēma,* the nymph who bears on her head a lighted torch: his own Polia (Wisdom). Polia represents Poliphile's private Venus, his personal version of universal love, just as Beatrice represents the love and knowledge of God for Dante.

Colonna may have been familiar with Ficino's equation of *voluptas* and *voluntas:* when *voluntas* expands to infinity, "penes bonum infinitum voluntas omnis est ipsa voluptas." He elsewhere defines *voluntas* as the "inclination of the mind to the good," and *voluptas* as that "which within the good, belongs to the will." [36] Colonna's work expresses allegorically what Ficino propounded as theory; in a spirit of *amor fati,* the mottoes on the walls of the Temple of Venus read: "Chacun est tiré de sa volupté," "Everyone is drawn by sensuality," and "Il fault que chacun face selon sa nature," "Everyone must act according to his nature." [37] Ficino was convinced that Plotinus frequently alluded to the passion of lovers not only to paraphrase the divine passion but also to show that *voluptas* should be reclassified as a noble passion.[38] The Neoplatonism of Colonna (that Dominican friar) is as strongly anti-ascetic as Ficino's: both try to infuse a little neopagan joy into their Christianity.

Thelemia guides Poliphile at a crucial period in his life: when he must decide which path to follow in the future. The Thélémites arrive at the abbey at a similar juncture: neophytes in life, they choose their future according to their *thelēma,* their free will. They live together in complete accord (for the harmony of Thélème is the harmony of Venus, too). They allow the most divine part of their natures to guide them, as did Poliphile, who followed Thélémie; their love for one another remains strictly platonic, truly harmonic charity in the Pauline sense and in the sense in which Ficino exalts ideal love between persons.[39] A desire to marry, while not a sin, is a step backwards. It lowers them from the ideal platonic balance, and they automatically leave the abbey. Their actions are regulated by a sort of social contract, a collective inner light which attunes them all to the same chord. In their "abode of Venus," they are secure in the love of God, for their abbey, like the Temple of the Bottle, houses a fountain of Grace. Thélème and the Temple of the Bottle may be conceived (like the kingdoms of the *Hypnerotomachia*) as states of the soul: the most perfect states man can attain on earth. Like Bacbuc and her companions, the true faithful of the abbey live amid the utmost abundance and opulence; not in sinful, physical *luxuria,* but in a spiritual paradise in "the fulness of God's house." [40]

Voluntas = Caritas = (celestial) *Voluptas.* Rabelais would have accepted this equation because both his Franciscan background and his Neoplatonic learning would have led him to the same conclusion.

Both of the two parallel traditions are perfectly fused in his utopian abbey.

Nature and Will under Ideal Conditions: Thélème

A humanist ideal of education, depicted in the training of Gargantua and implicit also in Thélème, entails the idea that, in complete freedom, an individual can maintain harmonic balance between soul and body. This was not merely a utopian dream, for all the best humanist educators put it into practice. By alternating physical and mental training (*mens sana in corpore sano*), man may attain his highest potential and become a citizen who can serve his community in peace or war, according to his own particular gifts.[41] Guarino Veronese and Vittorino da Feltre both subscribed to the notion that the dignity of man's spirit requires that he be freed from the duress of rote memorization, and that only in freedom can it experience the true joy of learning and discovery.[42] Liberal arts are the subjects to be imparted to the virtuous, i.e., the virile, the free, and well-born. So indispensable is liberty to virtue that for the Renaissance educator the two become synonymous.[43] Many Renaissance thinkers believed that a man will *always* choose the good if left to his own devices, for, with Ficino, they believe the will to be "an inclination of mind toward the good." Ficino theorizes that man seeks God always by an *instinctus essentialis;* he cannot be satisfied until he has reached that goal. He calls this instinct the desire (*conatus*) to deify oneself; it depends upon the Absolute which is within all of creation, but especially in man. God became man, Ficino believes, in order that man might become God.[44]

It goes without saying that these ideas of freedom and virtue (that freedom *is* virtue) readily apply to Rabelais's *Fay ce que vouldras*. But Rabelais clearly holds that for most humans more than an innate *instinct et aguillon* is necessary to achieve virtue, because, unlike the Thélémites, man normally cannot boast perfect union of his (fourfold) soul and body, and their harmony with the divine will. He is usually out of balance, owing either to inner discord or to external circumstances or to both. He must therefore seek divine guidance as well as that of his own good counsel. If he depends solely upon the will of God with no active participation himself, he may go astray, as does Bridoye (TL.xliii), who had successfully discovered the "will of

God over a period of more than forty years" by casting his dice! But at last he made an incorrect judgment, not because the dice failed to reveal the divine will but because his failing eyes misread them. Human weakness deceived him, but if he had consulted with his own reason as well as casting his dice, even this error might have been avoided.[45]

But far more than Bridoye, Panurge exemplifies for Rabelais the typical man who, out of harmony and blinded by human weakness, follows the urges of his lower nature.

Chapter 6
_____

Man: Panurge and Misdirected Will

Man's Nature: a "Fatal Destiny"?

Panurge is Rabelais's priapic protagonist, telling bawdy stories himself or providing the occasion for a scatological or venereal incident. By nature a lustful man, his character never changes in this respect throughout the four books in which he figures. He begins his Rabelaisian career with a series of bawdy stories, practical jokes, pranks, and seductions; he ends it in the Temple of the Bottle where Bacbuc's ritual purges his impure sexual appetites. His horizons are rarely raised above the level of the sensitive soul:[1] among the principal characters, he occupies the lowest rung of the ladder.

The tales Panurge tells and those told him are among the most memorable of the bawdy stories that have earned Rabelais a reputation for his gallic humor. In most of these tales, the "moral message" serves merely as an excuse as in Panurge's courtship of a great Parisian lady (P.xxi–xxii), or the story of Hans Carvel's ring (TL.xxviii.432–33). Certain stories contain a sound, "common-sense" message, as in "To prove that the Codpiece is the principal piece in a warrior's armour" (TL.viii). Panurge defends the practical notion that the individual may be sacrificed to the protection of the race. Thus the old warning to a soldier, "Stevie, look after the pot of wine" (the head, where the spirits dwell), should be modified to: "Stevie, look after the pot of milk, that is to say his testicles, in the name of all the devils in hell. When a man loses his head, only the individual perishes; but if the balls were lost, the whole human race would die out" (TL.viii.309). The concern of the little wife that her husband arm himself *completely* is, Panurge assures us, an altogether praiseworthy sentiment:

She saw her husband fully armed
But for his codpiece, going to war.
She said, 'My dear, in case you're harmed,
Arm that as well, that is most dear. (TL.viii.310)

Panurge's very obscene suggestion in "How Panurge demonstrated a
very new way of building the Walls of Paris" (P.xv) hides a similarly
commonsensical message. Panurge explains the invulnerability of walls
constructed of "les callibistrys des femmes," *entrelardés de* "bracque-
mars enroiddys," "the thing-o'-my bobs of the ladies" interlaced with
"stiff what-d'you-call-'ems." This wall, a Panurgical allegory, actually illustrates an earlier anecdote of Pantagruel who reports that when
Agesilaus was asked why a great city like Lacedemonia had no walls,
he pointed at the citizens of the city, so expert in the arts of war, and
said, "Here are the walls of the city" (P.xv.232). In his own way, Panurge proposes that, through a perpetual venereal bout, the citizens
produce enough "living stones" to protect the city.

Although Panurge provides Rabelais the occasion for much light-
hearted fun, and though sexual preoccupations may at times be justified as practical, Panurge becomes stuck in the quagmire of his indecision: Should he marry or not? Will marriage inevitably bring him
cuckoldry? His problem exemplifies an ethical dilemma already prefigured in *Gargantua*. The opposition between Picrochole and Grandgousier has already raised the question: does the nature of man entail the
rigorous determinism of a "fatal destiny" or can man, through right
will, through reason and temperance, escape an apparently unavoidable
fate?

Picrochole and Grandgousier: Prefigurations
of Panurge's Problem

In the Picrocholine war, Rabelais first plays with the balance of
power in human character between will and nature. Picrochole, the
prime mover of the furious attack on Grandgousier's lands and people,
seems predetermined to take the action he does. There can be no doubt
that he is aptly named, for when the incident between the *fouaciers* of
Lerné and the vine-tending shepherds was reported to him, he flew
into a rage and, without inquiring further into the trouble, ordered

total mobilization of every man, under threat of hanging (G.xxvi.81). His behavior remains consistently choleric, for even after his final defeat, he wanders angrily away, and as he crosses the water at Port Huaux, an old witch tells him that he will get his kingdom back "at the coming of the Cocklicranes. No one knows what has become of him since then. All the same I have been told that at present he is a miserable porter at Lyons, furious as ever" (G.xlix.144).

Although the undertow of Picrochole's nature seems particularly strong, he has nevertheless made a choice. Far from being caught in a dilemma, he is duty bound as a king to seek out the truth about the quarrel. But he allows his nature to gain the upper hand. Thinking only of his own power and glory, he attacks Grandgousier, who wrings his hands, weeps and laments that his oldest friend should thus attack him. He prays for divine inspiration and counsel, convinced that only the devil could have provoked Picrochole to such outrageous action. Perhaps his old friend has become mad, and God has chosen Grandgousier to "return him to the yoke of his holy will through good discipline" (G.xxviii; my trans.). Once self-discipline (which Grandgousier hopes to replace by his own "good discipline") has been relinquished, once he ceases to seek out the will of God, Picrochole, left only to his own choleric nature, is easily seduced by "the evil spirit."

The behavior of Picrochole contrasts repeatedly with that of Grandgousier, who prays for God's grace, aid, and counsel, for the knowledge and strength needed to attune Picrochole's corrupt will with the holy will. And while Grandgousier is praying, his messenger Ulrich Gallet takes all possible measures to convince Picrochole of the error of his ways. Upon Gallet's return, he finds Grandgousier kneeling bare-headed in a corner, praying that Picrochole's anger should cool and that he should return to reason without forcing Grandgousier to go to war. He eagerly asks Gallet for news of his friend, but his messenger must disappoint him: Pichrochole, having abandoned reason and moderation, has been forsaken by God (G.xxxii.95). Until Picrochole submits again to God's will, everyone around him must suffer. Grandgousier, good shepherd, seeks to bring back the lost sheep, but despite all protests, his former friend continues to attack so furiously that he is forced to write Gargantua for help. Following his own lower nature and seduced by evil influences, Picrochole subjects himself to the immutable laws of nature and of fortune, which will inevitably bring him to disaster (in the original astrological sense of the word).

Consequences of Panurge's Weakness

Picrochole's downfall begins with his free choice to follow his choleric nature. In like manner, Panurge begins the *Tiers Livre* as a free man with a certain natural inclination toward *voluptas*. His part in the book begins with chapter 2, "How Panurge . . . Ate His Wheat in the Blade," which remains his keynote throughout. He wants immediate enjoyment of every bodily pleasure without suffering any of the possible consequences. For the first time, the idea of marriage has entered his head, and the realization of a perpetual *combat vénérien* intrigues him so much that he becomes obsessed by it. He appears before Pantagruel in unusual garb. His right ear has been pierced "in the Jewish fashion" and in it is a small gold earring inlaid with a black flea. He wears a long robe made of five yards of cloth, he has left off his breeches and attached spectacles to his cap. Pantagruel finds all this very strange, and particularly misses the magnificent codpiece "on which he used to depend as on the holy Anchor for a last refuge from the shipwrecks of adversity." Panurge explains, "I have the flea in my ear . . . I want to marry" (TL.vii; my trans.). In calling the codpiece Panurge's holy anchor and last refuge, Rabelais is at the same time reminding the reader of Panurge's essentially priapic nature and poking fun at it. The anchor is a common emblem for Christ or the Christian faith, the only firm hold in an ocean of sin and uncertainty. Rabelais makes it clear that Panurge long ago substituted his own "anchor" for the true one. The meaning of the golden earring with the flea has been explained by Screech. To commemorate the Flight from Egypt, a Jewish slave owner was obliged to offer his slave freedom after seven years' service. If the slave refuses, "then you shall take an awl, and thrust it through his ear . . . and he shall be your bondman for ever" (Deut. 15:17). In his pierced ear, Panurge chooses to wear an earring engraved with the image of a flea: an odd adornment, since "to have the flea in one's ear" was a euphemism for "to burn with lust."[2] Panurge chooses to serve his appetites rather than God, subjecting his higher nature to his base impulses. Having done this, he can no longer follow the path of moderation which Pantagruel urges (TL.xiii.374). Once he has deviated from the golden mean, he is out of balance, a state which may lead to any sort of disorder, including wickedness, if the heart and mind are seduced away from moderation by the "evil spirit" ("si hors aequité par l'esprit maling est l'affection dépravée" [TL.viii.352]. In giving himself up to to his bodily urges, Panurge has fallen prey to the "evil spirit," as Pantagruel observes (TL.xix.394). So far, his case exactly parallels that of Picrochole. But, even though his logical pyrotechnics throughout the *Tiers Livre* reveal his ability to rationalize his pernicious behavior and to turn every gloomy prediction in his favor, he cannot *act* according to his reasonings. His mental efforts are to no avail, his will remains in suspension in a sort of limbo. While Picrochole acts before thinking, Panurge thinks incessantly but cannot act. Caught in his dilemma, Panurge delays the inevitable consequences of action but incurs the fatal effects of indecision: his youthful whimsy degenerates into obsession, his former gaiety and aplomb collapse into the whimpering, abject cowardice which he will exhibit during the tempest at sea.

How to Resolve a Dilemma:
Gargantua and Badebec

Pantagruel repeatedly urges Panurge to make his decision and resign himself to consequences which are beyond his control, and thus not suitable objects for the concern of a Christian man. Panurge's dilemma is a self-inflicted one. But even in the case of a dilemma imposed by external circumstances, a will properly attuned can reach a decision. Rabelais has already explored this situation: an absolute dilemma, resolved in a manner worthy of emulation.

Quand Pantagruel fut né, qui fut bien esbahy et perplex? Ce fut Gargantua, son père. Car, voyant d'un cousté sa femme Badebec morte, et de l'aultre son filz Pantagruel né, tant beau et tant grand, ne sçavoit que dire ny que faire, et le doubte que troubloit son entendement estoit assavoir s'il devoit plorer pour le dueil de sa femme ou rire pour la joye de son filz. (P.iii.181).

"When Pantagruel was born no one could have been more astonished and perplexed than his father Gargantua. For, seeing on the one
side his wife Badebec newly dead, and on the other his son Pantagruel
newly born, and so big and handsome, he did not know what to say or
do. His mind was troubled with the doubt whether he ought to weep in
mourning for his wife, or laugh out of delight at his son" (P.iii.177).
In this passage, Rabelais's style suggests the shuttle motion of Gargantua's feelings by the repetition of *d'un cousté . . . et de l'aultre*
(on the one side . . . and on the other), and through the antitheses,
morte-né, plorer-rire, deuil-joie (dead-born, weep-laugh, mourning-
delight). The dilemma is forcibly presented and developed: the absolute antinomy of death against life, unqualified grief struggling
against unqualified joy. In the face of such an emotional impasse,
reason is powerless, especially the dry, inhuman scholastic logic *in
modo et figura*:

> D'un costé et d'aultre il avoit argumens sophisticques qui le suffocquoy-
> ent, car il les faisoit très bien *in modo et figura;* mais il ne les pouvoit
> souldre, et par ce moyen demeuroit empestré comme la souriz empeigée
> ou un milan prins au lasset. (P.iii.181)

> "On either side he found sophistical arguments which took his breath
> away. For he framed them very well *in modo et figura,* but he could
> not resolve them. And consequently he remained trapped, like a mouse
> caught in pitch or a kite taken in a noose." (P.iii.177)

Like Panurge, Gargantua may deliberate all he likes, but the best
formal logic cannot help him make up his mind. He acts out his
dilemma, alternately weeping over his dead wife and laughing over
his newborn son, alternately asking God why he has been thus
punished and praising Him for the gift of a child. For the moment,
Gargantua is determined by his emotions; he has lost his freedom;
his will remains paralyzed; his humanity becomes concentrated in its
lowest habitation, the sensitive soul. Without grace, Gargantua cannot
see what he must will: without will, he cannot resolve his problem,
for when faced with a decision where each side has an equal claim
on reason, the mind without guidance merely wallows in a slough
of logical propositions, all equally probable. In such a situation, only
the will can choose one side over the other.[3]

In his natural delight over the birth of Pantagruel, Gargantua begins festive preparations, forgetting momentarily the loss of Badebec. She is soon recalled to him, however, and in desperation he invokes God: "Lord God, must I turn sad again?" (p. iii.178). The grace to resolve his dilemma is not long withheld. With a sudden exclamation, Gargantua breaks the deadlock: "By my faith as a nobleman, it's better to weep less and drink more!" (p. iii.178).

Gargantua's character, which Pantagruel inherits, is naturally joyous and tranquil. Acceptance of life as it comes is presented here, as at the end of book five, in the metaphor of "Trinch!," an idea closely related to "fay ce que vouldras." "My wife is dead. Well, in God's name . . . I shan't bring her back to life by my tears . . . I must think of finding another" (p. iii.178). Along with whole-hearted acceptance of life and of the divine will, Rabelais reminds the reader that the loss of a wife, like any other of life's reverses, must not be taken too seriously. This is in keeping with Rabelais's Pauline attitude toward marriage which Pantagruel interprets to Panurge in book three: "Let those that are married be as if they were not married; those who have wives be as if they had no wives" (TL.xxxv.386).[4] If a man has been properly disinterested in his wife from the beginning, her loss will not seem such a blow. This attitude toward wives is actually part of Rabelais's attitude toward this world as a whole: it must be thoroughly enjoyed, and yet not allowed to distract a man from the state of true inner joy which is proper to a good Christian.

Because he has decided to accept the inevitable, to choose joy rather than sorrow, Gargantua remains at home with the living, and, in the same spirit in which Jesus said, "Let the dead bury their dead" (Luke 9:60), he sends others to bury Badebec. He does not forget her entirely, but first composes an epitaph appropriately celebrating her beauty and virtue; a final tribute in which his moral dilemma, too, is laid to rest.

As soon as he gives himself over to *voluptas,* Panurge ceases to maintain the moral distance necessary to choose and then to take the consequences. As long as he remains thus bound by his appetites, he is a fool, mistaking *hepithumia* for *thelēma,* wandering far from the path which Gargantua and Pantagruel follow, and which every man should take.

How Foolish Is Panurge?

Freedom for Renaissance humanists meant escape from fear, superstition, and vice that dwarf the growth of the soul. Because Panurge voluntarily wears the chains of all three, he is a fool. It would be accurate to say that his vices (to which he is by nature vulnerable) give rise to his fears, which he attempts to quiet with his superstitions. His predicament is nowhere more poignantly illustrated than during the tempest at sea (QL.xviii-xxii).

The Fool according to Aulus Gellius

The Pantagrueline fleet passes nine cargo vessels loaded with monks of all descriptions, headed for the Council of Trent to "chew over the articles of faith against the new heretics" (QL.xviii.490). Panurge, filled with joy at this "good omen," superstitiously bribes the monks with liberal provisions of food, so that they will remember him in their devout prayers — which Gargantua had roundly condemned as mockery of God (G.xl.119). All the while Pantagruel remained pensive and melancholy. Frère Jean is about to ask him why he shows such unaccustomed irritation, when all at once, the ill-luck that Panurge had sought to avoid by magico-religious means falls upon them. As Marichal points out, greeting monks is in itself a bad omen.[5] Rabelais had exploited this idea before when Grandgousier, having defeated Picrochole's army, decides against pursuit. Gymnaste protests that Frère Jean is a prisoner of the enemy. " 'Do they have the monk?' asked Gargantua. ' 'Pon my honor, it will be their undoing' " (G.xliv; my trans.; cf. also G.xlv.130).[6] Meeting monks on the right side of the ship is a redoubled ill-omen, says Marichal, since in the "Ancien Prologue au Quart Livre," it is the *left* side which means good luck.[7] Jean later blames Panurge sharply for causing the storm, implicitly because of his truck with the ill-starred monks, *triply* ill-starred, since they are bound for the Council of Trent, boding no good for a ship-load of Evangelicals!

All the voyagers, though frightened, commend themselves to God and do their best to keep the ships afloat — all except Panurge who, collapsing like a heap of jelly, invokes all the saints to his aid, begs for confession, calls on the Virgin, wishes he were in the ship with the "good and blessed council-bound fathers . . . such fat and devout and jolly fellows they were, so sleek and so gracious." Frère Jean angrily shouts at him, "Come, you hangdog devil . . . in the name of the thirty legions of hell, come and help us!" But Panurge, immobilized by terror, merely whines in reply, "Let's not swear at this moment, my friend and father . . . To-morrow we'll swear as much as you like" (QL.xix.493). Panurge uses every "magic charm" in the Christian repertory; he falls prey to every superstition which Rabelais condemns. His hypocrisy is evident in his unwillingness to swear *now* — tomorrow, if you wish, but not just now, while we are all in actual danger!

At the height of the storm, Pantagruel cries out piteously: "Save us, Lord God, we are perishing. However, let it not be according to our wishes, but Thy will be done!" (QL.xxi; my trans.). Like a broken record, Panurge continues his cowardly accompaniment: "May God and the holy Virgin be with us! Alas, alas, I'm drowning! . . . True God, send me some dolphin to save me on land. . ." (QL.xxi; my trans.). Frère Jean swears at him and threatens, "If I come down there . . . I'll give you good proof that your balls hang from the arse of a cuckoldy calf!" (QL.xxi.498).

These reactions to danger typify the positions of the three main characters on Rabelais's "ladder." Pantagruel, while begging divine mercy, defers to the will of God as above that of any mortal (his words are patterned on those of Jesus in the Garden of Gethsemane). Panurge, overcome by panic, invokes the Virgin (as no other Rabelaisian hero ever does), and begs salvation for himself alone, forgetting everyone else. Jean, the simple monk, because of his purity of heart and purpose, automatically and courageously acts to save all on board (consistent with his defense of the abbey close). His fear is not even aroused by the terrible danger, for he is too occupied in cursing in disgust at his friend's degradation. Panurge's behavior recalls the role of the fool in an account of a storm at sea by Aulus Gellius, which became a favorite didactic *topos,* repeated by St. Augustine, by Folengo in his *Baldus,* and by Erasmus in *Naufragium.* In summarizing the story as told by Aulus Gellius, St. Augustine emphasizes the Stoic theory of *phantasiae.* These are impressions made on the mind by circumstances beyond our control and which, if yielded to, can lead astray (cf. Picrochole, led astray by "phantasmes ludificatoires"). The difference between a wise man and a fool, St. Augustine notes, is that the mind of the latter yields to such impressions, while the wise man (though he may suffer like Pantagruel) remains true to his principles and good judgment.[8] While the fool Panurge blubbers at his feet, Pantagruel, though frightened, clings to the mast and holds it firm.[9]

The Fool Who Prefers *Voluptas* to *Caritas*

From the beginning when Panurge gave in to his lust, he yielded himself up to his animal soul. Consistent in foolishness, he repeats the same mistake in the different circumstances of the storm. Ironically, his appetite for pleasure leads him into the most uncomfortable situations from the moment he attaches the flea to his ear until he receives absolution from the Bottle.

Panurge's misfortunes suggest that Rabelais's attitude towards hedonism, a position which he is usually supposed to champion, was essentially negative. Marsigli, Colonna, Ficino, Pico, Valla, and a host of other Renaissance writers agree that pleasure is a positive force in moral conduct, and that the God who endowed man with a desire for pleasure obviously intended him to enjoy life as much as possible. Marsigli, alleging Plato, attests that nature *is* God's will.[10] Rabelais, too, believes that pleasure is beneficial, for his Pantagruelistes do not lack for bodily comforts, and no physical luxury is absent from his abbey.

But Rabelais, through the examples of Picrochole and Panurge, modifies this idea, for both men are misled by their choleric or lustful natures. Both are deceived by *philautia* (self-love) as Screech reminds us.[11] Pantagruel tells Panurge, "I see that you are misled by philauty — by self-love, that is" (TL.xxix.369). In itself a natural force tending toward the betterment of a man's condition through pleasurable activity, misplaced self-love leads both fools to conclude that immediate sensual pleasure is better than ultimate happiness.

Panurge's Saving Grace

As Erasmus's Folly uses the word, the victims of philauty deceive themselves into a false happiness, a flabby, illusory paradise on earth. But Panurge in no way gives in to this sort of slackness, since he indefatigably seeks the truth. Within him there still remains an *instinct et aguillon* that pushes him from one prediction of his fate to another, since none of them carry the persuasive power of first principles. He remains, despite everything, an illustrious boozer, a sincere seeker driven by his desire to know the truth. His *philautia* blinds him to the truth when he is shown it; he must be granted a special gift of grace before his eyes can be opened. But meanwhile, driven by something analogous to Wessel Gansfoort's *displicentia propria,* an *inborn* dissatisfaction with one's own short-comings, he remains eternally restless until the ideal has finally been reached.[12] This *displicentia* provides Panurge so powerful a motive force that he convinces Pantagruel of the worth of his quest; in his fervor he carries along with him twelve ships and the entire Pantagrueline company. His desire to know is so imperious that he even forces heaven. In "Trinch!" he receives a clearer mandate than any Bacbuc can remember. It is he, and not his more virtuous companions, who merits a special revelation, precisely because he *is* a seeker. Even the misguided and deceived man may receive grace if he wants it badly enough.

One inborn trait offsets another. The *instinct et aguillon* of Thélème is Panurge's salvation.[13] There are no miracles: in his essential nature, he remains priapic and lustful, traits not evil in themselves, as long as they do not prevail. At last, he is able to throw off the chains of philauty to act, regardless of consequences. He has achieved his personal golden mean and is now able to drink the wine of *methē nēphalios.* Come what may, he will joyfully remain in the company of the good boozers.

The circle closes, the mortal plagued with misguided will may raise himself though the mystery of wine to the level of his lord, Pantagruel. Man's nature is good in itself; the world and the flesh are here for his enjoyment, but beware the monk! the devil lurks to deceive. Man must depend upon the grace of God for guidance, and then on his temperate reason. Good counsel without this grace leads nowhere: only direct communication from God breaks the deadlock. *Trinch!* is Rabelais's coincidence of opposites: in this word he embodies the Cusan paradox of ineffable wisdom beyond the grasp of human intelligence which is nevertheless communicated to a lowly man in all his human degradation and bestiality. It is not granted to Panurge's reason, but to his *foye* (liver: a possible pun?). Ineffable wisdom, because it surpasses human wisdom, is presented to human foolishness: to the lower man, the liver; and to a fool, Panurge.

Conclusion

Four major interpretations of Rabelais's works have coexisted throughout the four centuries since his lifetime. The first one, addressed to Rabelais in Nicolas Bourbon's *In Rabellum,* is later repeated by Montaigne.[1] Both dismiss Rabelais as a (rather longwinded) teller of bawdy and amusing tales — not quite the sort of thing our youth should be allowed to read. Their idea, that there is no "substantial marrow" at all, has been maintained in various forms, and has found a recent champion in Leo Spitzer.[2] A second interpretation, that Rabelais is a darkly hermetic writer, exploiting the orphic and cabalistic mysteries, has been upheld by many commentators and imitators, from his sixteenth-century adaptor into German, Johann Fischart, to the recent study of Probst-Biraben.[3] A third position, maintained during Rabelais's lifetime by reactionary churchmen and Protestant radicals alike, reads into Rabelais a calculated revolt against Christianity: Rabelais, a covert atheist, sought to ridicule the most sacred mysteries of the Christian faith. The chief modern proponents of this idea were the positivist scholar Abel Lefranc and his followers. More recent variations on this theme have come from the Marxist critics Lefevre and M. Bakhtin. In their view, Rabelais, a proto-Marxist who invented the communistic utopia of Thélème, addressed himself to the proletariat at the country fairs. Last, there are those who believe Rabelais to have been some kind of Christian: Gilson, Febvre, and Krailsheimer think him "liberal" but still orthodox; Telle and Saulnier see in him an Erasmian Evangelical; Screech reminds the twentieth-century *Rabelaisant* that Rabelais could be an Erasmian Evangelical *and* wholly orthodox, judged by the time in which he wrote; still others believe him to be a Protestant, as did Pierre-Antoine Le Motteux.

The evidence would seem best to justify the most moderate and obvious interpretation: Rabelais was a fervent Christian, who condoned neither Béda's nor Calvin's extremism. Rabelais never left the Church, though he at times felt hampered by it and certainly hoped to correct abuses within it through a return to the purity of early Christianity. His hostility to theological argument may indicate that Rabelais saw — as Franz Overbeck would later see — the contradictions between the refusal of the primitive Church to compromise with the secular world and the rationalization of such a compromise through the deadening spirit of theology. He incarnates his love of simple, straightforward humanity in Frère Jean, who defends the Vineyard, the Faith, with essential Christianity, the staff of the Cross. Jean scorns ritual and, although a monk, he agrees with Gargantua that there should be no intermediary between a man and his God; monks should be spiritually and physically active leaders of their communities. Since God is omnipresent, there would be no need for a church building, if mankind only knew how to remain in touch with Him. In Thélème, the inmates live according to God's will; the "house of God" is the abbey itself. Besides praying, the Rabelaisian Christian should revere and read the Scriptures, though he might misinterpret them if he is not given the grace to understand.

Although Rabelais satirizes the Golden Legend, repeating in many places his scorn for those credulous ones who believe such old wives' tales, he still believes in a hierarchy of souls above man (heroes and daemons); his patron Guillaume du Bellay was a hero; his giants are good daemons and even saviors. His optimism is apparent in his attitude toward heroes. *If* a man is free and well-born to begin with, he may become a hero (and, perhaps, a saint), not through miracle-working but through the greatness of his soul, his learning, his serenity, his faith.

Rabelais approaches closest to orthodoxy in the complex of ideas revealed in the symbolism of the wine. His Pantagruelistes remain in constant contact with the divine through the wine of the Scriptures, of prayer, or of the Eucharist. For Rabelais, winedrinking means the *actual* entry of the divine presence into a man, just as the ancients believed they were actually swallowing Bacchus or Apollo. In some sense, therefore, Rabelais believes in transubstantiation, though it is impossible to say whether he believed the formal communion service indispensable for a Eucharistic experience. The atmosphere of the "Propos," or of the "Festin devant Chaneph," confirms that formalism did not appeal to him nor appear necessary for communication with God. However, priests (or priestesses like Bacbuc) are still necessary to administer and explain the sacraments: thus Rabelais approves of some sort of institutionalized religion, while simultaneously rejecting the quibbles of theological casuistry.

The wine in Rabelais's barrel "from a living and perpetual source," his Christ/*logos* inside the Silenus, is a syncretic message, a combination of Christian and humanistic Neoplatonism. He goes far beyond the doctrines of Plato himself, who believed consciousness to be the supreme good. For Rabelais, truth is revealed to faith (*à la fois* with the immediacy of intuition, *par l'instinct et l'aguillon, au foye* and *à la foy*), not to reason, a faculty of which Rabelais is skeptical and at times contemptuous. Although Rabelais loves Plato and uses him abundantly, his attitude toward human wisdom is conditioned by fifteen centuries of Christian forebears. His statements on furor are close to Erasmus's skepticism vis-à-vis human knowledge in the *Praise of Folly,* similar to Agrippa's *De incertitudine et vanitate scientiarum,* and to Cusa's *Docta ignorantia*: "Man can know nothing perfectly . . . for the end of knowledge is completely hidden in God . . . ."[4] Far from condemning learning, Cusa (like Rabelais) merely warns the seeker that human knowledge has little or nothing to do with ultimate truth. Rabelais would accept this clear distinction between knowledge and wisdom: his Frère Jean incarnates it, for Jean is an ignorant but truly wise man. Knowledge concerns the things of this world, it is relative, and is naturally acquired; but wisdom, a knowledge of divine things, is a gift of grace.[5]

Rabelais's entire approach, his *serio ludere,* the grotesque mask, is deeply justified by his conviction that true wisdom often disguises itself as foolishness (the converse is not always true; not all fools are wise). Because he is the most foolish, Panurge receives the divine revelation; the "Propos des bien yvres," apparent gibberish, contains God's truth.

Rabelais accepts the idea, inherited from St. Francis, St. Thomas, and Ficino, that a man wills the good unless he is seriously misguided and seduced by the evil spirit; he believes that the Good is also the supremely pleasant (as in Thélème). In a peculiarly Renaissance fusion of Neoplatonist and Epicurean ideas, a blend which finds a parallel in the theology of the Evangelical mystics Sebastian Franck and Meister Eckhart, Rabelais suggests that union with God is a supreme *voluptas,* achieved by love (a function of the will) and not by knowledge or reason.

The essential goodness of man, which saves Panurge in the end, is an Evangelical inner light. This is the means by which the Thélémites coordinate their activities; this is what spurs Panurge to consult the *Dive Bouteille.* Centuries of Church Fathers called it *synderesis* or *displicentia propria,* the last remnant of uncorrupted man before the Fall. Gargantua and Pantagruel incarnate the pure light of Adam's innocence: Gargantua's emblem, the *androgyne,* epitomizes his role. The spark of *synderesis,* that *scintilla animae,* the soul's spark, akin to Rabelais's *theléma,* brings about *sobria ebrietas* through the divine draught of Spirit. Innate particularly in the free and the well-born, *theléma* is fostered by education. The training of Gargantua represents a synthesis of the best ideas of the Renaissance educators; Rabelais's abbey displays the results of the perfect education. But even in Thélème, man's natural, inner light needs a supplement. Although his will is spurred to follow the promptings of conscience, a man's final choice is free. Rabelais's heroes can make most of their decisions themselves, but at times, caught in a dilemma, they need divine help. His insistence on grace severs Rabelais from the classical philosophers and from their humanist imitators. He follows the Augustinian-Franciscan tradition: the wine represents divine grace and wisdom; the will urges man to accept it, but, since his will is free, a man may still reserve the right to refuse.

To the seeker, all things are revealed. The diligent dog will crack his bone, the boozer becomes drunk with wisdom, the frozen words melt. If we accept the axiom that Rabelais's work is a Silenus box, then his absurd metaphors, when examined with perseverance, will yield their precious drugs. Rabelais's winecask-Bacchus reveals a Christ within: the Dionysian furor reveals the experience of Pentecost.

On entering the temple of Bacchus, the seeker must purify himself of earthly desires before he can raise his eyes to the *divine* appetites. The allegory on the temple walls, Bacchus's victory over the wealth and power of India, echoes each man's conquest of the world. When he at last merits the divine revelation, he is told to drink the wine of life, for its heady draught is worth any risk. *Trinch!* commands each man to live according to God's will, which each must interpret in his own way. Some are born with the mission to parch the throats and peel the tongues of their fellowmen until they *must* drink the wine of wisdom; some are born with a hearty natural affinity for essential truth, and live in a state of grace above mere human wisdom. These may misquote the breviary stuff and still understand its essence. Others, blinded by self-love, may choose the wrong path, but, if they continue to seek a way out, they may be saved at last; the veriest fool often merits the highest honor. We end as we began, with the knowledge that all things are revealed to the true seeker. All mankind (and the more foolish the better) can be saved in the end. Rabelais's circular structure begins and ends with his exhortation to Everyman, the thirsty seeker: "Boozers . . . Trinch!"

Notes

Introduction

1. Etienne Gilson, "Rabelais franciscain," *Les Idées et les Lettres,* 2d ed. (Paris, 1955), pp. 197–241; "Notes médiévales au Tiers Livre de Pantagruel," *Revue d'Histoire Franciscaine,* 2(1925):72–88.

2. Lucien Febvre, *Le Problème de l'incroyance au XVIe siècle; la religion de Rabelais* (Paris, 1947).

3. Verdun L. Saulnier, *Le Dessein de Rabelais* (Paris, 1957); Michael A. Screech, *L'Evangélisme de Rabelais* (Geneva, 1959).

4. Rudolf Stadelmann, "Vom Geist des ausgehenden Mittelalters," *Deutsche Vierteljahrsschrift für Literaturwissenschaft und Geistesgeschichte.* Buchreihe, 15(1929): 110–12.

5. Saulnier; Screech. Cf. the work of E. V. Telle, and of Robert Marichal.

6. Rabelais characterizes the Geneva Protestants as "les Demoniacles Calvins, imposteurs de Genève" (QL. xxxii.629). For an account of his independent position vis-à-vis Luther, see Screech, pp. 18–37.

7. Robert Marichal, "L'Attitude de Rabelais devant le néoplatonisme et l'italianisme," *François Rabelais, 1553–1953* (Geneva, 1953), pp. 181–209, and Screech, *The Rabelaisian Marriage* (London, 1958), chap. 6.

8. The authors of the *Corpus Hermeticum,* inspired by Plato and Jewish wisdom literature, seek to explain the universe, both creator(s) and the hierarchies of creatures: "'Whence did the elements of nature come into being?' He [Poimandres] answered, 'They issued from God's Purpose, which beheld that beauteous world [the intelligible world] and copied it. The watery substance, having received the Word, was fashioned into an ordered world, the elements being separated out from it; and from the elements came forth the brood of living creatures.'" Libellvs I, 8b, p. 117. "And each god [i.e., one of the four elements], by his several powers, put forth that which he was bidden to put forth. And there came forth four-footed beasts and creeping things and fishes and winged birds, and grass and every flowering herb . . . . [And God ordained the] births of men, and bade mankind increase and multiply abundantly . . . And to this end did He make men, that they might contemplate heaven, and have dominion over all things under heaven . . ." Libellvs III, 3a–3b, p. 147. "He sent down man, a mortal creature made in the image of an immortal being, to be an embellishment of the divine body [the earth] . . . For it is man's

function to contemplate the works of God; and for this purpose was he made, that he might view the universe with wondering awe, and come to know its Maker." Libellvs IV, 2, p. 151. The above quotations are from *Hermetica,* vol. 1, ed. Walter Scott (London, 1968).

9. Erich Auerbach, *Scenes from the Drama of European Literature; Six Essays* (New York, 1959), pp. 11–76.
10. Cornelius Agrippa, *La Philosophie occulte* (The Hague, 1727), III, ii, 6.
11. Bernard Weinberg, *Critical Prefaces of the French Renaissance* (Evanston, Ill., 1950), pp. 63–64; my trans. Because of the similarity of the metaphors (the eagle and the marrow strongly suggests the dog and the marrow bone of Prologue G, Abel Lefranc believes that this text may have been one of Rabelais's sources. *Ed. Cr.* 1:10–11, n. 67.
12. Margaret Mann Phillips, *The "Adages" of Erasmus; a Study with Translation* (Cambridge, 1964), pp. 275–76.

Chapter 1

1. Wolfgang Raible, "Der Prolog zu *Gargantua* and der Pantagruelismus," *Romanische Forschungen* 78(1966):253–79.
2. Rabelais's "Pythagorean symbols" may allude to Erasmus's *Adage* I, i, 1: *Pythagorae symbola.* "Nam ea, temetsi prima . . . fronte superstitiosa quaepiam ac deridicula videantur, tamen si quis allegoriam eruat, videbit nihil aliud esse, quam quaedam recte vivendi praecepta." This reference strengthens the probability that Rabelais intends the reader to discover, behind his comic Silenic-bacchic mask, serious precepts for right living.
3. G. Mallary Masters, *Rabelaisian Dialectic and the Platonic-Hermetic Tradition* (State University of New York Press, 1969), pp. 16–17.
4. Walter Ong, *Ramus, Method and the Decay of Dialogue* (Cambridge, Mass., 1958), p. 311; Febvre, *Le Problème de l'incroyance;* McLuhan, *The Gutenberg Galaxy* (Toronto, 1962). Though Ong published his work on Ramus before McLuhan's book appeared, many of his ideas are heavily influenced by McLuhan who was a professor at the University of St. Louis, when Ong attended that institution.
5. The polarity of inner and outer, "cortex" and "medulla"; "escorce" and "mouelle" (as in the exegesis of Ezekiel 17:3–6), goes far back into the Middle Ages and probably into classical antiquity as well. For the extensive medieval background of this commonplace, see Henri de Lubac, *Exégèse médiévale* (Paris, 1959).
6. Rabelais's *crocz* and *pies* are pictorial symbols with the specific meaning: *croquez pie,* i.e., "drink the contents." The humanists, who believed hieroglyphics to represent the Divine Ideas, examined them with passionate interest, since they not only "pointed toward" a hidden truth but also actually participated in the power of the Idea. The sign then became confused with what it symbolized, the medium became the message. Pico believed that the ancient fathers chose symbols based on real insight into the structure of the world: a code of equivalence between sensible objects and their divine counterparts, e.g., fire, which is equivalent to the love of God. See Gombrich, "Icones Symbolicae, the Visual Image in Neo-Platonic Thought," *Journal of the Warburg and Courtauld Institutes* 11(1948):169.
7. Rabelais prefers "bouteille de Pandora" to "jar" or "box" (cf. Prologue to TL.

328; TL. iii.342). The only Roman writer who mentions Pandora's *pithos* or *dolium* (jar) is Porphyry (cf. Dora and Erwin Panofsky, *Pandora's Box* [New York, 1956], pp. 9–10), whose work was familiar to Rabelais (cf. C. J. Rawson, "Rabelais and Horace: A Contact in the *Tiers Livre,* chap. 3," *French Studies* 19[1965]: 377). Erasmus, too, mentions Pandora in three adages (1.1.31; 1.3.35; 2.4.12), though each time, her *pithos* becomes a *pyxis* (box). Panofsky believes that Erasmus began the misunderstanding (Pandora's *box* rather than her *jar*), which is current today. Reporting the contents of a letter from Panofsky, C. J. Rawson speculates that under Erasmus's influence, the size of the *pithos* was reduced to a mere *vasculum,* which may have suggested a bottle to Rabelais (Rawson, p. 377). Since Rabelais assimilates Pandora's container with his own work, he disregards the evils which have flown out, remembering only good hope, which he opposes to the despair in the Danaids' tub. It seems natural that she should exchange *pithos* for bottle, since his book is identified elsewhere as either a bottle or a barrel. Rabelais neither follows Erasmus slavishly nor does he make a merely fortuitous comic transformation of the *pyxis:* his choice of bottle forms another link in an unbroken metaphorical chain.

8. The use of living waters (*aquae vitae*) and wine as commonly interchangeable metaphors for spirit is borne out by a number of Old and New Testament passages, e.g., John 4:13–14, where Jesus speaks to a Samaritan woman at a well and asks her for a drink. He tells her, "Every one who drinks of this water will thirst again, but whoever drinks of the water that I shall give him will never thirst; the water that I shall give him will become in him a spring of water welling up to eternal life." The living waters in John 7 are also a metaphor for spirit, and have been so interpreted by the Fathers of the Church: St. Thomas Aquinas' compilation of commentaries on the Gospels by Doctors of the Church lists the opinions of St. Jerome, St. Augustine, St. Gregory the Great, and St. Chrysostom, all of whom explicate this text. The entire notion of the *Fons sapientiae,* which is at the bottom of the Revelation of the Bottle, depends upon this equation of water, wine, and spirit.

9. A covert reference to Lucian's *Dionysos, 7.*

10. A few examples: "My soul thirsts for God, for the living God." Ps. 42:2; "Blessed are those who hunger and thirst for righteousness . . ." Matt. 5:6; "Jesus said to her, 'Every one who drinks of this water will thirst again, but whoever drinks of the water that I shall give him will never thirst . . .'" John 4:13; "I am the bread of life; he who comes to me shall not hunger, and he who believes in me shall never thirst." John 6:35; "If any one thirst, let him come to me and drink. He who believes in me, as the Scripture has said, *Out of his heart shall flow rivers of living water.*" John 7:37–38.

11. Philo, III, par. 27 *ad Gen.* 16, 7, p. 198A, in Lewy, *Sobria Ebrietas* (Giessen, 1929), p. 20. Philo is commenting upon Proverbs 9:1–16, a text more concise and meaningful in the Vulgate than in any modern version: "Sapientia aedificavit sibi domum, excidit columnas septem. Immolavit victimas suas, miscuit vinum, et proposuit mensam suam . . . Et insipientibus locuta est: Venite, comedite panem meum, et bibite vinum quod miscui vobis."

12. *Republic* 2.376 in Jowett 1:639.

13. Phillips, p. 271.

14. Plato *Timaeus* 73 in Jowett 2:51.

15. Richard B. Onians, *The Origins of European Thought about the Body* (Cambridge, 1951), pp. 109–12. Rondibilis quotes Hippocrates' opinion that the grey cerebral matter and spinal fluid are the source of semen: "Il maintient grande portion de la géniture sourdre du cerveau et de l'espine du dours" (TL. xxxi.443).
16. Galen *On the Natural Faculties* 3.15.
17. Some interpreters have seen in the Prologue to TL a reference to the war between France and the forces of Charles V. Others believe that Rabelais refers to the struggle for reform within the Church. Both these ideas may be correct. It seems likely, too, that Rabelais is making war on more general human ills, like superstition, loss of faith, or depression.
18. Raible's argument that the substantial marrow of Rabelais is the curative power of laughter, would have found support in the fact that Rabelais transforms Plato's original comparison of Socrates with Silenus statuettes, which open up to reveal images of gods, into a medical comparison. The hidden treasure becomes precious drugs. Part of the evidence Raible *does* use to support his argument may be turned against it. Two of the authorities whom he quotes to prove the *medical* efficacy of laughter as a curative power, Boccaccio and Marguerite de Navarre, are more interested in theology than in physical cures. Raible's perspective appears limited by the twentieth-century bias in favor of empirical science and what we now consider good medical practice; see his "Der Prolog zu Gargantua und der Pantagruelismus," pp. 262–63.
19. Lewy, p. 39.
20. Lewy, pp. 55–56. The name *Isaac* in Hebrew is derived from the verb *to laugh,* since Abraham and Sarah both laughed skeptically when God announced the birth of their son. Abraham was one hundred, and Sarah ninety at the time (Gen. 17–18).
21. Erasmus, *Opera omnia* (Leyden, 1703), 2.774 f. Nicolaus Cusanus, in *De ludo globi,* expounds the theological implications to be found in a frivolous and laughable game of ball.
22. A. J. Krailsheimer, *Rabelais and the Franciscans* (Oxford, 1963), chaps. 3–6.
23. Wolfgang Kayser, *Das Groteske, seine Gestaltung in Malerei und Dichtung* (Oldenburg, 1957), pp. 21–22.
24. Edgar Wind, *Pagan Mysteries in the Renaissance* (New Haven, 1958), p. 190.
25. Plotinus distinguishes two forms of *Nous,* a rational one which is subordinate to the second, "loving *Nous.*" When the worshiper reaches the highest ecstasy, all intellectual clarity vanishes in a state which Plotinus compares to intoxication by nectar: "Stripped of its wisdom in the intoxication of the nectar, the Nous becomes loving; through its excess it becomes simpler and more joyful." Intoxication is better for the *Nous* than staid abstention from such revels. *Ennead* 6.7.35.
26. "*Hermes:* 'Now speech, my son, God imparted to all men; but mind he did not impart to all . . .' *Tat:* 'Tell me then, father, why did not God impart mind to all men?' *Hermes:* 'It was his will, my son, that mind should be placed in the midst as a prize that human souls may win.' *Tat:* 'And where did he place it?' *Hermes:* 'He filled a great basin with mind, and sent it down to earth; and he appointed a herald, and bade him make proclamation to the hearts of men: Hearken, each human heart; dip yourself in this basin, if you can, recognizing for what purpose you have been made, and believing that you shall ascend to Him who sent the basin down. Now those who gave heed to the proclamation, and dipped them-

selves in the bath of mind, these men got a share of *gnosis* [knowledge of God]; they received mind, and so became complete men.' " Libellvs IV, 4, p. 151, in *Hermetica,* ed. Scott.

27. Phillips, p. 269.

28. Also Henri Clouzot in *Ed. cr.* 1:15, n. 100, "Il est permis de ne pas croire rigoureusement que R. n'a employé à composer son roman que le temps de ses repas."

29. It has long been recognized that Rabelais's reference to Homer and Ennius recalls a specific passage in Horace: "Laudibus arguitur vini vinosus Homerus/Ennius ipse pater numquam nisi potus ad arma/prosiluit . . ." *Epist.* I, xix, line 6–8. Rabelais may have become aware of the classical ideas on the benefits of wine through the Erasmian adages *In vino veritas* (1.7.17), and *Aquam bibens nihil boni parias* (2.6.2). In the latter adage, Erasmus quotes Horace, who asserts that no poet can properly create unless inspired by wine: "Nulla placere diu, neque vivere carmina possunt,/Quae scribuntur aquae potoribus."

    For an interpretation of Prologue III which in part parallels my own, see Floyd Gray "Structure and Meaning in the Prologue to the *Tiers Livre,*" *L'Esprit Créateur* 3(1963):57–62.

30. The fool Trimalchio accurately reflects the Roman (as well as Greek) identification of wine and life: "The ancient Roman festival of the spirit of the year, Anna Perenna, on the Ides of March is now more intelligible. Its distinctive feature was that the assembled crowd drank wine 'and they pray for as many years as they take ladles full. . . . There you will find a man who drinks up the years of Nestor, a woman who has been made a sibyl by her cups' (i.e., very long-lived)." Onians, pp. 216, 221–24.

31. Charles Estienne, *Dictionarium latinogallicum* (Paris, 1561), defines *philologus,* referring to Cicero, as "Amateur des lettres."

32. Lewy, pp. 8–9.

33. It is amusing to note that business (busy-ness) is expressed negatively in Latin as *negotium,* a lack of (*nec-*)*otium.* In the minds of the ancients, leisure, far from evoking any such Puritan condemnation as "An idle mind is the devil's workshop," ranks far above *negotium,* since free time is necessary for any creative endeavor: "O dulce otium honestumque, ac panae omni negotio! pulchrius! o! mare! littus! verum secretumque *mouseion*! quam multa invenitis! quam multa dictatis!" Plin. 1. I, ep. 9.

34. Philo provides an early Neoplatonic parallel to Rabelais: "Every *immanently* cultured and learned sage perfects himself not through reflection or study, nor by painful labor, but at birth he immediately finds the road made plain which leads to heaven-sent wisdom. He may drink this wisdom undiluted; it refreshes him, and he remains, in the truest sense of the word, in a state of sober inebriation . . . This . . . [sage] is Isaac!" *De fuga atque inventione* par. 166 I 571M, in Lewy, pp. 8–9; my trans.

35. Jean Guiton mentions "L'Ecolier limousin," Panurge's first appearance, Thaumaste, "La Sybille de Panzoust," "L'Oracle de la Dive Bouteille," as so many episodes in which the word is protagonist, "Le Mythe des paroles gelées," *Romanic Review* 31(1940):9.

36. Panurge, the prankster, coward, and misguided sinner, stubbornly seeks the truth until he finds it. Pantagruel considers his cause worthy enough to mount an expe-

dition to the Dive Bouteille to seek an answer to Panurge's unanswerable question. Panurge's final triumph, clearly foreshadowed in book four, is consummated in book five.

37. The difference between written and spoken words was not something observed by Rabelais alone. The Count in Castiglione's *Il Cortegiano* comments, perhaps alluding to the commonplace, "Verba volant scripta manent," "Ché pur, secondo me, la scrittura non è altro che una forma di parlare, che resta ancor poi che l'omo ha parlato, e quasi una imagine o piú presto vita delle parole: e però nel parlare, il qual, subito uscita che è la voce, si disperde, son forse tollerabili alcune cose che non sono nello scrivere; perché la scrittura conserva le parole, e le sottopone al giudicio di chi legge, e dá tempo considerarle maturamente." *Opere,* a cura di G. Prezzolini (Milan, n.d.), pp. 90–91.

38. Guiton, p. 12. Guiton does not report the considerable difference in tone between the two authors. Rimbaud's line is a sarcastic comment upon the sweetish romanticism of the *"bons" poètes,* while Rabelais relates a "straight-forward" myth.

39. The worlds are not infinite in number, nor one, nor five, but one hundred and eighty-three, arranged in the form of a triangle, each side of the triangle having sixty worlds; . . . The inner area of the triangle is the common hearth of all, and is called the Plain of Truth, in which the accounts *logoi,* the forms, and the patterns of all things that have come to pass and of all that shall come to pass rest undisturbed; and round about them lies Eternity, whence Time, like an ever-flowing stream, is conveyed to the worlds. Opportunity to see and to contemplate these things is vouchsafed to human souls once in ten thousand years if they have lived goodly lives; and the best of the initiatory rites here are but a dream of that highest rite and initiation . . . (*De defectu oraculorum* 22).

40. Then Gideon said to God, "If thou wilt deliver Israel by my hand, as thou hast said, behold, I am laying a fleece of wool on the threshing floor; if there is dew on the fleece alone, and it is dry on all the ground, then I shall know that thou wilt deliver Israel by my hand, as thou hast said." And it was so. When he rose early next morning and squeezed the fleece, he wrung enough dew from the fleece to fill a bowl with water. Then Gideon said to God, "Let not thy anger burn against me, let me make trial only this once with the fleece; pray, let it be dry only on the fleece, and on the ground let there be dew." And God did so that night; for it was dry on the fleece only, and on all the ground there was dew.

41. Antiphanes said humorously that in a certain city words congealed with the cold the moment they were spoken, and later, as they thawed out, people heard in the summer what they had said in the winter; it was the same way, he asserted, with what was said by Plato to men still in their youth; not until long afterwards, when they had become old men, if ever, did most of them come to perceive the meaning (*De defect. oracul.* 22).

42. Ovid *Meta.* 11.50.

43. Rabelais consistently misspells the Arimaspians of Herodotus and Pliny, calling them "Arismapiens."

44. An alternate translation suggested by Norman O. Brown (based on *nēphalieuō* and *leibō*), "those who make a libation without wine," also might suggest the gods as well (e.g., Homer *Iliad* 1.595), who drink nectar, not wine, from Vulcan's bowl. The term which Philo Judaeus invented to describe the ecstasy of the believer in communion with God, *methē nēphatios,* is based on the same root word. Rabelais

meant *Nephelibates* to carry associations of holiness or saintliness for the initiate. Saulnier presents an entirely different interpretation of the myth. The *Nephelibates* are the cloud-flying griffons from whom the *Arismapiens* take their gold. (cf. Pliny and Herodotus. Neither authority actually mentions a war; they only say that the Arimaspians *take* their gold from the griffons.) Saulnier believes the Nephelibate-griffon to signify the forces of Emperor Charles V, since the griffon is similar to the Austrian eagle; the Arimaspians are the northern Protestants. Rabelais offers no personal opinion on the outcome of the battle because, in accordance with the tacit agreement among Evangelicals, he has decided to remain silent. His words are therefore "frozen." "Le Silence de Rabelais et le mythe des paroles gelées," *François Rabelais, 1553–1953* (Geneva, 1953), pp. 233–47.

45. "Torche, lorgne" form part of a battle cry. In the fifteenth and sixteenth centuries, *lorgner* meant to strike violently, as in this quotation from Coquillart: "Torsche, lorgne, depesche, rue" (Grandsaignes d'Hauterive, s.v. *lorgner*). These cries add little to the meaning of the passage, but they heighten the warlike atmosphere.

46. Rabelais is credited with giving literary currency to *Goth* as a term of general abuse, cf. E. S. de Beer, "Gothic: Origin and Diffusion of the Term; the Idea of Style in Architecture," *Journal of the Warburg and Courtauld Institutes* 11(1948): 144. The two passages quoted from Rabelais seem to typify his two most important uses of Goth.

47. "Motz de gueule" plays on the ambiguity of the word *gueule* which is at the same time a heraldic term for red (gules) and very impolite slang for mouth. In the latter sense, "motz de gueule" would mean swear words or blasphemies.

48. Augustin et Porphire nous sont témoins que les Platoniciens ont mis trois personnes en Dieu, dont ils nomment la premiere le Pere de l'univers; la seconde le Fils, et premier entendement . . . la troisiéme Esprit, ou Ame du monde. . . .

Plotin et Philon enseignent que le Fils de Dieu est le premier esprit, c'est-à-dire, le divin entendement procedant du Pere, de la même maniere que le Verbe ou la Parole sans personne qui parle, ou comme une lumiere d'une autre lumiere; c'est pourquoi il a été appelé le Verbe, la Parole, et la splendeur du Pere. *Phil. occ.* 3.7.26.

49. "Les noms propres des choses, sont certains rayons que l'on trouve presens partout, qui gardent leur force autant que l'essence de la chose domine en elles. . . . Toute voix . . . signifie d'abord par une influence d'harmonie céleste, ensuite par l'imposition de l'homme . . . ; quand les deux significations se rencontrent . . . pour lors ce nom se rend très-efficace à agir, ayant une double vertu . . . la naturelle et la volontaire." *Phil. occ.* 1.70.197–98; my trans.

50. *Phil. occ.* 1.70.199.

Chapter 2

1. Phillips, *The "Adages" of Erasmus,* pp. 271–76.

2. Francis Cornford, *The Origin of Attic Comedy* (London, 1914), pp. 103–104; also F. Nietzsche, *Die Geburt der Tragödie aus dem Geiste der Musik,* passim.

3. One authority believes that Orphism is linked to the Dionysiac cult in the way a religion is related to its sects, as in the case of Christianity to Lutheranism. Orphism would represent a branch of the Dionysian religion centering around the personality and deeds of a reformer, Orpheus. The reform movement eventually became

a new and separate religion, paralleling the original development of Christianity. Vittorio D. Macchioro, *From Orpheus to Paul* (New York, 1930), p. 137.

4. Augustine, *De civ. Dei* 7.21 ff.

5. For the following choice of texts illustrating the "Song of the vine" and their interpretation, I am indebted to Jean Daniélou, *The Lord of History* (London, 1958).

   "My beloved had a vineyard on a very fertile hill. He digged it and cleared it of stones, and planted it with choice vines; he looked for it to yield grapes, but it yielded wild grapes . . . And now I will tell you what I will do to my vineyard. I will remove its hedge, and it shall be devoured; I will break down its wall, and it shall be trampled down . . . For the vineyard of the Lord of hosts is the house of Israel, and men of Judah are his pleasant planting; and he looked for justice, but behold, bloodshed; for righteousness, but behold, a cry!" Isa. 5:1–7.

6. "There was a householder who planted a vineyard . . . and let it out to tenants. . . . When the season of fruit drew near, he sent his servants to the tenants, to get his fruit; and the tenants took his servants and beat one, killed another, and stoned another. Again he sent other servants . . . and they did the same to them. Afterward he sent his son to them, saying, 'They will respect my son.' . . . And they took him and cast him out of the vineyard and killed him. When therefore the owner of the vineyard comes, what will he do to those tenants?" Matt. 21: 33–40.

7. St. Zeno, *Tractatus* 2.28 (*Patrologia Latina* 11:471–72), in Daniélou, p. 180.

8. "I am the true vine, and my Father is the vinedresser. Every branch of mine that bears no fruit, he takes away, and every branch that does bear fruit he prunes, that it may bear more fruit . . . As the branch cannot bear fruit by itself, unless it abides in the vine, neither can you, unless you abide in me. I am the vine, you are the branches . . . If a man does not abide in me, he is cast forth as a branch and withers; and the branches are gathered, thrown into the fire and burned." John 15:1–7.

9. Masters, "The Hermetic and Platonic Tradition in Rabelais' *Dive Bouteille*," *Studi Francesi* 28 (1966):22.

10. Helen North, *Sophrosyne; Self-knowledge and Self-restraint in Greek Literature* (Ithaca, 1966), p. 330.

11. F. Antal, "The Maenad and the Cross," *Journal of the Warburg and Courtauld Institutes* 1(1937):71–73.

12. "On the Dignity of Man," *The Renaissance Philosophy of Man,* ed. Ernst Cassirer (Chicago, 1948), p. 234.

13. "Il faut remarquer que chacune de ces ames [célestes] suivant la philosophie d'Orphée, a deux vertus, l'une qui consiste dans la connoissance, l'autre qui consiste a vivifier et gouverner son corps. En ce sens Orphée apelle dans les spheres célestes la premiere vertu Bacchus, il apelle l'autre Muse: C'est de là que personne ne s'ennivre par quelque Bacchus, qui n'ait été marié auparavant à sa Muse. On distingue donc, et on met neuf Bacchus auprès des neuf Muses." *Phil. occ.* 2.58.413.

14. Wind, *Pagan Mysteries,* p. 155.

15. Wind, pp. 161–62.

16. Cesare Ripa, *Iconologia* (Perugia, 1764–1767), 1:321. Ripa, though a seventeenth-century scholar, collected iconological data already commonplace in the Renaissance.

17. Ripa, I, 321.
18. Wind, "Dürer's 'Männerbad': a Dionysian Mystery," *Journal of the Warburg and Courtauld Institutes* 2(1938–39):269–71.
19. In *Vit. Apoll.* 2.35f., Philostratos syncretizes all traditions of inspiration: "Consider me, too, O King, and all those who drink water, as filled with the spirits of gods. For we are possessed by the Nymphs, and are Bacchantes of sobriety." Lewy, p. 70; my trans.
20. Philo explains religious inspiration with Dionysian metaphors: "The mind of man . . . flies up . . . following wisdom [and] strives for pure, spiritual being. While contemplating the Archetypes and Ideas of those objects perceptible to the senses which it has seen below — Archetypes and Ideas which are immeasurably beautiful things — it is seized by a sober drunkenness, and becomes ecstatic like those possessed by the Corybantic spirit. A further nostalgia and a higher desire take possession of the mind; it thinks to draw near to the presence of God." *De opificio mundi* 70, in Lewy, pp. 22–23; my trans.
21. Ariosto's *Orlando Furioso*, which parodies the same principle by applying it to profane love, illustrates that furor was a widespread commonplace in the Renaissance.
22. Ficino, *Op. omnia* (Basel, 1576), p. 498. Ficino's regime employs almost the same means as does Dionysian purification in Dürer's *Männerbad* where wine, music, and sweet odors are all represented as beneficial. Most humanists, including Rabelais, make little or no distinction between the four Platonic furors; Agrippa speaks of the Apollonian and Dionysian furors in the same chapter without any clear differentiation.
23. "Aristote appelle cette devination fureur, et veut qu'elle vienne de l'humeur melancolique . . . il dit, que les Sybilles, les Bachides, . . . sont devenus devins, et Poëtes par leur humeur melancholique . . . cette humeur . . . qui s'apelle naturelle et blanche, laquelle quand elle est excitée et allumée . . . excite la fureur . . . sur-tout quand elle est aidée de quelque influence céleste, particulierement de Saturne. . . ." *Phil. occ.* 1.60.169–70.
24. Pierre d'Aban, *Les Oeuvres magiques de Henri-Corneille Agrippa* (Rome, 1744).
25. Nietzsche summarizes the ancient Greek idea of divination: "Die uralte heilige Tempelmusik, die sich an Orpheus und Musaeus knüpft, ist nicht agonal . . . (Pausanius 10.7). Diese Art der Musik und Poesie kommt von den *Thraciern* namentlich zu den Griechen. Die *Orakelpoesie* glaubt durch den Rhythmus die Zukunft zu erzwingen; so wie das Wort buchstäblich ausgesprochen wurde, bindet es die Zukunft. *Chrēsmoi* "Nothwendigkeiten," *fata* "Aussprüche." Der Hexameter soll in Delphi erfunden sein, pythischer Vers." *Gesch. der griech. Lit.*, lectures 1875–76 (Munich; Musarion-Ausg., 1922), 5:221.
26. "Ciceron s'en tenant au sentiment des Stoiciens, assûre que la prédiction de l'avenir n'apartient qu'aux dieux. Et Ptolomée l'Astrologue parle ainsi; il n'y a que ceux qui sont inspirez de la divinité, qui puissent prédire les particularitez de l'avenir. Pierre l'Apôtre appuye ces sentimens, en disant: La prophetie n'est jamais arrivée à l'homme quand il a voulu; mais quand les hommes ont été inspirez du St. Esprit, ils ont parlé comme les saints personnages de Dieu. . . . Il y a trois sortes de descentes de cette nature, à sçavoir, la fureur, le ravissement, et le songe. . . ." *Phil. occ.* 3.45.206–07.
27. "Nous devons donc après nous être bien preparez par une bonne vie nous presenter, et nous donner à l'amour de Dieu, et à la religion, et en cet état dans un as-

soupissement de tous les sens, et une tranquilité d'esprit attendre cette divine am-
broisie, ce nectar divin, nectar, dis-je que le Prophete Zacharie appelle un vin qui
fait porter fruit aux vierges, loüant et adorant le Bacchus élevé par dessus les cieux,
le Souverain des Dieux, le Roi du Sacerdoce, l'auteur de la regeneration celebré
par les anciens Prophetes, sous le tître de deux fois né, de qui nous recevons des
dons divins." *Phil. occ.* 3.1.2.

28. One of the definitions of Bacchus current in Rabelais's time is simply *vin*. This
usage is based upon the mythological metonymies to be found in Horace, Vergil,
Ovid, and others (cf. Estienne, or Lewis and Short, s.v. *Bacchus*). This definition
remains valid today, even for English speakers (cf. *Webster's New International
Dictionary,* s.v. *Bacchus*). Rabelais was also aware of the rhetorical use of the god's
name. During his discussion of Pantagruelion, he reports that, at the moment of
death, certain hanged men cried out that Pantagruel had them by the throat. But
this is a mere solecism, taking the invention for the inventor, or a "figure syn-
ecdochique, . . . comme on prend Cérès pour pain, Bacchus pour vin" (TL. li. 506).

29. Panurge's madness is a cleverly feigned rhetorical device, using the idea that there
is truth in madness in order to convince his hearer. Rabelais possibly uses Panurge's
furor to parody the Protestant idea of Divine grace *lent* to the sinner, who is in
God's *debt* for it.

30. Panurge's *philautia* (self-love) is evident in his very syntax. He obsessively repeats
the subject pronoun ("je . . . je . . . je . . ."), in marked contrast to Pantagruel's
sober, classical, and objective reply. Instead of being possessed by the god, he is
self-possessed.

31. *Timaeus* 71, in Jowett, 2:50.

32. "Faut-il, pour davant icelles [Intelligences coelestes] saige estre, je dis sage et
praesage par aspiration divine et apte à recepvoir bénéfice de divination, se oublier
soy-mesmes, issir hors de soy-mesmes, vuider ses sens de toute terrienne affection,
purger son esprit de toute humaine sollicitude et mettre tout en nonchaloir. Ce
que vulgairement est imputé à folie" (TL. xxxvii.462).

33. This passage echoes the practice of the *sottie,* familiar to Rabelais, who himself had
belonged to a *société joyeuse* at the University of Montpellier, ca. 1530. The *sottie,*
probably a descendent of the *festum stultorum* (a Church festival), is brilliantly
represented by the plays of Pierre Gringore, e.g., *Le Prince des Sots,* a play produced in 1512, where Gringore, in his role of La Mère Sotte, satirized the Church
in the person of the Pope, Jules II. Petit de Julleville, *Le Théâtre en France* (Paris,
1923), pp. 60–65.

34. Because she was once punished by Jupiter who suspended her in the air and amid
the clouds by a golden chain (cf. *Iliad* 15.18–21), Juno became the symbol for
air in the graphic representation of the four elements (cf. Plutarch, *Isis et Osiris*
32; Cicero, *De natura deorum* 2.26). Tervarent, 227–28.

35. Plattard, in "L'Ecriture sainte," takes this attitude.

36. *Webster's New International Dictionary* definition of symposium, "a drinking party,
esp. one following a banquet and providing music, singing and conversation," fits
the "Propos" very well.

37. As in the case of Triboullet who is "Fol de haulte game," i.e., in harmony with
the spheres, Pantagruel's studies raise him to a celestial level.

38. Verdun Saulnier, seeking early sixteenth-century instances where *hausser le temps*
is used synonymously with *boire,* finds only one in Mathurin Cordier (1530). A
little later, Guillaume Bouchet and Brantôme exploit the same idiom. Saulnier

speculates that, by mid-century, the two expressions had become equivalent. "Le Festin devant Chaneph," *Mercure de France* 320(1954):656.

39. Saulnier, pp. 652–54, 656–66.

40. Saulnier, in "Le Festin," examines the context of this chapter at length, showing how Rabelais opposes the feast on board his Evangelical ship to the abuses of the Isle of Chaneph (hypocrisy), where Pantagruel and his companions do not deign to land. Saulnier correctly shows that Rabelais is opposing the true faith, symbolized by the divine feast, to the abusive religion of the hypocrites whom he vilifies throughout the five books.

41. The Horatian Epistle I, v, also represents wine as cure-all, with no disadvantages: "quid non ebrietas designat? operta recludit, spes iubet esse ratas, ad proelia trudit inertem, sollicitis animis onus eximit, addocet artis. fecundi calices quem non fecere dissertum? contracta quem non in paupertate solutum?" (ll. 16–20)

42. The *Encyclopaedia Britannica* (11th ed.) informs us that "The only really definite and mature art-form denoted by the word *motet* is that of the sixteenth-century pieces of ecclesiastical music in one or two . . . continuous movements, for the most part on Biblical or other ecclesiastical prose texts. . . . The title of motet is also occasionally loosely used for non-ecclesiastical works. . . . [but] the most important kind of motet is that which is intimately connected with the solemn mass for a particular holy day."

43. "Anima certe, quia spiritus est, in sicco habitare non potest, ideo in sanguino fertur habitare." Augustine, *Quaest. Novi et Veteris Testamenti* (qu. 23, *Patrologia latina* 35, col. 2229).

44. Cf. "quod cum spe divite manet in venas animumque meum, quod verba ministret" (Horace, *Epist.* 1.15.19 ff.). The belief was also widespread that the blood was the seat of the soul (Onians, p. 63). Since the soul's habitation may be either the blood or the "hollow veins" of the respiratory system, the wine our revelers drink is pure food for the spirit: "Cestuy entre dedans les vènes: la pissotière n'y aura rien." ("Vinum recipiunt inanibus venis" Seneca, *Epist. Mor.* 122.6; "potionem inanibus venis rapit," Arnobius, *adv. Nat.* 5.6.) The *grenoillière* where the dry soul takes refuge of course means a froggy marshland, but, according to Godefroy in the fifteenth and sixteenth centuries it also means a tavern where there is no shortage of spirits.

45. In Genesis 14:18, Melchisedek, priest and king, meets the victorious warrior Abraham with a gift of bread and wine. Philo Judaeus interprets his gift as of the Holy Spirit, and makes Melchisedek a high priest of the *logos* (Philo, *Leg. alleg.*, par. 79 and 82). The high priest is, by implication, a wine steward. Likewise, Origen, basing himself on John 15:5, where Jesus tells his disciples: "I am the vine, you the branches," explicitly calls Christ a Wine Steward, who offers mankind the inebriating wine of *logos* (Lewy, pp. 21–22; 120). Philo describes the relation between the blessed soul and the *logos* as a relation between drinker and wine steward: "For who pours drink from the holy ladle of true joy into the happy, perfect soul, which offers its understanding as its holiest chalice, if not the *logos*, God's wine-steward and leader of the divine symposium, who is identical to the drink itself, but himself undiluted wine, refreshment, spice, praise, and gladness, and, to use poetic words, the ambrosian elixir of joy and delight." Philo, *Quod omnis probus liber sit*, 12 ff., in Lewy, pp. 19–20; my trans. Here is abundant evidence of the traditional and orthodox Christian nature of Rabelais's similes.

46. Godefroy gives the definition "du temple."

47. According to Clouzot, Malindi is "au XVIe siècle la ville extraordinaire et lointaine par excellence" (*Ed. cr.* 1:59). An El Dorado, notes Boulenger (p. 19); in other words, an earthly paradise where the inhabitants constantly imbibe the spirits. Historically, Vasco da Gama erected a pillar at Malindi, on the coast of East Africa, when he visited the port in 1498. Milton refers to the city as "Melind" in *Paradise Lost*.
48. Rabelais ambiguously refers to the tears of Christ and to Lagrima Christi, a muscatel grown on the slopes of Vesuvius.

Chapter 3

1. Spitzer, "Rabelais et les rabelaisants," *Studi Francesi* 12(1960):423; my trans.
2. Most of my interpretations of these Dionysian symbols derive from Ripa's *Iconologia* 1:320–25, as well as from Juan E. Cirlot, *A Dictionary of Symbols* (New York, 1962), and Guy de Tervarent, *Attributs et symboles dans l'art profane, 1450–1600* (Geneva, 1958). An amusing common-sense account of Bacchus' conquest of India is given by Polyaenus in his *Stratagems of War*, trans. Shepherd (London, 1796): "Bacchus, in his Indian expedition, to gain admittance into the cities, instead of gleaming armour, habited his troops in white linen and deers' skins. Their spears were adorned with ivy, and the points of them concealed under a Thyrsus. His orders were given by cymbals and tabrets, instead of trumpets: and, intoxicating his enemies with wine, he engaged them in dancing. (This might have been effected by presents of wine and invitations to festivity, or by feigned flights, and stores of wine purposely left in his camp. In rude times, and among a barbarous people, either stratagem might be practiced with success. But the former seems to be the deception in this place alluded to.) From hence was derived the institution of the orgies of Bacchus, which are only commemorations of this, and whatever stratagems else that General practiced in his conquest of India, and the rest of Asia" (1.i.5). "Pan, a general under Bacchus, was the first who reduced to a regular system the marshalling of an army: he invented the phalanx, and ranged it with a right and left wing; from whence he is usually represented with horns. Victory always sat upon the strongest sword, till he pointed out the way to conquest by artifice and manoeuvre.
   In the midst of a barren desert, Bacchus was by his scouts informed, that an immense army of the enemy were encamped a little above him. The intelligence was alarming; but he soon found himself relieved from his embarrassment, by a ready expedient of Pan, who ordered the whole army, in the silence of the night, on a signal given, to set up a loud and general shout. The surrounding rocks, and the cavity of the forest re-echoed the sound, and imposed on the enemy an apprehension that his forces were infinitely more numerous than they were; and, seized with a general consternation, they abandoned their camp, and fled. From the circumstances of this stratagem the nymph Echo has been feigned by the poets to be the mistress of Pan; and from hence also all vain and imaginary fears are termed Panics" (1.ii.6–7).
3. Cirlot, p. 144. Lewis and Short inform us that "Bacchus, as a giver of courage, is represented with horns, Tib. 2, 1–3; Hor. C.2, 19, 30."
4. Ripa, 1:315.
5. Tervarent, p. 241.

6. Tervarent, pp. 153–55.
7. *Rabelaisian Dialectic*, p. 23.
8. Thomas Taylor, *The Theoretic Arithmetic of the Pythagoreans* (Los Angeles, 1934), p. 178.
9. The early Christian commemoration of the Last Supper was not at all formal, and since Greek *koinōnia* meant simply "community" or "gathering," any feast within or without the Church could be a "eucharistic" meal. Early Christians commemorated the Last Supper also with the feast of *Agapē*, a love-feast which became so abusively lavish that the practice was stopped in favor of a simpler, more formal celebration. St. Paul chides his flock for their lax practices in the *Agapē* feast: "So then when you meet together, it is no longer possible to eat the Lord's Supper. For at the meal, each one takes first his own supper, and one is hungry, and another drinks overmuch. Have you not houses for your eating and drinking?" 1 Cor. 11:20–22. In returning to the *simplicitas* of the early Church, Rabelais represents the Last Supper simply as a communal meal.
10. For an analysis of the Neoplatonic number symbolism, and of the symbolism involved in the geometry and materials used in the *lampe admirable* and the *fontaine phantasticque*, see Masters, "The Hermetic and Platonic Tradition in Rabelais' *Dive Bouteille*," *Studi Francesi* 28(1966):15–29. The one hundred steps are broken down by Rabelais into 1, 2, 3, 4, 9, 8, 27; the seven degrees of the Platonic psychogeny which represents purification of the soul and attainment of the highest spiritual state.
11. Masters ("The Hermetic and Platonic Tradition," pp. 19–20) suggests that the Lantern "la mye du grand M. P. Lamy," "la plus divine . . . plus docte, plus saige," stands for Plato to whom Pierre Lamy first introduced Rabelais. Masters further believes that for Rabelais, Plato points the way, but does not enter the circle of ultimate truth. ("The Platonic and Hermetic Tradition and the *Cinquiesme Livre* of François Rabelais" [Ph.D. diss., the Johns Hopkins University, 1964], p. 88). The Platonic guide has taken them as far as human reason can go. The company now enters the realm of revealed knowledge. The Christian tradition that natural reason and revealed religion form a continuous whole goes back to Paul, Rom. 1:18–20; 2:14–15.
12. Cf. Euripides' *Bacchae*.
13. Peter's prophecy is meant to recall those texts in the Old Testament which describe the last days more graphically: "I will send fire on Magog, and on those who dwell securely in the coastlands; and they shall know that I am the Lord" Ezek. 39:6–8. "I will bring distress on men, so that they shall walk like the blind, because they have sinned against the Lord; their blood shall be poured out like dust, and their flesh like dung. Neither their silver nor their gold shall be able to deliver them on the day of the wrath of the Lord. In the fire of his jealous wrath, all the earth shall be consumed. . . ." Zeph. 1:17–18.
14. At his most "devout" moment, during the storm at sea, Panurge invokes Jupiter and God in one breath: "Pleust à Dieu . . . que maintenant . . . je feusse en terre ferme bien à mon ayse! O que troys et quatre foys heureulx sont ceulx qui plantent chous! . . . O que petit est le nombre de ceulx à qui Juppiter a telle faveur porté qu'il les a destinez à planter chous!" (QL. xviii.593)
15. Wind, *Pagan Mysteries*, p. 158.
16. Phillips, p. 275.

17. Cornford, p. 103. In Hellespont and other areas influenced by Lampsakos, Dionysus and Priapus were considered identical, Priapus was depicted wearing the ivy wreath or grape vines in his hair, he carried the thyrsos and the wine flash. In his poetic incarnation, he always remained separate from Dionysus, but accompanied him constantly in the guise of servant or teacher, as Silenus, Pan, or the satyrs. Priapus has been worshiped as a "pantheistic" god of the universe, identified with Helios, with the Cosmos, or as Omnipotent (*potens pollens invictus*), as the Creator (*pater rerum, genitor et auctor orbis*), as Nature and Pan (*Physis ipsa Panque*), as the highest god whom Jupiter and the others serve. Thus Priapus, too, assumes the roles both of Pan and of Proteus. Roscher III, 2979–2980.

18. *Ennead* 3.v; Plato's *Symposium* and Ficino's *Commentary,* as well as his *De amore.*

19. Colonna, *Songe de Poliphile,* p. 48; my trans.

20. Rabelais's play with food as a symbol for those things which excite men to seek out wisdom, and with wine as a symbol for divine knowledge may derive from the relation of Latin *sapio* to French *sapience,* whence comes a direct connection between the sense of taste and wisdom. In Latin antiquity, the connection was commonplace, for *sapio, sapientia* meant good taste in the sense of discernment, discretion, prudence, intelligence, wisdom, philosophy. K. Weinberg in "Nietzsche's Paradox of Tragedy," *Yale French Studies* 38(1967):251–66, gives a summary of Nietzsche's brief but excellent analysis of the interconnection: "To the mind of the Ancients, the esthetic experience rated above all other forms of knowledge. The sense of taste in particular, as the most subtle tool of *touch* and *testing,* for them was so closely related to the idea of 'wisdom' that 'the Greek word which designates the *sage* etymologically belongs to *sapio* I taste, *sapiens* the one who is tasting, *sisyphos* the man with the keenest taste; an acute feeling out through tasting [*herausschmecken*], a significant aptitude for *distinguo* by the palate: this was the specific art of the philosopher, such as popular consciousness saw it'" (Nietzsche, Schlechta ed., 3:363, par. 3; my trans.). The use of *sapio* in the *Vulgate* remains true to the original classical sense of "to suggest, to be inspired by," "quia non sapis ea quae Dei sunt . . ." Matt. 16:23; Mark 8:33 (quoted by Lewis and Short, p. 1629). Spanish has always maintained the equivalence between taste and wisdom since *sabe* can either mean "it tastes of . . ." or "he (she) knows"; Medieval French authors also took the connection for granted: "Li cinkismes vertus del entendement si est apielee sapience et cis ki l'a *sapiens,* c'est auques a dire savourans, car cis ki sapiens est, il saveure ce k'il set par la vraie connissance k'il a des sciences et des ars." Jean d'Arkel, *Li Ars d'amour* 2:159, Petit, quoted by Godefroy, 7:314. As in the "Propos" episode, "gouster le bon vin" in Rabelaisian terms is strictly equivalent to the experience of divine inspiration.

21. "The Platonic and Hermetic Tradition and the *Cinquiesme Livre* of François Rabelais." (Ph.D. diss., Johns Hopkins University, 1964), p. 26.

22. Tervarent, p. 309.

23. Dante's Beatrice, who first appeared to him when both were nine years old (*Vita nuova,* I), is a figure of theology, guiding the poet through the nine heavens: "Questo numero fu ella medesima . . . Lo numero del tre è la radice del nove, perocchè senza numero altro, per sè medesimo moltiplicato, fa nove . . . Dunque se il tre è fattore per sè medesimo del nove, e lo fattore dei miracoli per sè medesimo è tre cioè Padre, Figliuolo e Spirito santo, li quali sono tre ed uno, questa donna fu accompagnata dal numero del nove a dare ad intendere, che ella era un nove, cioè

un miracolo, la cui radice è solamente la mirabile Trinitade" (*Vita nuova,* XXX). Rabelais's purifying ritual, in typically ridiculous guise, has strongly Christian and theological connotations.

24. *Phil. occ.* 2.12.256.
25. Taylor, p. 201.
26. *Phil. occ.* 2, chap. 14.
27. The *épilénie,* as presented here, differs from the version in the Ed. Pl., where the base formed by the repetition of verses 4–8 has been omitted. Masters vouches for the greater authenticity of the above version, since that is how the Jean Martin edition (1565) presented the poem. "The Platonic and Hermetic Tradition," p. 178.
28. Cirlot, pp. 107–108.
29. Lewy, pp. 12–13. Some of Philo's Old Testament sources may be Proverbs 9:1–6, "Wisdom has built her house, she has set up her seven pillars, she has slaughtered her beasts, she has mixed her wine, she has also set her table," etc. See the stories of Hagar and the angel, and Moses' staff for other fountains in the Old Testament.
30. "Dum homo habet magnam sitim, appetit frigidum et humidum ["tant beau, tant cler et tant froid au cueur d'esté"]. Spiritus enim exterioris hominis inflammatus desiderat refrigerium: ita Paulus [1 Cor. 16:18] gratias agebat illis, qui spiritum suum refriguerunt. Dum homo habet magnam sitim in spiritu interioris hominis, tunc desiderat sapientiam. Nam intellectus ex caritate, quam habet ad veritatem aeternam miro zelo accenditur et inflammatur et desiderat refrigerium contra hanc sitim spiritualum." *Cusanus Texte* (Heidelberg, 1936/37), pp. 122, 124.
31. Cusa, p. 124; my trans.: "De primo puteo qui est naturae animalis et altus, bibit pater, filii, et pecora; de secundo, qui altior in orizonte naturae, bibunt 'filii hominum,' tantum, scilicet ratione vigentes, et philosophi vocantur; de tertio, qui altissimus, uti canimus, 'Tu solus altissimus, Iesu Christi.' In illi profundissimo puteo est fons sapientiae; quae praestat felicitatem et immortalitatem."
32. The heptagon, shape of the carbuncle which surmounts the fountain, is the shape of the philosophers' stone: the squared circle. Masters quotes the *Rosarium philosophorum* to substantiate this: "Out of man and woman make a round circle [the androgyne] and extract the quadrangle from this end and from the quadrangle the triangle. Make a round circle and you will have the philosophers' stone." "The Platonic and Hermetic Tradition," p. 28.
33. Cusa, p. 132; my trans. "Qui bibit spiritum, bibit fontem scaturientem. Spiritus enim est quasi scintilla ignis Dei, qui dicitur 'ignis consumens,' qui cum in terram mittitur, fit fons emanans ignem. . . ."
34. Cusa, pp. 154, 156; my trans. "Christus vocatur 'petra deserti'. . . . Verbum in petra fuit thesaurus Dei apertus ad dandum vivas aquas. Aqua illa tam largiter fluens habuit initium in verbo seu imperio omnipotentis."
35. For an account of the confusion of the functions of heart, stomach, and liver in ancient Greece and Rome, see Onians, pp. 84 ff.
36. Two earlier poems, "trophées" (p. xxvii), resemble this poem in form and, in a sense, in content. After their first victory against the invading Dipsodes, the defenders of Utopia celebrate with a feast. Pantagruel erects a trophy and composes a poem to commemorate the battle, while Panurge celebrates the feast:

(A)

Ce fut icy qu'apparut la vertus
De quatre preux et vaillans champions,
Qui de bon sens, non de harnois vestuz,
Comme Fabie ou les deux Scipions,
Firent six cens soixante morpions,
Puissans ribaulx, brusler comme une escorce.
Prenez-y tous, roys, ducs, rocz et pions,
Enseignement que engin mieulx vault que force:
Car la victoire,
Comme est notoire,
Ne gist que en heur.
Du consistoire
Ou règne en gloire
Le hault Seigneur,
Vient, non au plus fort ou greigneur,
Ains à qui luy plaist, com' fault croire.
Doncques a chevanche et honneur
Cil qui par foy en luy espoire.

Here was displayed the valour bright
Of four knights, worthy men of brawn,
Who with no armour but their wit
(Like Fabius and the Scipios twain)
Six hundred and sixty lice did burn
Like chaff, all hefty rogues and coarse,
By this learn, king, duke, rook, and pawn,
That trickery's worth more than force.
For victory,
Says History,
Doth only lie
With that domain
In which doth reign
The Lord on high.
So not to strong or great 'tis given,
But those He loves, so we believe,
Those who place faith and hope in Heaven,
Fame, gain and glory do receive.

168

(B)

Ce feut icy que mirent à baz culz
Joyeusement quatre gaillars pions,
Pour bancqueter à l'honneur de Bacchus
Beuvans à gré comme beaulx carpions,
Lors y perdit râbles et cropions
Maistre levrault, quand chascun si efforce.
Sel et vinaigre, ainsi que scorpions,
Le poursuivoyent, dont en eurent l'estorce;
Car l'inventoire
D'un défensoire
En la chaleur,
Ce n'est que à boire
Droict et net, voire
Et du meilleur,
Mais manger levrault, c'est malheur,
Sans de vinaigre avoir mémoire;
Vinaigre est son âme et valeur;
Retenez-le en poinct péremptoire.

'Twas here that squatted in delight
Four merry boozers on the lawn,
Feasting and pledging Bacchus' might,
Drinking their fill like carp at dawn.
Here Master Leveret came to mourn
The loss of chaps and chine, perforce,
With vinegar and salt chased down,
Scorpions they carried in their stores.
The Inventory
Defensory
Against the heat,
Is drinking just
The best, which must
Be swallowed neat.
To vinegar must thought be given
Since hare without it makes you grieve,
For vinegar's its soul and leaven,
A lack that nothing can retrieve.

Both of these votive offerings of thanks belong to the long tradition of figure poems recently investigated by Masters, "Rabelais and Renaissance Figure Poems," *Etudes rabelaisiennes* 8(1969):53–68. These poems were originally inscribed on votive monuments, and therefore followed the shape of the monument. Later, the poems lost any connection with monuments, and became monuments in themselves. Part of the Christian tradition, figure poems are assimilated to Renaissance beliefs about hieroglyphics as *figurae* which participate in the power of the Word they convey. Rabelais knew about this tradition, since an infolio edition of Rabanus Maurus, a figure-poet, was published in 1503, and many of Rabelais's contemporaries practiced the form (e.g., Jean Thenaud and Salmon Macrin). Maurus freely invented forms for his figure poems which represent angels, the king, a monk, or Jesus, but which are all related to a basic cruciform (Masters, pp. 56–59). Rabelais likewise exercises his imagination by inventing an original symbol: the bottle-poem. Masters compares all three poems to the Ionian altar form; they could also be related to Maurus's cruciform poems. I believe it would be consistent with Rabelais's bacchic imagery if he intended all three to be viewed as wineglasses. (The wineglass figures prominently along with the bottle and the lantern as ensigns for Pantagruel's ships: QL. i.)

The *trophées* are reversed examples of Silenic jesting. The serious paean of praise to God is given first; Panurge's poem is a comic echo, in which the deity evoked to correspond to the "hault Seigneur" is Bacchus; feasting and drinking stand in place of the "good fight." While Pantagruel commemorates wit and ingenuity which overcome brute force and overwhelming numbers, Panurge reminds the cook that without art, food is tasteless: salt and vinegar must be added to the rabbit stew, or it will be flat.

Though the usual situation is reversed here, and the serious meaning precedes the parody, both are nonetheless present.

37. Rabelais repeatedly stresses that Panurge listens to the oracle with one ear only, and that the wine of the holy fountain is "one-eared wine" or "wine *for* one ear" (*du vin à une oreille*). The reader is reminded of the birth of Gargantua through his mother's left ear. A number of critics (Lefranc, Febvre, Screech) have pointed out that Gargantua's birth through the ear parodies the iconological representation of the Annunciation to Mary — Christ's conception — through the left ear. The parallel with the divine revelation to Panurge seems obvious: Mary received the incarnate Word through the ear, and Panurge in the same way receives the divine Word which resolves his dilemma. Rabelais here plays covertly with a theme which is overt in G.vi: the similarity adds another bit of evidence for the authenticity of this portion of the *Cinquiesme Livre*.

38. Cf. *Homil. in Gen 14:4 ad Gen. 26:30* (ed. Baehrens, pp. 125 ff.), in Lewy, p. 20.

39. *Comment. in Cant. III* (ed. Baehrens, pp. 184 ff.), in Lewy, pp. 124–25.

40. Scotus, *Rep. par.,* 1, 4. *Sententiarum,* d. viii, "De sacramente altaris," qu. 1.

41. Most of the material on the symbolism of the blood is drawn from Emile Mâle, *L'Art religieux de la fin du moyen âge en France* (Paris, 1925), pp. 108–22.

42. As the sixteenth century advances, representations of the mystical winepress, which earlier had included symbols of the Passion, the Eucharist, and of baptism, begin to employ the Eucharist symbols as a means of combating the Protestant heresies, and includes symbolic representations of the scriptures and of the Church as well.

Figure 2, a sixteenth-century engraving, shows figures from the Old Testament cultivating the vineyard while the apostles gather the grapes. But it is Jesus himself, instead of grape clusters, who lies beneath the press; it is His blood which pours into the vat. The Scriptures, symbolized by a wine barrel on a wagon drawn by the Lion (St. Mark), the ox (St. Luke), the eagle (St. John), and the angel (St. Matthew), distribute the wine of the message throughout the world. The Church, symbolized by the four Fathers, puts aside barrels of the blood-wine, while a pope and a cardinal store them away in a wine cellar to be distributed to the faithful. The real presence is here confirmed dogmatically.

43. Henri de Lubac, *Corpus mysticum; l'Eucharistie et l'eglise au Moyen Age* (Paris, 1949), p. 32.

Chapter 4

1. Krailsheimer, *Rabelais and the Franciscans*, pp. 304–305.

2. According to Thomas Taylor, 9 was considered by the Pythagoreans a final, consummate number because it "flows around the other numbers like an ocean." It is also said to resemble the horizon. *The Theoretic Arithmetic of the Pythagoreans*, p. 201. Rabelais couples these Pythagorean connotations with the Christian symbolism of 9 to convey the idea that the *livret* beneath the flasks contains final and consummate truth.

3. For an amusing and instructive explanation of Gargamelle's pregnancy, see Screech, "Eleven-Month Pregnancies: a Legal and Medical Quarrel," in *Etudes rabelaisiennes* 8(1969):93–106.

4. Febvre, pp. 168 ff. Screech elaborates Febvre's point in *L'Evangélisme de Rabelais*, p. 15: one should have *faith*, but not be *credulous*.

5. *Symposium* 189–90, in Jowett 1:316.

6. *Rabelaisian Dialectic*, pp. 19–23.

7. Bruno Snell, *The Discovery of the Mind* (Cambridge, Mass., 1953), p. 2.

8. The Larousse *Français-anglais* dictionary offers these expressions: "*Avoir qqch. pour des nèfles*, to get sth. dirt-cheap; *des nèfles!*, nothing doing!; U.S. nuts!" Similar expressions with *mesles* may have been current in the sixteenth century.

9. See Screech, "Some Stoic Elements," pp. 77–80 for further treatment of this passage.

10. "The Platonic and Hermetic Tradition," p. 83.

11. "Apres les choeurs des esprits bienheureux est placé immediatement ensuite l'ordre animastique, que les Theologiens Hebraïques nomment Issim, hommes fort robustes; et les Mages des gentils les apellent héros ou demi-dieux, ou dieux demones. St. Fulgence . . . croit qu'ils sont ainsi nommez, parce qu'ils ne sont pas jugez dignes du ciel . . . , et que cependant ils meritent plus que la terre pour le respect de la grace, comme autres fois Priape, Hippo, Vertumnus. . . . Quant à nos saints héros nous croyons que le pouvoir qu'ils ont leur est donné de Dieu . . . . De ce nombre qui va presqu'à l'infini, il y en a douze principaux, qui sont les douze Apôtres de Christ. . . ." *Phil. occ.* 3.34.138–41.

12. Screech examines the Evangelical meaning of the Thaumaste episode in "The Meaning of Thaumaste," *Bibliothèque d'Humanisme et Renaissance* 22(1960):62–72.

Chapter 5

"Frère Jean, Servant of Bacchus" is a revised version of my article "Frère Jean Evangélique," in *Modern Language Review* 66(1971): 298–305.

1. Marcel de Grève, "Les Érudits du XVIIe siècle en quête de la clef de Rabelais," *Etudes rabelaisiennes* 5(1964):48–53.
2. Grève, p. 50.
3. Jean's outcry is also reminiscent of Matthew 25:37, when Jesus, distinguishing the saved from the damned, tells his disciples that those who gave him drink when he was thirsty will be saved. The disciples ask, "Domine, quando . . . dedimus tibi potum?" Jesus replies, "Quamdiu fecistis uni ex his fratribus meis minimis, mihi fecistis" (Matt. 25:40). This association would place Jean in the company of the "least of these, Jesus' brothers." Those who refuse charity to these "brothers" are to be damned: "Sitivi et non dedistis mihi potum" (Matt. 25:42).
4. W. F. Smith traces Rabelais's allusion to Erasmus, *Adage* III, 2:37, *"Pontificalis caena* . . . Caeterum quod de pastoribus scriptum est, Peccata populi comedetis [Hosea 4:8]" "Rabelais et Erasme," *Revue des études rabelaisiennes* 6(1908):221.
5. Hugo Rahner, *Greek Myths and Christian Mystery* (London, 1963).
6. See Huguet, s.v. "dextre" and Du Cange, s.v. "dexter."
7. Attributed to Socrates in *Liber de vita et de moribus philosophorum et poetarum,* 30, *De Socrate philosopho;* see Screech, "Some Reflexions on the Abbey of Thelema," *Etudes rabelaisiennes* 8(1969):110. Plato's threefold soul becomes fourfold in Alexandrian thought: intellectual, rational, animal, vegetative.
8. Screech, "Some Reflexions," pp. 113–14.
9. Marichal, *Etudes rabelaisiennes* 5(1964):76–77.
10. "Cependant il est impossible de ne pas avoir l'impression qu'il y a dans l'énumération un ordre descendant et que la *chapelle* est moins noble que la *garde-robbe,*" Marichal, p. 77.
11. Marichal, p. 162.
12. "*The Graces* . . . otherwise called Charities, that is thanks. Whom the poetes feyned to be the Goddesses of all bountie and comeliness, which therefore (as sayth Theodontius) they make three, to wete, that men first ought to be gracious and bountiful to others freely, then to receive benefits at other mens hands curteously, and thirdly to requite them thankfully: which are three sundry Actions in liberalitye." This gloss on Seneca and Servius from the *Shepheardes Calender* is quoted in Edgar Wind, *Pagan Mysteries,* pp. 33–34.
13. Augustine *De Trinitate* 6.10.12; 8.10.14; 9–15.
14. Landino, "Commento sopra la commedia di Dante," on Dante 1.2, in E. Gombrich, "Botticelli's Mythologies," *Journal of the Warburg and Courtauld Institutes* 8(1945): 34.
15. Wind, p. 40.
16. Wind, p. 41.
17. "Circulus . . . prout in Deo incipit et allicit, pulchritudo: prout in mundus transiens ipsum rapit, amor; prout in auctorem remeans ipsi suum opus coniungit, voluptas. Amor igitur in voluptatem a pulchritudine desinit." Ficino, *De amore* 2.2, in Wind, p. 50.

18. Although Colonna's illustrator simplified the lower parts of the fountain as described in the text, his representation of the Graces and the cornucopia seems quite accurate: "Sopra il quale [uno oblongo calice inverso] excitata era una artificiosa arula, supposita alle tre Gratie nude: di finissimo oro, alla proceritate communa, l'una com l'altra adhaerentise, dalle papille delle tate delle quale l'aqua surgente stillava subtile, quale virgule . . . Et ciascuna di esse nella mano dextera teniva una omnifera copia, la quale sopra del suo capo alquanto excedeva: et daposcia tutte tre le aperture elegantemente convenivano in una rotondatione et hiato paremente inseme coeunte; cum fructi et fronde varii pendenti fora . . . Daposcie il solertissimo artifice fusore, per non impedire uno cubito cum l'altro, cum signo di pudicitia le statue cum la leva mano occultavano la parte digna di copertura." Colonna, *Hypnerotomachia Poliphili* (Padua, 1964), pp. 81–83.

19. Rabelais's Graces repeat in a different version the liberal and selfless giving and receiving of love which the androgyne emblem allegorizes.

20. Ficino, *De amore* 3.3, in Wind, p. 41.

21. Wind, p. 39.

22. Wind, p. 74.

23. *Altercazione* 4.104 f., in Wind, p. 59.

24. *Rabelaisian Marriage,* pp. 30–34. Screech bases himself, in part, on E. Telle's article "Thélème et le paulinisme matrimonial érasmien," *François Rabelais: 1553–1953* (Geneva, 1953), pp. 112 ff. Screech admits that a modified Venus could have relevance for Rabelais, "The Abbey could be a Humanist and Evangelical exploitation of the traditional theme of a *séjour de Vénus.* If so, Rabelais must have had some reformed Venus in mind. She was sometimes reformed in the Renaissance into a kind of patroness of chaste wedlock. Certainly Thelema is no easy sojourn of venerial delights." p. 32.

25. *De civ. Dei* 11.30.241.

26. *Phil. occ.* 2.9.238; my trans.

27. Taylor, *The Theoretic Arithmetic of the Pythagoreans* (Los Angeles, 1934), pp. 192–94.

28. Telle gives a rather extreme venerial interpretation of the significance of 6, and concludes that Rabelais was a rabid opponent of celibacy as a virtue. In this way, Rabelais would have committed greater heresy than either Calvin or Luther. Screech considerably modifies this position, but still uses Thélème as a massive example of Rabelais's favorable attitude toward women and marriage, even though the inmates must leave the abbey after the wedding ceremony.

29. Screech, *Rabelaisian Marriage,* p. 28.

30. Per Nykrog, "Thélème, Panurge et la dive bouteille," *Revue d'histoire littéraire de la France* 65(1965):391.

31. Kurt Weinberg, "Zum Wandel des Sinnbezirks von 'Herz' und 'Instinkt' unter dem Einfluβ Descartes'," *Archiv für das Studium der neueren Sprachen und Literaturen* 203(1966):7. To illustrate the contemporary notion of instinct, the following excerpt from Agrippa on the *furor:* "L'on dit . . . que l'humeur mélancholique est si imperieuse que par son feu . . . elle fait venir les esprits célestes dans les corps humains, par la presence et *l'instinct* ou l'inspiration desquels . . . les hommes étoient transportés, et disaient plusieurs choses admirables." *Phil occ.* 1.60.170; italics mine.

32. Etienne Gilson, *Jean Duns Scot* (Paris, 1952), p. 578. In a polemic ironically

reminiscent of theological arguments satirized by Rabelais himself, Marcel Françon takes Nykrog to task for being slipshod in his definition of *thelēma* which does *not* refer to the spontaneous and thoughtless impulses of concupiscence, *hepithumia*, but to a "rational appetency." Desire is thus divided in two, a base and a noble desire, lust and *thelēma*. Cf. his "Thélème," *Annali dell' Instituto Universitario Orientale*, Romance section 8(1966):257–59.

33. Nykrog, p. 389.
34. Françon, "Francesco Colonna's *Poliphili Hypnerotomachia* and Rabelais," *Modern Language Review* 50(1955):52–55.
35. I have used the first French edition, *Hypnerotomachie, ou Discours du songe de Poliphile*, ed. Jean Martin (Paris, pour Jacques Kerver, 1546; newly published by the Club des Libraires de France, 1963), pp. 41–50, to summarize Poliphile's encounter with Telemia.
36. Ficino, *Opera omnia* (Basel, 1576), pp. 881, 108.
37. Colonna, p. 75.
38. Ficino, p. 1793.
39. Scotus believes that Grace and *caritas* differ only by formal, not essential distinction. Consequently, Grace (*charis*), like charity, has its seat in the will (*thelēma*). Avery R. Dulles, *Princeps concordiae; Pico della Mirandola and the scholastic tradition* (Cambridge, 1941) p. 124. The mystical use of the Graces (and Venus) as the emblem of Thélème seems even more appropriate.
40. Pico, *Opera* 1.320.
41. Cf. Plato, *Republic,* and Diogenes rolling his tub in the Prologue to TL.
42. Nesca Adeline Robb, *Neo-platonism of the Italian Renaissance* (London, 1935), pp. 41–42.
43. Cf. Pier Paolo Vergiero, *De ingenuis moribus* (Padua, 1918), pp. 15 ff.; Maffeo Vegio, *De educatione liberorum* 839 ff. 15.1622, in Robb, pp. 41–42.
44. Ficino, p. 305.
45. For a detailed study of the trial of Bridoye, see Screech, "The Legal Comedy of Rabelais and the Trial of Bridoye in the *Tiers Livre de Pantagruel*," *Etudes rabelaisiennes* 5(1964):175–95.

Chapter 6

1. This term is used throughout to refer to the lower two souls in the classical tetrad of intellective, rational, animal and vegetative souls.
2. *Ed. Scr.*, p. 63; also Screech, *Rabelaisian Marriage*, pp. 80, 124.
3. According to the Franciscan doctrine, the will alone chooses; reason merely weighs (cf. Gilson, *Jean Duns Scot*, p. 601). Ficino's idea of will is almost identical: will alone may choose among the alternatives presented by reason, the deliberating faculty (*consultare*) (cf. Kristeller, *The Philosophy of Marsilio Ficino*, p. 258). The agreement between medieval Franciscan and Renaissance Neoplatonic notions is due to their common debt to St. Augustine. Rabelais, as a Franciscan friar, was ideally placed to assimilate Neoplatonism to his basic fund of ideas.
4. Screech, *Rabelaisian Marriage*, chaps. 5–7.
5. Marichal, "Quart Livre Commentaires," *Etudes rabelaisiennes* 5(1964):78.
6. According to Littré, in the sixteenth century *bailler le moine*, "to give the monk," meant to bring bad luck.

7. Marichal, p. 78.

8. *De civ. Dei* 9; 4.175–76.

9. Odysseus, tied to the mast, is the only man aboard his ship who hears the Siren's song. He escapes death and yet has full knowledge of it. Clement of Alexandria and later Christian exegetes interpret this as the Christian man who needs not stop his ears against temptation, but resists it by holding tight to the mast, depicted in the form of a cross. Hugo Rahner, *Greek Myths and Christian Mystery* (London, 1963), "Odysseus at the Mast," pp. 328–86. Pantagruel, like Odysseus, cleaves to the Cross, and is saved.

10. See Luigi Marsigli, *Commentary on Petrarch's Canzone "Italia Mia"* (Bologna, 1863).

11. Cf. Screech, *Rabelaisian Marriage,* chap. 4.

12. "Der Hauptantrieb des Menschen, der ihn zu Edlem drängt, ist das Bestreben sich von den eigenen 'Unlustgefühlen' (*displicentia propria*) zu befreien, die mit einem unvollkommenen Zustand unausweichlich verbunden sind. Dieser Aufschwung ist ein durchaus natürlicher Vorgang, eine seelische Spekulation möchte man sagen: die lästige Unruhe hört nie auf, so lange das Ideal nicht erreicht ist. . . ." Stadelmann, pp. 191–92.

13. The *instinct et aguillon* and the *displicentia propria* may be assimilated to the Patristic idea of *synderesis.* Synderesis should mean "preservation," but is used by the Fathers and mystics in a way unjustified by etymology. It stands for that remnant of soul which retains the purity of the sinless state before the fall. It becomes identified with the Neoplatonic notion of an impeccable "soul-center." St. Bonaventure calls it "apex mentis seu scintilla." For Hermann of Fritzlar, it is "a power or faculty in the soul, wherein God works immediately, without means and intermission." Ruysbroeck calls it a natural will toward the good. Meister Eckhart speaks of a *Funkelein* within the soul which cannot be extinguished. St. Thomas calls it the highest activity of moral sense; Jean Gerson lists it among the three faculties of man: it is intellect or natural light which comes directly from God. The other two faculties are the understanding (or reason) which mediates between *synderesis* and the third faculty, sense-consciousness. James Hastings, *Encyclopedia of Religion and Ethics* (New York, 1908–1926), 12:157. It is this faculty which drives Panurge onward until he can be restored to proper balance by the divine command, *Trinch!*

Conclusion

1. Montaigne believes *Pantagruel* to be *un livre* "simplement plaisant" (2:10).

2. Spitzer, "Rabelais et les 'rabelaisants,' " *Studi Francesi* 12(1960):401–23. Spitzer's position is that Rabelais's meaning is irrelevant to his literary art, and that the critic should limit his perspective to the aesthetic and stylistic qualities of the work at hand. The rest is intellectual history or sociology.

3. Probst-Biraden, *Rabelais et les secrets de Pantagruel* (Nice, 1949).

4. Cusa, *Apologia doctae ignorantiae* H.II; 3, 15, 17; my trans.: "Nihil perfecte homo noscere poterit . . . finis enim scientiae Deo tantum reconditus est. . . ."

5. Eugene F. Rice, "Nicholas of Cusa's Idea of Wisdom," *Traditio* 13(1957):261–363.

Selected Bibliography

PRIMARY SOURCES

Editions of Rabelais

Rabelais, François. *OEuvres complètes.* Edited by Jacques Boulenger and Lucien Scheler. Paris: Pléiade, 1955.

——————. *OEuvres.* Edited by Abel Lefranc. 2d ed., rev. 6 vols. Paris: Champion, 1913–55.

——————. *Gargantua.* Edited by M. A. Screech. Geneva: Droz, 1970.

——————. *Pantagruel.* Edited by V. L. Saulnier. Geneva: Droz, 1965.

——————. *Le Tiers Livre.* Edited by M. A. Screech. Geneva: Droz, 1947.

——————. *Le Quart Livre.* Edited by Robert Marichal. Geneva: Droz, 1947.

——————. *The Histories of Gargantua and Pantagruel.* Translated by J. M. Cohen. Baltimore: Penguin Books, 1955.

Versions of the Bible

Bible. *The Holy Bible.* RSV. New York: Nelson, 1952.

——————. *The Jerusalem Bible.* Garden City, N.Y.: Doubleday, 1966.

——————. *Biblia sacra.* Vulgate edition. 4 vols. Rome: Catholic Book Agency, 1955.

Other Texts

Aban, Pierre d'. *Les OEuvres magiques de Henri-Corneille Agrippa.* Liège, 1788.

Agrippa von Nettesheim, Heinrich Cornelius. *La Philosophie occulte.* The Hague: R. C. Alberts, 1727.

Aquinas, Thomas. *Catena in quatuor Evangelia, ad plurima exempla comparata et emendata.* 2 vols. Venice: Bettinelli, 1746.

Ariosto, Ludovico. *Orlando Furioso.* Venice: Misserini, 1630.

Augustinus, Aurelius. *OEuvres.* Edited and translated by B. Roland-Gosselin. 25 vols. Paris: Desclée, De Brouwer, 1936.

————. *De civitate Dei.* 2 vols. Leipzig: Tauchnitus, 1825.

————. *The City of God.* Edited and abridged by Vernon J. Bourke. New York: Image Books, 1958.

Aulus Gellius. *The Attic Nights.* Translated by John C. Rolfe. 2 vols. London. Heinemann, 1927–28.

Castiglione, Baldassare. Giovanni della Casa. *Opere.* Edited by G. Prezzolini. Milan: Rizzoli, n.d.

Cicero, Marcus Tullius. *Scripta quae manserunt omnia.* 8 vols. Leipzig: Teubner, 1961–66.

Colonna, Francesco. *Hypnerotomachia Poliphili.* Edited by G. Pozzi and L. A. Ciapponi. 2 vols. Padua: Antenore, 1964.

————. *Le Songe de Poliphile.* Paris: Les Librairies Associés, 1963.

Dante, Alighieri. *La Vita Nuova.* Edited by C. Witte. Leipzig: Brockhaus, 1876.

Des Periers, Bonaventure. *Cymbalum mundi.* Edited by Peter H. Nurse. Manchester: University of Manchester, 1958.

Du Moulin, Antoine. *La Vertu et propriété de la quinte essence de toutes choses.* Translated by Jean de Roquetaillade. Lyons, 1581.

Duns Scotus, Joannes. *Commentaria oxoniensis ad IV. libros magistri sententiarum.* vols. 17, 21. Florence: S. Bonaventura, 1912.

————. *Opera omnia.* New ed. vols. 22–24. Paris: L. Vivès, 1894.

Erasmus, Desiderius. *The "Adages" of Erasmus.* Translated by Margaret Mann Phillips. Cambridge, Eng.: Cambridge University Press, 1964.

————. *The Education of a Christian Prince.* Translated by Lester K. Born. New York: Columbia University Press, 1936.

————. *Opera omnia.* 10 vols. in 11. Lyons: P. Vander, 1703–06.

————. *The Praise of Folly.* Translated by Hoyt Hopewell Hudson. Princeton, New Jersey: Princeton University Press, 1941.

Euripides. *Electra, The Phoenecian Women, The Bacchae.* Chicago: Chicago University Press, 1959.

Ficino, Marsilio. *Opera omnia.* 2 vols. Turin: Bottega d'Erasmo, 1959.

Fischart, Johann. *Geschichtsklitterung (Gargantua).* 1575, 1582 and 1590. Reprint. Edited by A. Alsleben. Halle: Niemeyer, 1891.

Folengo, Teofilo, *Marcaronées (Macaronaei opus quod inscribitur Baldus).* Florence, 1941.

Galenus. *OEuvres anatomiques, physiologiques et médicales.* 2 vols. Paris: Baillière, 1854–56.

Giorgio, Francesco. *De Harmonia mundi totius, cantica tria.* Venice: B. de Vitalibust, 1525.

Gringore, Pierre. *Le Prince des Sots.* In Picot, Emile. *Recueil général des Sotties.* Paris: Firmin-Didot, 1912.

Hebreo, Leone. *Diálogos de amor.* Translated by the Inca Garcilaso de la Vega. Buenos Aires: Espasa-Calpe, 1947.

Hermes Trismegistus. *Corpus hermeticum.* Edited by A. D. Nock and translated by A.-J. Festugière. 2d ed. 2 vols. Paris. Société les Belles Lettres, 1960.

——————. *Hermetica.* Edited by Walter Scott. 4 vols. London: Dawsons, 1968.

Herodotus. [*Works*]. Translated by A. D. Godley. 4 vols. London: Heinemann, 1921–24.

——————. *The Histories.* Translated by Aubrey de Selincourt. Baltimore: Penguin Books, 1954.

Hippocrates. [*Works*]. Translated by W. H. S. Jones. 4 vols. London: Heinemann, 1923–31.

Horatius Flaccus, Quintus. *Opera.* Oxford: Talboys, 1838.

Lucianus Samosatensis [*Works*]. Translated by A. M. Harmon. 8 vols. London: Heinemann, 1913–67.

Macrobius, Ambrosius Aurelius Theodosius. *Commentary on the Dream of Scipio.* Translated by William Harris Stahl. New York: Columbia University Press, 1952.

Migne, Jacques Paul. *Patrologiae cursus completus* [*Patrologiae graecae*]. 161 vols. in 106. Turnhout: Brepols, 1964.

——————. *Patrologiae cursus completus* [*Patrologiae latinae*]. 271 vols. Paris: Migne, 1844–49.

More, Thomas. *Utopia.* 1516. Reprint. Leeds, Eng.: Scholar Press, 1966.

Nicolaus Cusanus. *Opera.* 1514. Reprint. 3 vols. Frankfurt am Main: Minerva, 1962.

——————. *Cusanus-Texte.* Edited by Josef Koch. Heidelberg: C. Winter, 1936–37.

Origenes. *Werke.* Edited by Paul Koetschau. 11 vols. Leipzig: Hinrich, 1899–1935.

"Ovide moralisé:" *poème du commencement du 14e siècle.* Edited by C. de Boer. 5 vols. Amsterdam: J. Muller, 1915–38.

Ovidius Naso, Publius. [*Opera*]. Edited by Rudolph Merkel and R. Ehwald. 3 vols. Leipzig: Teubner, 1910–12.

Paracelsus. *Four Treatises.* Translated by C. Lilian Temkin. Baltimore: Johns Hopkins Press, 1941.

——————. *Selected Writings.* Translated by Norbert Guterman. New York: Pantheon Books, 1951.

Petrarca. *Petrarch's Secret, or The Soul's Conflict with Passion: Three Dialogues.* Translated by William H. Draper. London: Chatto and Windus, 1911.

Philo Judaeus. [*Works*]. Translated by F. H. Colson and G. H. Whitaker. 10 vols. London: Heinemann, 1930.

Philostratus, Flavius. *Opera auctiora.* Edited by C. L. Kayser. Hildesheim: Olms, 1964.

Pico della Mirandola, Giovanni Francesco. *Opera omnia.* 2 vols. Basel: H. Patrina, 1572–73.

——————. *On the Imagination.* Translated by Harry Caplan. New Haven: Yale University Press, 1930.

Plato. [*Works.*]. Translated by H. N. Fowler. 9 vols. London: Heinemann, 1921–28.

——————. *Dialogues.* Translated by Jowett. Chicago: Encyclopedia Britannica, 1952.

——————. *Plato's Cosmology: the Timaeus of Plato.* Translated by Francis MacDonald Cornford. London: Routledge and Paul, 1937.

Plinius Secundus, C. *Historia mundi.* Basel: Frobenius, 1530.

——————. *Natural History.* 10 vols. Cambridge, Mass.: Harvard University Press, 1938–63.

Plotinus. *Opera.* Edited by Paul Henry and Hans Rudolf Schwyzer. Oxford: Clarendon Press, 1964.

Polyaenus. *Stratagems of War.* Translated by Dr. Shepherd. 2d ed. London: George Nicol, 1796.

Ripa, Cesare. *Iconologia.* 5 vols. Perugia, 1764–67.

Thenaud, Jean. *La Saincte et trescrestienne Cabale.* Published in part in Blau, J. L. *The Christian Interpretation of the Cabala in the Renaissance.* New York: Columbia University Press, 1944.

Weinberg, Bernard. *Critical Prefaces of the French Renaissance.* Evanston, Ill.: Northwestern University Press, 1950.

SECONDARY SOURCES

Antal, F. "The Maenad under the Cross." *Journal of the Warburg and Courtauld Institutes* 1(1937):71–73.

Arenas, A. F. "*Hypnerotomachia Poliphili.* Estado actual de la investigación en torno al libro escrito por el domínico Francisco Colonna." *Revista de Archivos, Bibliotecas y Museos* 78(1960):641–64.

Auerbach, Erich. *Mimesis; the Representation of Reality in Western Literature.* Garden City, N.Y.: Doubleday, 1957.

——————. *Scenes from the Drama of European Literature; Six Essays.* New York: Meridian Books, 1959.

Beer, E. S. de. "Gothic: Origin and Diffusion of the Term; the Idea of Style in Architecture." *Journal of the Warburg and Courtauld Institutes* 11(1948):143–62.

Berk, Philip R. "Evangelical Irony: Allegory and Design in Rabelais." Ph.D. dissertation, University of Pittsburgh, 1969.

Blau, Joseph Leon. *The Christian Interpretation of the Cabala in the Renaissance.* New York: Columbia University Press, 1944.

Cirlot, Juan Eduardo. *A Dictionary of Symbols.* New York: Philosophical Library, 1962.

Cornford, Francis MacDonald. *The Origin of Attic Comedy.* London: Arnold, 1914.

Daniélou, Jean. *The Lord of History; Reflections on the Inner Meaning of History.* Translated by Nigel Abercrombie. London: Longmans, 1958.

Delaruelle, L. "Ce que Rabelais doit à Erasme et Budé." *Revue d'Histoire Littéraire* 11(1904):220–62.

Dorez, Léon. "Des origines et de la diffusion du 'Songe de Poliphile,'" *Revue des Bibliothèques* (1896), pp. 239–83.

Du Cange, Charles DuFresne. *Glossarium Mediae et Infimae Latinitatis.* 10 vols. Niort: Faure, 1883.

Dulles, Avery Robert. *Princeps Concordiae: Pico della Mirandola and the Scholastic Tradition.* Cambridge, Mass.: Harvard University Press, 1941.

Encyclopaedia of Religion and Ethics. Edited by James Hastings. 13 vols. Edinburgh: T. & T. Clark, 1908–27.

Febvre, Lucien. *Le Problème de l'incroyance au XVIe siècle; la religion de Rabelais.* Rev. ed. Paris: A. Michel, 1947.

Françon, Marcel. "Francesco Colonna's *Poliphili Hypnerotomachia* and *Rabelais.*" *Modern Language Review* 50(1955):52–55.

—————. "Thélème." *Annali dell' Instituto Universitario Orientale,* Romance Section 8(1966):257–59.

Gilson, Etienne. *Jean Duns Scot; introduction à ses positions fondamentales.* Paris: Vrin, 1952.

—————. "Notes médiévales au *Tiers Livre de Pantagruel.*" *Revue d'histoire franciscaine* 2 (1925):72–88.

—————. "Rabelais franciscain." *Les Idées et les lettres.* 2d ed. Paris: Vrin, 1955.

Godefroy, Frédéric. *Dictionnaire de l'ancienne langue française et de tous ses dialectes du IXe au XVe siècle.* 10 vols. Paris: Vieweg, 1881.

Gombrich, Ernst Hans Josef. "Botticelli's Mythologies; A Study in the Neo-Platonic Symbolism of his Circle." *Journal of the Warburg and Courtauld Institutes* 8(1945): 7–60.

—————. "Icones Symbolicae, the Visual Image in neo-Platonic Thought." *Journal of the Warburg and Courtauld Institutes* 11(1948):163–92.

Grandsaignes d'Hauterive, Robert. *Dictionnaire d'ancien français, moyen âge et Renaissance.* Paris: Larousse, 1947.

Gray, Floyd. "Structure and Meaning in the Prologue to the *Tiers Livre.*" *L'Esprit Créateur* 3(1963):57–62.

Greene, Thomas M. *Rabelais; a Study in Comic Courage.* Englewood Cliffs, N.J.: Prentice-Hall, 1970.

Grève, Marcel de. "Les Érudits du XVIIe siècle en quête de la clef de Rabelais." *Etudes rabelaisiennes* 5(1964):41–63.

Guiton, Jean. "Le Mythe des paroles gelées." *Romanic Review* 31(1950):3–15.

Gundersheimer, Werner L. "Erasmus, Humanism and the Christian Cabala." *Journal of the Warburg and Courtauld Institutes* 26(1963):38–52.

Haydn, Hiram Collins. *The Counter-Renaissance.* New York: Grove Press, 1960.

Hopper, Vincent Foster. *Medieval Number Symbolism.* New York: Columbia University Press, 1938.

Huguet, Edmond. *Dictionnaire de la langue française du seizième siècle.* 7 vols. Paris: Champion, 1925–67.

Huizinga, Johann. *The Waning of the Middle Ages.* New York: Longmans, Green, 1949.

Kayser, Wolfgang. *Des Groteske; seine Gestaltung in Malerei und Dichtung.* Oldenburg: Gerhard Stalling, 1957.

Krailsheimer, Alban J. *Rabelais and the Franciscans.* Oxford: Claredon Press, 1963.

——————. "The Significance of the Pan Legend in Rabelais' Thought." *Modern Language Review* 56(1961):13–23.

Kristeller, Paul Oskar. *The Philosophy of Marsilio Ficino*. New York: Columbia University Press, 1943.

Lebegue, Raymond. "Rabelais, the Last of the Erasmians." *Journal of the Warburg and Courtauld Institutes* 22(1952):193–204.

Lewy, Hans. *Sobria ebrietas; Untersuchungen zur Geschichte der antiken Mystik*. Giessen: Topelmann, 1929.

Lubac, Henri de. *Corpus mysticum; l'eucharistie et l'église au moyen âge*. 2d ed., rev. Paris: Aubier, 1949.

——————. *Exégèse médiévale; les quatre sens de l'écriture*. 4 vols. Paris: Aubier, 1959–64.

Macchioro, Vittorio D. *From Orpheus to Paul; a History of Orphism*. New York: Holt, 1930.

McLuhan, Marshall. *The Gutenberg Galaxy; the Making of Typographic Man*. Toronto: University of Toronto Press, 1962.

Mâle, Emile. *L'Art religieux de la fin du moyen âge en France*. Paris: A. Colin, 1925.

Marichal, Robert. "L'Attitude de Rabelais devant le néo-platonisme et l'italianisme." *François Rabelais, 1553–1953*. Geneva: Droz, 1953, pp. 181–209.

——————. " 'Quart Livre,' commentaires." *Etudes rabelaisiennes* 5(1964):65–162.

Masters, George Mallary. "The Hermetic and Platonic Tradition in Rabelais' *Dive Bouteille*." *Studi Francesi* 28(1966):15–29.

——————. "The Platonic and Hermetic Tradition and the *Cinquièsme Livre* of François Rabelais." Ph.D. dissertation, The Johns Hopkins University, 1964.

——————. "Rabelais and Renaissance Figure Poems." *Etudes rabelaisiennes* 8 (1969):53–68.

——————. *Rabelaisian Dialectic and the Platonic-Hermetic Tradition*. Albany: State University of New York Press, 1969.

Nietzsche, Friedrich Wilhelm. *Gesammelte Werke*. 23 vols. Munich: Musarion Verlag, 1920–29.

North, Helen. *Sophrosyne; Self-Knowledge and Self-Restraint in Greek Literature*. Ithaca: Cornell University Press, 1966.

Nykrog, Per. "Thélème, Panurge et la Dive bouteille." *Revue d'histoire littéraire de la France* 65(1965):385–97.

Ong, Walter J. *Ramus, Method and the Decay of Dialogue; from the Art of Discourse to the Art of Reason*. Cambridge, Mass.: Harvard University Press, 1958.

Onians, Richard Broxton. *The Origins of European Thought about the Body, the Mind, the Soul, the World, Time and Fate*. Cambridge, Eng.: Cambridge University Press, 1951.

Panofsky, Dora and Erwin. *Pandora's Box; the Changing Aspects of a Mythical Symbol*. New York: Pantheon Books, 1956.

Plattard, Jean. "L'Ecriture sainte dans l'oeuvre de Rabelais." *Revue des études rabelaisiennes* 8(1910):257–330.

Popkin, Richard Henry. *The History of Scepticism from Erasmus to Descartes.* Assen: Van Gorcum, 1960.

Probst-Biraben, J. H. *Rabelais et les secrets de Pantagruel.* Nice, 1949.

Rahner, Hugo. *Greek Myths and Christian Mystery.* London: Burns and Oates, 1963.

Raible, Wolfgang. "Der Prolog zu Gargantua und der Pantagruelismus." *Romanische Forschungen* 78(1966):253–79.

Rawson, C. J. "Rabelais and Horace; a Contact in the Tiers Livre, chap. III." *French Studies* 19(1965):373–78.

Rice, Eugene F. "Nicholas of Cusa's Idea of Wisdom." *Traditio* 13(1957):261–363.

Robb, Nesca Adeline. *Neo-Platonism of the Italian Renaissance.* London: Allen and Unwin, 1935.

Roscher, Wilhelm Heinrich, *Ausführliches Lexikon der Griechischen und Römischen Mythologie.* 6 vols. Leipzig: Teubner, 1884–1937.

Saulnier, Verdun L. *Le Dessein de Rabelais.* Paris: Société d'Editions d'Enseignement Supérieur, 1957.

——————. "Le Festin devant Chaneph, ou la confiance dernière de Rabelais." *Mercure de France* 320(1954):648–66.

——————. "Le Silence de Rabelais et le mythe des paroles gelées." *François Rabelais, 1553–1953.* Geneva: Droz, 1953, pp. 233–47.

Screech, Michael A. "Eleven-Month Pregnancies." *Études rabelaisiennes* 7(1969):93–106.

——————. *L'Evangélisme de Rabelais.* Geneva: Droz, 1959.

——————. "The Legal Comedy of Rabelais and the Trial of Bridoye in the *Tiers Livre de Pantagruel.*" *Études rabelaisiennes* 5(1964):175–95.

——————. *The Rabelaisian Marriage.* London: Arnold, 1958.

——————. "Some Reflexions on the *Abbey of Thelema.*" *Études rabelaisiennes* 8 (1969):109–14.

Seznec, Jean. *The Survival of the Pagan Gods: The Mythological Tradition and Its Place in Renaissance Humanism and Art.* New York: Pantheon, 1953.

Smith, W. F. "On the Authenticity of the Fifth Book of Rabelais." *The Modern Quarterly of Language and Literature* 1(1898–99):283–89.

——————. "Rabelais et Erasme." *Revue des études rabelaisiennes* 6(1908):215–64; 375–78.

Snell, Bruno. *The Discovery of the Mind; the Greek Origins of European Thought.* Translated by T. G. Rosenmeyer. Cambridge, Mass.: Harvard University Press, 1953.

Söltoft-Jensen, H. "Le Cinquième Livre de Rabelais et le "Songe de Poliphile.' " *Revue d'histoire littéraire de la France* 3(1896):608–12.

Spitzer, Leo. "Rabelais et les 'rabelaisants.' " *Studi Francesi* 12(1960):401–23.

Stadelmann, Rudolf. "Vom Geist des ausgehenden Mittelalters." *Deutsche Vierteljahrsschrift für Literaturwissenschaft und Geistesgeschichte* 15(1929).

Taylor, Thomas. *The Theoretic Arithmetic of the Pythagoreans.* Los Angeles: Phoenix Press, 1934.

Telle, Emile V. "Thélème et le Paulinisme matrimonial érasmien." *François Rabelais: 1553–1953.* Geneva: Droz, 1953, pp. 104–19.

Tervarent, Guy de. "Attributs et symboles dans l'art profane, 1450–1600." *Dictionnaire d'un langage perdu,* vol. 1. Geneva: Droz, 1958.

Villey-Desmesrets, Pierre Louis Joseph. *Marot et Rabelais.* Paris: Champion, 1923.

Weinberg, Kurt. "Nietzsche's Paradox of Tragedy." *Yale French Studies* 38(1967): 251–66.

——————. "Zum Wandel des Sinnbezirks von 'Herz' und 'Instinkt' unter dem Einfluss Descartes.'" *Archiv für das Studium der neueren Sprachen und Literaturen* 203(1966):1–31.

Wind, Edgar. 'Dürer's 'Männerbad': A Dionysian Mystery." *Journal of the Warburg and Courtauld Institutes* 2(1938–39):269–71.

——————. *Pagan Mysteries in the Renaissance.* New Haven: Yale University Press, 1958.

Index

Aban, Pierre d', *see* Pierre d'Aban
Adonis, 99
Aeschylus, 65
Affaire des Placards, 117
Agesilaus, 136
Aglaia, 120
Agon, 46, 161
Agrippa, Heinrich Cornelius von Nettesheim, 20, 43, 47, 48, 51, 52, 80, 105, 123, 124, 149, 161, 173
Alcibiades, 23
Alexander the Great, 29, 30, 74
Allegory, 24, 35, 37, 47, 70, 73, 105, 118, 132, 136, 151, 173
Amor, 120, 122
Androgyne, 99–100, 150
Apollo, 50, 69, 96, 100, 119, 122, 149, 161
Aquinas, Thomas, see Thomas Aquinas, St.
Ariosto, Lodovico, 161
Aristophanes, 100
Aristotle, 29, 40, 51
Arkel, Jean d', 166
Arnobius, 163
Atheism, 17, 147
Atlas, 61
Augustine, St., 19, 43, 46, 64, 119, 123, 124, 143, 144, 150, 155, 163, 174; referred to as Hippo, 106
Aulus Gellius, 142, 143

Bacchus, 28, 45, 46, 47, 48, 50, 51, 52, 53, 61, 65, 66, 70, 71, 72, 73, 74, 75, 76, 77, 78, 79, 84, 86, 88, 95, 99, 103, 104, 105, 107, 119, 149, 150, 154, 159, 161, 162, 164, 166, 170

Bakhtin, M., 147
Béda, Noel, 148
Benedictine, 92, 107
Boccaccio, Giovanni, 31, 156
Bonaventure, St., 175
Botticelli, Sandro, 122
Bouchet, Guillaume, 162
Boulenger, Jacques, 35
Bourbon, Nicolas, 147
Brantôme, Pierre de, 162
Brown, Norman O., 158
Brutus, 69
Budé, Guillaume, 18

Cabala, Cabalists, 20, 97, 147
Calvin, John, Calvinist, 18, 109, 148, 173
Capella, Martianus, 123
Castiglione, Baldassare, 158
Castor and Pollux, 99
Cato, 65
Cathay, 74
Chanson de Roland, 115
Charles V, emperor, 159
Chrysostom, St., 155
Cicero, 51, 157, 161
Cirlot, Juan E., 164
Clement of Alexandria, 47, 123, 175
Clouzot, Henri, 164
Coincidentia oppositorum, 77, 85, 145
Colonna, Francesco, 70, 76, 120, 121, 130, 131, 132, 144, 173
Coquillart, Guillaume, 159
Cordier, Mathurin, 162
Corpus Hermeticum, 20, 153
Cusa, Nicholas of, 17, 20, 47, 84, 85, 90, 145, 149, 156, 167

Dante Alighieri, 73, 131, 166

185

Florence M. Weinberg is associate professor of French and Spanish literature at Saint John Fisher College, Rochester, New York. She received her B.A. from Park College (1954), her M.A. from the University of British Columbia (1963), and her Ph.D. from the University of Rochester (1968).

The manuscript was edited by Marguerite C. Wallace. The book was designed by Richard Kinney. The text typeface is Linotype Granjon designed by George W. Jones about 1928; and the display face is Weiss italic designed by Emil Rudolf Weiss about 1926.

The text is printed on Oxford Paper Company's Rhodes Text paper and the book is bound in Columbia Mills' Fictionette Natural Finish cloth over binders boards. Manufactured in the United States of America.